OMNIVM LVX CIVIVM

BOSTON
PUBLIC
LIBRARY

On Dickinson

On Dickinson

The Best from *American Literature*

Edited by Edwin H. Cady and Louis J. Budd

Duke University Press   Durham and London 1990

All the poetry of Emily Dickinson is reprinted by
permission of the publishers and the Trustees of
Amherst College from *The Poems of Emily Dickin-
son,* edited by Thomas H. Johnson, Cambridge,
Mass.: The Belknap Press of Harvard University
Press, Copyright 1951, © 1955, 1979, 1983 by The
President and Fellows of Harvard College.

© 1990 Duke University Press
All rights reserved
Printed in the United States of America
on acid-free paper ∞
Library of Congress Cataloging in Publication Data
appear on the last printed page of this book.

Contents

Series Introduction

From Vol. 1, no. 1, in March 1929 to the latest issue, the front cover of *American Literature* has proclaimed that it is published "with the Cooperation of the American Literature Section [earlier Group] of the Modern Language Association." Though not easy to explain simply, the facts behind that statement have deeply influenced the conduct and contents of the journal for five decades and more. The journal has never been the "official" or "authorized" organ of any professional organization. Neither, however, has it been an independent expression of the tastes or ideas of Jay B. Hubbell, Clarence Gohdes, or Arlin Turner, for example. Historically, it was first in its field, designedly so. But its character has been unique, too.

Part of the tradition of the journal says that Hubbell in founding it intended a journal that should "hold the mirror up to the profession"—reflecting steadily its current interests and (ideally) at least sampling the best work being done by historians, critics, and bibliographers of American literature during any given year. Such remains the intent of the editors based at Duke University; such also through the decades has been the intent of the Board of Editors elected by the vote of members of the professional association—"Group" or "Section."

The operative point lies in the provisions of the constitutional "Agreements" between the now "Section" and the journal. One of these provides that the journal shall publish no article not approved by two readers from the elected Board. Another provides that the Chairman of the Board or, if one has been appointed and is acting in the editorial capacity at Duke, the Managing Editor need publish no article not judged worthy of the journal. Historically, again, the members of the successive Boards and the Duke editor have seen eye-to-eye. The Board has tended to approve fewer than one out of every ten submissions. The tradition of the journal dictates that it keep a slim back-log. With however much revision, therefore, the journal publishes practically everything the Board approves.

Founder Hubbell set an example from the start by achieving the almost total participation of the profession in the first five numbers of *American Literature*. Cairns, Murdock, Pattee, and Rusk were involved in Vol. 1, no. 1, along with Boynton, Killis Campbell, Foerster, George Philip Krapp, Leisy, Mabbott, Parrington, Bliss Perry, Louise Pound, Quinn, Spiller, Frederick Jackson Turner, and Stanley Williams on the editorial side. Spiller, Tremaine McDowell, Gohdes, and George B. Stewart contributed essays. Canby, George McLean Harper, Gregory Paine, and Howard Mumford Jones appeared as reviewers. Harry Hayden Clark and Allan Gilbert entered in Vol. 1, no. 2. Frederic I. Carpenter, Napier Wilt, Merle Curti, and Grant C. Knight in Vol. 1, no. 3; Clarence Faust, Granville Hicks, and Robert Morss Lovett in Vol. 1, no. 4; Walter Fuller Taylor, Orians, and Paul Shorey in Vol. 2, no. 1.

Who, among the founders of the profession, was missing? On the other hand, if the reader belongs to the profession and does not know those present, she or he probably does not know enough. With very few notable exceptions, the movers and shakers of the profession have since the beginning joined in cooperating to create and sustain the journal.

The foregoing facts lend a special distinction to the best articles in *American Literature*. They represent the many, often tumultuous winds of doctrine which have blown from the beginnings through the years of the decade next to last in this century. Those articles often became the firm footings upon which present structures of understanding rest. Looking backward, one finds that the argonauts were doughty. Though we know a great deal more than they, they are a great deal of what we know. Typically, the old best authors wrote well—better than most of us. Conceptually, even ideologically, we still wrestle with ideas they created. And every now and again one finds of course that certain of the latest work has reinvented the wheel one time more. Every now and again one finds a sunburst idea which present scholarship has forgotten. Then it appears that we have receded into mist or darkness by comparison.

Historical change, not always for the better, also shows itself in methods (and their implied theories) of how to present evidence, structure an argument, craft a scholarly article. The old masters were far from agreed—much to the contrary—about these matters.

But they are worth knowing in their own variety as well as in their instructive differences from us.

On the other hand, the majority of *American Literature*'s authors of the best remain among us, working, teaching, writing. One testimony to the quality of their masterliness is the frequency with which the journal gets requests from the makers of textbooks or collections of commentary to reprint from its pages. Now the opportunity presents itself to select without concern for permissions fees what seems the best about a number of authors and topics from the whole sweep of *American Literature*.

The fundamental reason for this series, in other words, lies in the intrinsic, enduring value of articles that have appeared in *American Literature* since 1929. The compilers, with humility, have accepted the challenge of choosing the best from well over a thousand articles and notes. By "best" is meant original yet sound, interesting, and useful for the study and teaching of an author, intellectual movement, motif, or genre.

The articles chosen for each volume of this series are given simply in the order of their first publication, thus speaking for themselves and entirely making their own points rather than serving the compilers' view of literary or philosophical or historical patterns. Happily, a chronological order has the virtues of displaying both the development of insight into a particular author, text, or motif and the shifts of scholarly and critical emphasis since 1929. But comparisons or trend-watching or a genetic approach should not blur the individual excellence of the articles reprinted. Each has opened a fresh line of inquiry, established a major perspective on a familiar problem, or settled a question that had bedeviled the experts. The compilers aim neither to demonstrate nor undermine any orthodoxy, still less to justify a preference for research over explication, for instance. In the original and still current subtitle, *American Literature* honors literary history and criticism equally—along with bibliography. To the compilers this series does demonstrate that any worthwhile author or text or problem can generate a variety of challenging perspectives. Collectively, the articles in its volumes have helped to raise contemporary standards of scholarship and criticism.

This series is planned to serve as a live resource, not as a homage to once vibrant but petrifying achievements in the past. For several sound reasons, its volumes prove to be weighted toward the more recent articles, but none of those reasons includes a presumed superiority of insight or of guiding doctrine among the most recent generations. Some of the older articles could benefit now from a minor revision, but the compilers have decided to reprint all of them exactly as they first appeared. In their time they met fully the standards of first-class research and judgment. Today's scholar and critic, their fortunate heir, should hope that rising generations will esteem his or her work so highly.

Many of the articles published in *American Literature* have actually come (and continue to come) from younger, even new members of the profession. Because many of those authors climb on to prominence in the field, the fact is worth emphasizing. Brief notes on the contributors in the volumes of their series may help readers to discover other biographical or cultural patterns.

Edwin H. Cady
Louis J. Budd

On Dickinson

Early Criticism of Emily Dickinson

Anna Mary Wells

I

WHEN Emily Dickinson appeared upon the literary horizon in this decade, she was greeted as a discovery of twentieth century critics. The revelation of an overlooked genius is always a pleasure, since it reveals not only the excellence of our own taste but also the obtuseness of someone else. And it is a source of particularly solid satisfaction to a modern critic to discover a mistake or an oversight on the part of our Victorian literary grandparents. Therefore, when in 1924 Conrad Aiken called hers "perhaps the finest poetry by a woman in the English language,"[1] the book reviewers, at least, were inclined to overlook the fact that William Dean Howells had spoken similarly of it in 1891:

If nothing else had come out of our life but this strange poetry, we should feel that in the work of Emily Dickinson, America, or New England rather, had made a distinctive addition to the literature of the world, and could not be left out of any record of it. This poetry is as characteristic of our life as our business enterprise, our political turmoil, our demagogism or our millionaires.[2]

It is not difficult to understand why this should be. The attitude of most of Emily Dickinson's poetry is closer to what we choose to call modern than to the general conception of what people were thinking in the eighteen-nineties. The flippancy of many of the religious poems, the epigrammatic brevity of all, and the unexpected mingling of sardonic wit with sentiment find numerous parallels in the work of our contemporary poets.

> Heavenly Father, take to Thee
> The supreme iniquity
> Fashioned by thy candid hand
> In a moment contraband.
>
> Though to trust us seems to us
> More respectful, we are dust.

[1] Conrad Aiken, "Emily Dickinson," *The London Bookman*, LXVII, 8 (October, 1924).
[2] W. D. Howells, "Poems by Emily Dickinson," *Harper's Magazine*, LXXXII, 318.

We apologize to thee
For thine own duplicity.[3]

The idea of this poem is not unique in the literature of the century; it suggests Mark Twain's *The Mysterious Stranger*. Emily Dickinson was not an iconoclast, nor, so far as her thinking went, was she solitary, although her poetry was not of the type popularly associated with the years between 1830 and 1886 when she lived.

II

The outline of her life story is widely known, partly because it is one which offers scope for a good deal of romantic speculation. Daughter of a New England family long connected with Amherst college, she lived all her life in Amherst, the last thirty years in a seclusion which the village, and later the world, regarded as mysterious. None of the many explanations which have been offered for this have been accepted as entirely satisfactory.[4] In her teens and early twenties she left the town a few times: for a year at South Hadley Female Seminary, for visits in Boston or concerts in Northampton, and once for a winter in Washington and Philadelphia, where she was reported to have had a tragic love affair.[5] She lived

[3] Emily Dickinson, *Complete Poems of Emily Dickinson* (Boston: Little, Brown and Co., 1924), p. 298.

[4] In addition to the explanation in the official biography mentioned below, we have the statement of Mrs. M. L. Todd in the introduction to *Poems of Emily Dickinson,* Second Series (Boston: Roberts Brothers, 1892), that she "lived in seclusion from no love disappointment," but that her way of life was "the normal blossoming of a nature introspective to the last degree." Mrs. Todd was a personal friend of Emily Dickinson, but it is of course possible that she was not informed of all the facts in the poet's life. Colonel T. W. Higginson, in his paper on Emily Dickinson published in *Carlyle's Laugh,* admits that she puzzled him, and quotes her as having said when he asked her whether she ever felt the want of company or employment, "I never thought of conceiving that I could ever have the slightest approach to such a want in all future time." A Mrs. T. A. Eliot, in a somewhat rambling article of personal reminiscences published in the Sunday *Oregonian* (Portland, Oregon), on March 19, 1899, states that the Dickinson family were noted for eccentricities, and implies that Miss Dickinson may have been mildly insane. Other articles of personal reminiscence offer variations of the official love story. (Cf. "Reminiscences of Emily Dickinson," by C. B. Green in *The Bookman* for November, 1924, and "Emily Dickinson," by L. F. Abbott, an Amherst undergraduate from 1877 to 1881, in *The Outlook,* CXL, 211-213.) Jean Catel attempted a psychoanalytical analysis of the situation in an article entitled "Essai d'analyse psychologique" in *The Revue Anglo-Americaine* for October, 1924 (II, 394), but ended by admitting that the biographical material was insufficient. *"On devine qu'une pieuse et regrettable reticence nous voile l'essentiel."* Conrad Aiken's suggestion, which seems to me rather penetrating, is that her early life gave her so little intellectual companionship worthy of her that she turned in upon herself, and that later she enjoyed being an enigma and deliberately exaggerated her effects. (Conrad Aiken, "Emily Dickinson," *The Dial,* LXXVI, 301-308.)

[5] Martha Dickinson Bianchi, *Life and Letters of Emily Dickinson* (Boston and New York: The Houghton Mifflin Co., 1924).

on this continent in company with Emerson, Thoreau, Poe, Hawthorne, Longfellow, Lowell, Whittier, Whitman, and Melville, and
into the time when these were succeeded by Henry James, Howells,
Mark Twain, and Bret Harte. Transcendentalism was in its most
flourishing period during the decade in which she was growing to
maturity. As Conrad Aiken has pointed out,[6] *Moby Dick, The Scarlet Letter,* and *Leaves of Grass* were all published during her early
maturity. But the probabilities are that she never saw any of the
three except *The Scarlet Letter.* She wrote once to a friend who inquired about her reading: "You speak of Mr. Whitman. I never read
his book, but was told it was disgraceful."[7] On another occasion she
wrote to Colonel Higginson, who had inquired what she liked: "He
[her father] buys me many books, but begs me not to read them because he fears they joggle the mind."[8]

What other people were writing during her own time, then, had
comparatively little effect on her, although she seems to have absorbed something of the spirit of Transcendentalism. Her taste,
formed by what opportunities she had for reading, was more cath-
olic than discriminating.[9] *Dream Days* by Ik Marvel was one of her
favorite contemporary books. During a vacation from the South
Hadley Female Seminary she wrote that she had been reading *Evan-
geline, The Princess,* and *The Twins and Heart* by Tupper,[10] and
had liked them all. She admired the poetry and prose of Helen Hunt
Jackson,[11] her personal friend and author of *Ramona* as well as of
that celebrated fifth-reader classic, "October's Bright Blue Weather."
Yet along with these preferences she knew and enjoyed the Brown-
ings, George Eliot, Poe, Hawthorne, Keats, Sir Thomas Browne, the
Bible (particularly the book of Revelation), DeQuincey, Tennyson,
Plato, Dante, the Brontés, Wordsworth, and Dickens, among others
whom she mentions.[12] Of Shakespeare she said, "After Shakespeare

---

[6] Conrad Aiken, "Emily Dickinson," *The Dial,* LXXVI, 301-308.

[7] Bianchi, *op. cit.,* p. 239.

[8] Thomas Wentworth Higginson, "Emily Dickinson" in *The Atlantic Monthly,* LXVIII,
446 (October, 1891). This entire paper was republished in his volume, *Carlyle's Laugh, and
Other Surprises* (Boston: The Houghton Mifflin Co., 1909).

[9] Bianchi, *op. cit.,* p. 82.   [10] *Ibid.,* p. 136.

[11] *Ibid.,* p. 372. In a letter from Emily Dickinson to Helen Hunt Jackson dated March,
1885, the poet praises *Ramona,* which she had just finished reading.

[12] These references occur throughout the letters. For those mentioned here see Bianchi's
Life and Letters of Emily Dickinson, pp. 276, 294, 302, 318, 327, 240, 287, 311. There are
many others.

is any other writer needed?"[13] She quoted from many of these in her letters, particularly from Dickens and Shakespeare. It is hard to understand just what Conrad Aiken meant by the "meagreness of literary allusion"[14] in her letters.

Many attempts have been made to show literary influences in her work. She has been compared most frequently, I suppose, to Blake. But neither in her own time nor in ours have critics seen much relation to others writing at her own time. That may be the reason why one reviewer of the *Collected Poems* in 1924 said, with a blithe disregard for the facts, that her poetry was "first published, thanks to the persistence of a niece," and that her family were "fortunately too unintelligent even of its ultimate value to burn the poetry as the poet had requested, and so the bundle of priceless lyrics, tied up with bits of blue ribbon were allowed to repose in a drawer undisturbed."[15] The same injustice to her family is implied in the subtitle to the volume of poems most recently issued, *Further Poems of Emily Dickinson, Withheld from Publication by Her Sister Lavinia*.[16] The evidence of the early volumes of Miss Dickinson's work indicates that it is to this sister Lavinia that we owe their publication in the 1890's, and that the poems not published at that time were rejected by the editors as inferior to the best rather than withheld from consideration.[17] Another recent reviewer, equally careless of fact, has said, "She never dreamed of her potential pinions."[18]

[13] Bianchi, *op. cit.*, p. 294.   [14] Conrad Aiken, *op. cit.*

[15] J. G. Fletcher, "Woman and Poet," *The Saturday Review of Literature,* I, 77 (August 30, 1924).

[16] Boston: Little, Brown and Company, 1929.

[17] In the introduction to the first series, published by Little, Brown and Company in Boston in 1901 (first published by Roberts Brothers, 1891), Colonel Higginson, co-editor with Mrs. Mabel Loomis Todd, said, "This selection from her poems is published to meet the desire of her personal friends, and especially of her surviving sister." For the second series, referred to in footnote 4, Mrs. Todd wrote the introduction. She said: "Without important exception, her friends have generously placed at the disposal of the Editors any poems they have received from her; and these have given the obvious advantage of comparison among several renderings of the same verse. To what further rigorous pruning her verses would have been subjected had she published them herself we can not know." Finally, in the introduction to the third series, published by Roberts Brothers in 1896, Mrs. Todd said, "The intellectual activity of Emily Dickinson was so great that a large and characteristic choice is still possible among her literary material, and this third volume is put forward in response to the repeated wish of the admirers of her peculiar genius." These three passages seem to me to indicate clearly the coöperation of surviving members of Miss Dickinson's family in this first publication. The last one at least suggests that the editor did not see fit to publish all the available material in the third volume.

[18] Mildred Wasson, "Victory Comes Late to Emily Dickinson," *Literary Digest International Book Review,* vol. III, no. 12, p. 780 (November, 1925).

III

This romantic and popular account of the survival of neglected manuscripts has little if any basis in fact. The family of Emily Dickinson seems to have joined with her friends in urging her to publish her poems while she still lived; visitors considered it a great honor to be allowed to hear some of them read; her sister Lavinia and her sister-in-law Susan treasured every scrap they could find, as did most of the friends to whom she sent verses in letters, and her first volume of poems was published less than five years after her death, largely through the efforts of a man who had admired her work greatly during her lifetime, Colonel Thomas Wentworth Higginson.[19] Helen Hunt Jackson wrote back to Amherst in 1884:

My dear friend—

What portfolios full of verses you must have! It is a cruel wrong to your day and generation that you will not give them light.

If such a thing should happen as that I should outlive you, I wish you would make me your literary legatee and executor. Surely after you are what is called "dead," you will be willing that the poor ghosts you have left behind should be cheered and pleased by your verses, will you not?[20]

Samuel Bowles, editor of the Springfield Republican, called the author of these poems "part angel and part demon."[21] And Emily Dickinson herself, although she consistently refused to publish, had a fair notion of her own rarity. "All men say 'what' to me but I thought it a fashion,"[22] she confided once to Colonel Higginson, and a number of the poems, particularly those in *The Single Hound*, express a sort of intellectual vanity.

[19] The *Life and Letters of Emily Dickinson* is authority for the statement that the poems used to be read to visitors in the Dickinson family. Many letters to Colonel Higginson tell of attempts of various individuals to get Miss Dickinson to publish her poems. Colonel Higginson, in the article cited, quotes two letters asking him to advise her not to publish her poems, so that she may quote him in her refusal. Another letter from her in the same article says, "Two editors of journals came to my father's house this winter and asked me for my mind, and when I asked them 'why' they said I was penurious and they would use it for the world." In a letter to another friend, quoted on p. 281 of the *Life and Letters*, Miss Dickinson said: "Of Miss P. I know but this dear. She wrote me in October, requesting me to aid the world by my chirrup more. Perhaps she stated it as my duty, I don't distinctly remember, and always burn such letters so I cannot obtain it now. I replied declining." This would seem to indicate that such letters were not unusual.

[20] Quoted in the introduction to *Poems of Emily Dickinson*, Second Series.

[21] Bianchi, *op. cit.*, p. 81.

[22] T. W. Higginson, *op. cit.*, p. 449.

IV

Her friendship with Colonel Higginson was one of the most curious in all literary history. In 1862, having admired his articles in *The Atlantic Monthly*, she sent him a note expressing her admiration and a desire for criticism. He was at the time prominent in Boston literary circles, and a friend of many of the most famous writers of the nineteenth century. His account of the effect which her poetry had on him may be found in the *Atlantic* for October, 1891, in the article from which I have already quoted, which was published after Miss Dickinson's death:

> The impression of a wholly new and original genius was as distinct on my mind at the first reading of these four poems as it is now after thirty years of further knowledge.[23]

The four poems, untitled as hers usually were, were those beginning "Safe in their Alabaster Chambers," "The Nearest Dream Recedes Unrealized," "I'll Tell You How the Sun Rose," and "We Play at Paste," which Colonel Higginson singled out for comment.

> We play at paste
> Till qualified for pearl
> Then drop the paste
> And deem ourself a fool.
>
> The shapes, though, were similar,
> And our new hands
> Learned gem tactics
> Practicing sands.

According to the popular view of nineteenth century literary criticism, Colonel Higginson should have said: "Pearl does not rhyme with fool; 'ourself' is a grammatically incorrect form; the first stanza is iambic and the second won't scan." Instead he said: "This comprises in its eight lines a truth so searching that it seems the condensed experience of a long life." It is characteristic of all his criticism of Miss Dickinson to appreciate her insight and her epigrammatic brilliance, although he seems never to have appreciated fully her emotional qualities. He wrote her immediately, commending the

[23] *Ibid.*, p. 445.

poetry, pointing out some of its flaws, and suggesting that she delay to publish until she had written somewhat longer.

> At first I tried a little—a very little—to lead her in the direction of rules and traditions, but I fear it was only perfunctory and she interested me more in her—so to speak—unregenerate condition. I soon abandoned all attempt to guide this extraordinary nature, and simply accepted her confidence, giving as much as I could of what interested her in return.[24]

That Colonel Higginson understated here his own importance in the life of Miss Dickinson is amply testified by her letters to him. They continued to correspond to the end of her life. He sent her books to read, and suggested emendations in her poetry, which she almost never adopted although she called him "teacher" in her letters. Her gratitude to him was tremendous. She said once:

> Of our greatest acts we are ignorant. You are not aware that you saved my life.[25]
> You speak of Pippa Passes. I never heard anyone speak of Pippa Passes before. You see my posture is benighted.[26]

Her attitude toward him was always humble and eager. Her niece, Mrs. Bianchi, suggests that there was a touch of mockery in it;[27] if so, I think it must have been mixed with a good deal of genuine feeling, for she told him many things about herself, her family, and her emotions that add considerably to our meager stock of biographical information. One of the most famous descriptions of her is in a letter to him in answer to one of his containing a request for a photograph. It contains the often-quoted line, "eyes the color of sherry the

---

[24] *Ibid.*, p. 448. [25] *Ibid.*, p. 452. [26] *Ibid.*, p. 448.

[27] Mrs. Bianchi (*op. cit.*, p. 71) says: "It was in 1862 also that her literary philandering with Colonel T. W. Higginson began through a stray note of admiration from her for his article in the Atlantic Monthly on the Procession of the Flowers sent her by Sister Sue. Her family viewed the ensuing correspondence between them as a diverting interlude rather than a serious instruction, for, though she addressed him as Dear Master with an outward show of docile humility she never changed one line to please him. Their relations seem to have remained as a comedy version of Browning's Statue and the Bust." On p. 72 Mrs. Bianchi adds: "His letters to her, and there were many of them, she labelled to be burned upon her death; her chivalry outrunning his publication of her little impulsive notes to him, published with his own comment." The grounds for Mrs. Bianchi's objection to this publication are not clear, since she herself permitted the inclusion of these, along with many more personal letters in the *Life and Letters of Emily Dickinson*.

guest left in the bottom of the glass."[28] Many of her ideas about literature, life, and religion were phrased succinctly for one of the few
persons who she thought could understand them. It was to him that
she said of her family: "They are religious except me, and address
an eclipse every morning whom they call Father."[29] She explained
to him also why she felt as she did about association with people.
"They talk of hallowed things aloud and embarrass my dog."[30] Beyond the approbation of a few chosen friends she shunned any sort
of publicity. Her half humorous contempt for humanity and her
recognition of her own superiority are expressed in a number of
poems.

> I'm nobody. Who are you?
> Are you nobody, too?
> Then, there's a pair of us—don't tell!
> They'd banish us, you know.
>
> How dreary to be somebody!
> How public, like a frog,
> To tell your name the livelong day
> To an admiring bog![31]

She boasted of

> Eternity's disclosure
> To favorites, a few,
> Of the colossal substance
> Of immortality.[32]

The correspondence with Colonel Higginson also throws a good
deal of light on another question which has vexed critics ever since
her work was first published. The argument still continues: did
Emily Dickinson write awkwardly, ungrammatically, and with
faulty rhymes because she was unable to do better, or because her
artistic purpose demanded that she write so? The modern critic tends
toward the belief that every irregularity was conscious and of artistic
purpose. Susan Miles, in *The London Mercury* for February, 1926,

---

[28] Higginson, *op. cit.*, p. 447.   [29] *Ibid.*, p. 446.   [30] *Ibid.*, p. 449.
[31] Emily Dickinson, *Complete Poems*, p. 17.
[32] *Ibid.*, p. 268.

says that the irregularities express a world which does not dovetail properly, and goes on to analyze and classify the near-rhymes into three-quarter rhymes, half-rhymes, and non-rhymes, and to demonstate that in each case the sense of the verse demands exactly as close an approximation to rhyme as the poet chose. I very much doubt whether Emily Dickinson herself ever worked out any system of rhyme approximations. Poetry for her was always connected with emotion rather than cerebration, and her interest in form was only spasmodic. She did speak of it occasionally in answer to suggestions from Colonel Higginson:

> You think my gait spasmodic. I am in danger, sir. You think me uncontrolled. I have no tribunal.
> Are these more orderly? I thank you for the truth.
> When I try to organize, my little force explodes, and leaves me bare and charred.[33]

But when left to herself, her questions were of a different sort. In her first letter to Colonel Higginson she said, "Should you think it breathed, and had you leisure to tell me, I should feel quick gratitude."[34] Again she asked, "Have I told it clear?" and "Are they faithful?"[35] Her explanation of the reason she desired instruction shows the same interest in expressiveness rather than traditional correctness of form:

> An ignorance, not of customs, but if caught with the dawn or the sunset see me, myself the only kangaroo among the beauty, sir, if you please, it afflicts me, and I thought instruction would take it away.[36]

It was only to remove this affliction that she cared for instruction. Her famous definition of poetry shows the same emotional attitude:

> If I read a book, and it makes my whole body so cold no fire can ever warm me, I know that it is poetry. If I feel physically as if the top of my head were taken off, I know that it is poetry. These are the only ways I know. Is there any other way?[37]

I think that unless we refuse to believe she was sincere in this, we cannot believe she had a reasoned technique. She did have, however, what Colonel Higginson called "an ear which had its own tenacious

---

[33] Higginson, *op. cit.*, pp. 447, 448.
[34] *Ibid.*, p. 445.
[35] *Ibid.*, p. 446.
[36] *Ibid.*, p. 448.
[37] *Ibid.*, p. 453.

fastidiousness."[38] She did not undervalue her taste. She worked for simplicity, clarity, precision. Her refinement led frequently to obscurity, but it was always the obscurity of extreme condensation, not that of a hazy idea.

In 1886 she died, leaving neither a literary executor nor any instructions about the disposition of her poetry. Five years later Colonel Higginson and Mrs. Mabel Loomis Todd, an Amherst friend, jointly edited a selection from her poems. Neither of them expected that Emily Dickinson would ever have a large audience; they published the volume for the sake of the few who might care for it. While they were working on it, Colonel Higginson wrote to Mrs. Todd:

> You are the only person who can feel as I do about the extraordinary thing we have done in recording this rare genius. I feel as if we had climbed to a cloud, pulled it away and revealed a new star behind it.[39]

No one was more surprised than the editors when the volume ran through six editions in six months. The interest in the bizarre which characterized the nineties may in part have accounted for some of this; the criticism appearing in various periodicals suggests other reasons for its popularity. Almost all of such criticism used as its starting point Colonel Higginson's modest but unapologetic introduction:

> Such poetry must inevitably forfeit whatever advantage lies in the discipline of public criticism and the enforced conformity to accepted ways. On the other hand, it may often gain something through the habit of freedom and the unconventional utterance of daring thoughts.[40]

Two sentences in particular from this article have been quoted many times in discussions of Miss Dickinson's work:

> Her verses are like poetry pulled up by the roots, with rain, dew and earth still clinging, giving a freshness and fragrance not otherwise to be conveyed.
>
> When a thought takes one's breath away, a lesson in grammar seems an impertinence.

The introduction closed with a quotation from John Ruskin: "No

---

[38] Introduction to *Poems of Emily Dickinson*, First Series.
[39] Mary T. Higginson, *Thomas Wentworth Higginson: The Story of His Life* (1914), p. 368.
[40] Introduction to *Poems of Emily Dickinson*, First Series.

weight nor mass nor beauty of execution can outweigh one grain or fragment of thought."

One of the surprising things about nineteenth century criticism of Miss Dickinson is this insistence on the intellectual content of her verse rather than its melody. In spite of frequent irregularities, many of the poems linger in the memory for almost no other reason than that they slip off the tongue as simply and melodiously as nursery rhymes.

V

The publication of this volume called forth a number of magazine articles. Poole's *Index* lists eleven about the work of Miss Dickinson before 1900, and there were numerous newspaper reviews in addition to these. William Dean Howells, Thomas Bailey Aldrich, and Bliss Carman were among the prominent men who wrote of her work. Howells gave it praise almost as unstinted as Colonel Higginson's. One of his statements about it I have already noted.[41] He said also: "She could not have made such poetry without knowing its rarity, its singular worth. No doubt it was a radiant happiness in the twilight of her hidden, silent life."[42] Howells also made an attempt, as many modern critics have, to relate the abnormality of her life to her poetry:

There is no hint of what turned her life in upon itself, and probably this was its natural evolution or involution from tendencies inherent in the New England or the Puritan spirit. The experience of a New England college town has brought more knowledge of death than of life. The Puritan longing for sincerity, for veracious conduct, which in some good New England women's natures is almost a shriek is apparent in her.

Here he quotes in substantiation:

> I like a look of agony
> Because I know 'tis true,
> Men do not sham convulsions,
> Nor simulate a throe.[43]

Conrad Aiken, some thirty years later, finds in the same stanza evidence of a "morbid passion."[44] To Howells this emotional abnor-

---

[41] See p. 243.   [42] Howells, *op. cit.*
[43] *Complete Poems of Emily Dickinson*, p. 186.
[44] Conrad Aiken, "Emily Dickinson," *The Dial*, LXXVI, 301-308.

mality seemed to explain the strangeness of form: "The soul of an abrupt, exalted New England woman speaks in such brokenness." Yet his final conclusion was that the New England of her heredity and her environment could not explain her. He summed up the idea with a quotation from Whistler:

There never was an artistic period. There never was an art loving nation. But there were moments, and there were persons, to whom art was dear, and Emily Dickinson was one of these persons, one of these moments in a national life, and she could as well happen in Amherst, Massachusetts as in Athens, Attica.[45]

But the chorus of praise was not universal. Thomas Bailey Aldrich in an article in the Contributor's Column of *The Atlantic Monthly,* later reprinted as one of the *Ponkapog Papers,* set earnestly to the task of correcting the taste which could find anything admirable in work which was faulty grammatically. He could find no excuse for her "impossible rhyme, involved significance, and incoherence and shapelessness."[46] He showed that by a very slight rearrangement of her verse a rhyme could often be secured. One stanza originally ran thus:

> I taste a liquor never brewed,
> From tankards scooped in pearl;
> Not all the vats upon the Rhine
> Yield such an alcohol.[47]

Aldrich suggested this emendation:

> I taste a liquor never brewed
> In vats upon the Rhine:
> No tankards scooped in pearl could yield
> An alcohol like mine.

This certainly has the advantage of an impeccable rhyme, and the ease with which it could have been secured makes its absence a sharp annoyance to the critic. It seems to me that the very ease with which this stanza, and many other similar ones, can be changed to a con-

---

[45] Howells, *op. cit.*

[46] *The Atlantic Monthly,* LXIX, 143 (January, 1892). This is an unsigned article in the Contributor's Column; the fact that it is incorporated in the paper on Emily Dickinson in *Ponkapog Papers* indicates that it is the work of Aldrich.

[47] *Complete Poems of Emily Dickinson,* p. 14.

ventional form shows that Miss Dickinson did not really want to achieve regularity of form. Susan Miles, in the article[48] aleady mentioned, chose fifteen or twenty such stanzas, altered them as Aldrich did in this one, and attempted to show that in each case the regular version was less effective than the original irregular one. Aldrich continued:

If she had mastered the rudiments of grammar and gone into metrical training for about fifteen years, she might have been an admirable lyric poet of the second magnitude. Pulling up by the roots is a very poor way to treat either flowers or poetry. An eccentric, dreamy, half-educated recluse in a New England village cannot, with impunity, set at defiance the laws of gravitation and grammar. If Miss Dickinson's disjecta membra are poems, Shakespeare is a prolonged imposition, and Tennyson is an error.

This grouping of Tennyson and Shakespeare is interesting. A single concluding line reveals more specifically Aldrich's standard: "An ungrammatical thought does not, as a rule, take one's breath away."

An article in *The Boston Transcript,* evidently printed soon after this time, reprints much of Aldrich's article and reveals incidentally how great the interest in Miss Dickinson's poetry was.

The Atlantic Monthly is, if not the last, almost the last, of our periodicals that care enough for literature, pure and simple, to criticise it without fear and without favor, and without regard to the fads of the time—Browningese, Ibsenese, or, to come to the latest, Dickinsonese, which is now a mild epidemic in New England. Miss Dickinson was a Massachusetts woman whose life was passed in reading and writing—in reading earnest, profound books which she was unable to digest, and in writing what she mistook for poetry, and what to the irreverent mind sounds like the worst parts of Emerson and Blake.[49]

The fact that comparison of Emily Dickinson's fame with that of Browning and Ibsen was not considered out of proportion is another interesting commentary on her position in the literary con-

[48] Susan Miles, "The Irregularities of Emily Dickinson," *The London Mercury,* February, 1926.

[49] This quotation is from an undated, unsigned clipping headed *Boston Transcript* in the possession of the Jones Library, Amherst. The custodian has very generously given me access to the library's collection of material about Miss Dickinson. The fact that this clipping comments on an article appearing in the *Atlantic* for January, 1892, indicates that it was published soon after that time.

sciousness of the 1890's. In any case the "mild epidemic" endured long enough to justify the printing of two more volumes of poems, the Second and the Third Series, and the issuing of a volume of letters. The Third Series was not published until 1896, and was edited by Mrs. Todd alone. The joint editorship continued through the second volume, but this time Mrs. Todd wrote the introduction. The phrasing of some parts shows a remarkable similarity to the editorials in *Poetry: A Magazine of Verse* appearing some twenty years later.

> Her verses all show a strange cadence of inner rhythmical music. Lines are always daringly constructed, and the thought-rhyme appears frequently—appealing, indeed, to an unrecognized sense more elusive than hearing.[50]

An unsigned review of the volume of letters in *The Nation* for December, 1894, epitomized the two attitudes toward her which even now divide critics. The reviewer asked whether "these letters are a precious legacy of genius for which we have to thank the scrupulous industry of Mrs. Todd and the generosity of Miss Lavinia Dickinson," or the "abnormal expression of a woman abnormal almost to the point of disease." The answer, he says, "involves an endless controversy about standards of taste."

A review of the letters and poetry by Ella Gilbert Ives in *The Boston Transcript* summarized the attitude of the literary world toward Emily Dickinson in the first decade after her death:

> Those who cling to the old order and regard perfect form as essential to greatness have had their fling at her eccentricities, her blemishes, her crudities; they place her with the purveyors of raw materials to the artistic producers of the race. They deny her rank with the producers of permanent beauty and value. Others such as hail a Wagner, a Whitman, or a Turner as an originator of new types, and a contributor of fresh streams of life blood to art or literature accept Emily Dickinson as another proof of nature's fecundity, versatility, and daring.[51]

In 1896 Bliss Carman said of her:

> The conviction remains that Emily Dickson's contribution to English poetry (or American poetry if you prefer to say so) is by far the most important made by any woman west of the Atlantic. It is so by reason of

---

[50] *Poems of Emily Dickinson*, Second Series (Boston: Roberts Brothers, 1892).

[51] Undated clipping in the collection of the Jones Library.

its thought, its piquancy, its untarnished expression. She borrowed from no one; she was never common place, always imaginative and stimulating, and finally the region of her brooding was that sequestered domain where our profoundest convictions have their origin, and whence we trace the Puritan strain within us.[52]

This suggestion that Emily Dickinson should be classified as a Puritan, frequently reiterated since, is particularly interesting in view of her frankly avowed attitude toward the religion in which she was brought up. Bliss Carman defined what he meant thus:

For this New England woman was a type of her race. A life-long recluse, musing on the mysteries of life and death, she had that stability of character, that strong sanity of mind, which could hold out against the perils of seclusion, unshaken by solitude, undethroned by doubt. It would never, I feel sure, occur to anyone with the least insight into the New England conscience (with its capacity for abstemiousness, its instinct for being always aloof and restrained rather than social and blithe) to think of Emily Dickinson as peculiar or her mode of life as queer.

VI

Until 1900, then, discussion of Emily Dickinson in the magazines was fairly plentiful. It was after the turn of the century that for fifteen years she became almost as obscure as she had been during her life. Stedman's *An American Anthology*[53] represented her by twenty short verses. After that most histories of American literature ignored her altogether or added her name in an appendix. George Willis Cooke issued a volume called *Poets of Transcendentalism*[54] in 1903 with no mention of her. It has many poems which show interesting resemblances to hers. Her obscurity, her strange metrics, and her passionate individualism find parallels in it; and her simplicity and sincerity emerge in contrast to it.

In 1914 Emily Dickinson's niece, Martha Dickinson Bianchi, published a fourth volume of poems entitled *The Single Hound*,[55] made up largely of little personal verses sent to her sister-in-law or found in

[52] Undated clipping from unnamed paper in the collection of the Jones Library. The name of Bliss Carman is signed.

[53] E. C. Stedman, *An American Anthology* (1900), pp. 320-322.

[54] G. W. Cooke, *Poets of Transcendentalism* (1903).

[55] Emily Dickinson, *The Single Hound*, ed. by M. D. Bianchi (Boston: Little, Brown and Co., 1914).

letters to other friends. The renaissance of interest in American poetry which was in its first flush at that time made the welcome of these poems sure. It was the fifteen years of obscurity between 1900 and 1915 that led to the popular misconception that no one before our own generation had appreciated Emily Dickinson. The complete lapse of her reputation during this period is indicated in a brief article in *The Forum* for March, 1912, called "Three Forgotten Poetesses." This lumps her with Amy Levy and Emma Lazarus, with the patronizing assurance that all three "poetesses" had much matter worth reading. Of the criticism one sentence is sufficiently typical: "Thought is what one finds from the top to the bottom of every page."

Mrs. Bianchi's book, like the earlier ones, included a biographical and critical preface. This added very little to existing information about Miss Dickinson. It was an appreciation rather than a criticism. "She scintillated with star-dust," and "apocrypha and apocalypse met in her" are fairly typical comments from it.

From the time of the publication of *The Single Hound* (1914), interest in Emily Dickinson grew steadily until in 1924 it was great enough to justify the publication of a volume of collected poems, including all that had been published in the 1890's as well as the contents of *The Single Hound*. The title of this volume, *Complete Poems of Emily Dickinson*, made the appearance in 1929 of *Further Poems of Emily Dickinson*[56] a surprise. The introduction to this last volume does not make clear where the poems it contains have been during the past forty years, although the subtitle places the responsibility on Miss Lavinia Dickinson. No information as to the discovery of long-hidden manuscripts is included. These volumes have achieved a greater popularity than Miss Dickinson herself or Colonel Higginson would ever have considered possible. Histories of American literature give her from a page to a chapter; most anthologies include her, and a number of important critics have written about her. Gamaliel Bradford included her in his *Portraits of American Women* in 1919. Herbert Gorman gave her a chapter in his *Procession of Masks* published in 1923, and Clement Wood a chapter in his *Poets of America* in 1925. To trace the history of criticism of her work after 1915 in any detail would call for a good deal longer paper than this one.

[56] Boston: Little, Brown and Co., 1929.

Her permanent place in American literature has certainly not yet been assigned. One reviewer of the *Complete Poems*[57] suggests that we are still in a period of too great upheaval in the matter of poetic technique to form any permanent judgment. Whatever her final place, whether these poems are "a few showers of sibylline leaves more curious than anything else in our minor poetry"[58] or "the finest poetry by a woman in the English language,"[59] she remains one of the most interesting of our minor poets.

[57] Edward Sapir, "Emily Dickinson, A Primitive," *Poetry: A Magazine of Verse*, XXVI, 97-105.
[58] Katherine Lee Bates, *American Literature* (Chautauqua Press, 1917).
[59] Conrad Aiken. See footnote 1.

Emily Dickinson's Earliest Friend

George F. Whicher

I

IN dealing with the biography of a poet as vividly personal as Emily Dickinson the temptation to make her life fit the pattern suggested by her lyrics is all but irresistible. Small wonder, therefore, that the love and renunciation of which her poems so feelingly speak should be considered central in her experience. But Emily herself, conscious that the transmutation of actual experience into works of art often involves substitutions and intensifications which deprive the product of any assured value as a record of fact, protested that she was not to be identified with the speaker in the first person of her verses. Her warning should not be lightly passed over. A sound treatment of her life will begin by seeking to understand her story as she has literally recorded it in her letters. Not until this has been done shall we be warranted in looking for a connection between her poems and her personal history.

From a careful reading of her own factual statements it is difficult to avoid two leading impressions: first, that not one man, but several men in succession were of great importance to her; and, second, that tenderly as she was attached to them all, the relationship that she demanded of each in turn was not that of lover, but of teacher. Not for nothing was she brought up in a New England college town.

Four men were explicitly recognized by Emily Dickinson as her "tutors." In her second letter to Thomas Wentworth Higginson, who was the fourth and last, she described her relation to the other three in words characteristically charged with pedagogical implications:

I went to school, but in your manner of the phrase had no education. When a little girl, I had a friend who taught me Immortality; but venturing too near, himself, he never returned. Soon after, my tutor died,

and for several years my lexicon was my only companion. Then I found
one more, but he was not contented I be his scholar, so he left the land.[1]

One looks into the two biographical studies published by Emily
Dickinson's niece for an interpretation of this key to the poet's inner
development, but one looks in vain. Two other biographers, Miss
Josephine Pollitt and Miss Genevieve Taggard, have fully recognized
the importance of the passage, but their identifications of the "one
more" who "was not contented I be his scholar" are in flat contra-
diction to each other, and neither will stand the test of critical examination. Both Miss Pollitt and Miss Taggard agree, however, in
regarding Leonard Humphrey, the principal of Amherst Academy
from 1846 to 1848, as one of Emily's acknowledged masters, though
they are uncertain whether to identify him as the "friend who
taught me Immortality" or the "tutor" of her letter. In fact, they
imply that he was both. They assume, moreover, that when in her
later correspondence she referred without naming names to her
"earliest friend" or her "dying tutor," Emily meant Humphrey.
On the basis of these assumptions it has been possible to construct a
considerable romance out of Emily's relation to the young schoolmaster.[2]

Miss Pollitt and Miss Taggard were, of course, right in pointing
out that Emily's mind had been profoundly stimulated by a friendship formed in her later teens, and with the evidence available in
1930 it was natural that they should conclude that Humphrey was
the kindling spirit. What could be learned of his character sup-
ported the inference; he was a promising and pious young man, and
he was in a position to teach Emily. But new evidence has recently
come to light which identifies Emily's earliest friend and mentor
beyond a shadow of doubt, and which justifies the assertion that
Leonard Humphrey, though he held a place in her esteem, was not
her most trusted counselor.

Early in 1854 Emily wrote to the Rev. Edward Everett Hale,
then pastor of the Church of the Unity, Worcester, to ask informa-

[1] M. L. Todd, *Letters of Emily Dickinson* (New York, 1931), p. 273. Hereinafter referred
to as *Letters*.

[2] Josephine Pollitt, *Emily Dickinson, the Human Background of her Poetry* (New York,
1930), pp. 51 ff. Genevieve Taggard, *The Life and Mind of Emily Dickinson* (New York,
1930), pp. 59 ff.

tion about the last moments of a man who was dear to her. Like others brought up in the Puritan faith she held the belief that God's elect, as the solemn moment of death approached, would reveal by hopeful signs their confidence in their soul's eternal welfare. It made a difference that they should be "willing to die." This belief in which she was nurtured, and not sentiment or morbid curiosity, was the reason for Emily's lifelong interest in deathbed details. It was for such evidences of the spiritual state of her friend that she wrote to Hale the following letter of inquiry:[3]

Amherst, Jan. 13th [1854].

Rev. Mr. Hale,—

Pardon the liberty, Sir, which a Stranger takes in addressing you, but I think you may be familiar with the last hours of a Friend, and I therefore transgress a courtesy which, in another circumstance, I should seek to observe. I think, Sir, you were the Pastor of Mr. B. F. Newton, who died sometime since in Worcester, and I have often hoped to know if his last hours were cheerful, and if he was willing to die. Had I his wife's acquaintance, I w'd not trouble you, Sir, but I have never met her, and do not know where she resides, nor have I a friend in Worcester who could satisfy my inquiries. You may think my desire strange, Sir, but the Dead was dear to me, and I would like to know that he sleeps peacefully.

Mr. Newton was with my Father two years, before going to Worcester, in pursuing his studies, and was much in our family. I was then but a child, yet I was old enough to admire the strength, and grace, of an intellect far surpassing my own, and it taught me many lessons, for which I thank it humbly, now that it is gone. Mr. Newton became to me a gentle, yet grave Preceptor, teaching me what to read, what authors to admire, what was most grand or beautiful in nature, and that sublime lesson, a faith in things unseen, and in a life again, nobler and much more blessed.

Of all these things he spoke—he taught me of them all, earnestly, tenderly; and when he went from us, it was as an elder brother, loved indeed very much, and mourned and remembered. During his life in Worcester he often wrote to me, and I replied to his letters. I always asked for his health, and he answered so cheerfully that, while I knew

[3] Listed by Thomas F. Madigan in his catalogue, *The Autograph Album*, I, 50 (Dec., 1933), and there quoted in part. The present owner of the letter has courteously permitted me to examine a photostat. The year of date is added, presumably by Hale. I have regularized the punctuation, but left the capitals as in the original.

he was ill, his death indeed surprised me. He often talked of God, but I do not know certainly if he was his Father in Heaven. Please, Sir, to tell me if he was willing to die, and if you think him at Home. I should love so much to know certainly that he was today in Heaven.

Once more, Sir, please forgive the audacities of a Stranger, and a few lines, Sir, from you, at a convenient hour, will be received with gratitude, most happy to requite you sh'd it have opportunity.

Yours very respectfully,

Emily E. Dickinson

P.S. Please address your reply to Emily E. Dickinson, Amherst, Mass.

In Emily Dickinson's published letters there is no mention of Mr. B. F. Newton of Worcester. His name has only once been linked with hers in any of the books written about her, and that in a purely casual connection presently to be cited. Yet her letter to Hale leaves no doubt of the importance of his influence at the most impressionable period of her life. Moreover, the friend who taught her "a faith in things unseen, and in a life again, nobler and much more blessed," can hardly be other than the "friend who taught me Immortality" of her letter to Higginson. The man to whose early instruction Emily Dickinson so warmly acknowledged her indebtedness should no longer elude the attention of her biographers. I have here brought together such facts about him as I have been able to gather.

II

Benjamin Franklin Newton (March 19, 1821-March 24, 1853), fifth child and elder son of Benjamin Newton, Jr., and Sabra (Titus) Newton, was born in Worcester, Mass., where his family had lived for three generations. On his father's side he was descended from Richard Newton, who came from England about 1638 and settled in Sudbury. His mother was presumably the daughter of Jonah and Sarah (Smith) Titus of Sutton, Mass.[4]

Of his early life and education I have been unable to find any record. His grandfather was a farmer and had been, briefly, a private soldier in the Revolution. Probably his father remained a tiller of the soil. "Benjamin F. Newton was never graduated at

[4] F. P. Rice, *Worcester Births,* etc. (Worcester, Mass., 1894). E. N. Leonard, *Newton Genealogy* (De Pere, Wis., 1915), p. 133.

college." He "came into the profession [of law] mature in years."[5]
It is a fair inference from these statements that he enjoyed few
advantages and had a long struggle to win his professional status.

Newton is not known to have visited Amherst before he became
a law student in the office of Dickinson & Bowdoin, probably in the
autumn of 1847. That was the year when Emily was attending
Mount Holyoke Seminary. She does not mention her father's new
student in the long letter that she wrote to Abiah Strong describing
her Thanksgiving vacation, but he must have taken part in the
merrymakings of those four happy days. One is tempted to see an
allusion to the beginning of their intimacy in a letter written "on a
snowy Sunday morning in 1848" to Susan Gilbert:

> I've found a beautiful new friend and I've told him about dear Susie
> and promised to let him know you so soon as you shall come.[6]

The young men in Edward Dickinson's office were always welcome
at his house, where books and reading often formed a subject of
conversation. Others beside Newton took an interest in the literary
education of the Dickinson girls. Elbridge G. Bowdoin, the junior
member of the firm, was responsible for introducing them to *Jane
Eyre*. Emily told Higginson in 1870 that when she and Lavinia
were "little things in short dresses" one of her father's students had
expressed surprise that they were unacquainted with the works of
Lydia Maria Child; he "used to bring them books and hide in a
bush by the door."[7] This student may have been Newton or another. We have Emily's word, however, that of all the young men
who frequented the Dickinson house—cousins, law-students, class-
mates of her brother, and tutors from the college—Ben Newton
became particularly dear to her. He was the guide of her taste and
the awakener of her mind. The quality of his influence can be
gauged by the fact that he gave her in 1849, perhaps as a parting

[5] *Addresses before the Members of the Bar of Worcester County* (Worcester, Mass.,
1879), pp. 142 and 206.

[6] M. D. Bianchi, *Emily Dickinson Face to Face* (Boston, 1932), p. 179. I assume that
this letter was written late in January or early in February when Emily was at home between terms. If it refers to Newton, it could hardly have been written as late as December,
for by that time Susan Gilbert would undoubtedly have met him.

[7] *Letters*, pp. 136 and 287. In later life Emily habitually spoke of her first twenty-five
years as her "little girl" hood; Higginson's imagination may have added the short dresses.

gift, a copy of Emerson's *Poems*.[8] This would indicate a considerable advance from the novels of Mrs. Child.

In the winter of 1849-1850 Newton returned to Worcester to complete his legal studies in the office of Benjamin F. Thomas, a grandson of Isaiah Thomas and an extremely successful lawyer, who had recently resigned as Judge of Probate to enter upon "a large and for those days lucrative practice." In the course of the year Judge Thomas's student was admitted to the bar and set up for himself.[9]

His next move appears difficult to explain. On June 4, 1851, B. F. Newton, Esq., of Worcester was married to Miss Sarah Warner Rugg "of Boston." The marriage took place in Fitchburg, and the bride, one of many daughters of Ephraim and Betsey (Warner) Rugg, was a native of the town of Lancaster, Mass.[10] She was nearly twelve years older than her husband. One would like to know more of the circumstances of this marriage than can be gleaned from genealogies and old newspaper files. Newton was already an ailing man, stricken by tuberculosis. He may have taken in marriage a woman who was willing to nurse him. There were no children. His wife survived him by nearly half a century.

The newly married pair settled in Southbridge Street, Worcester, and Newton, dying by inches, kept on with his legal work. In May, 1852, upon the division of the old Southern District, he was appointed State Attorney for the Middle District (Worcester County).[11] Less than a year later he was dead.

The resolutions adopted by the Worcester County Bar the day following his death show that Newton, in his brief professional career, had won the full confidence and esteem of his colleagues. He was regretted as a man generally beloved.

Resolved, That the members of the Bar . . . have received with deep

[8] Bianchi, *op. cit.*, p. 114.

[9] *Worcester Directory*, 1850 and 1851. W. T. Davis, *Bench and Bar of the Commonwealth of Massachusetts* (Boston, 1895), II, 448. R. Olney, "Memoir of Benjamin F. Thomas, LL.D.," *Mass. Hist. Soc. Proc.,* 2. XVI, 297 (Oct., 1900).

[10] *The Massachusetts Spy*, June 11, 1851. Leonard, *loc. cit.*, refers to a marriage of Benjamin F. Newton "of Providence, R. I." and Sarah M. Newton, intention filed at West Boylston, Oct. 8, 1841; this might conceivably be a first marriage, but is more probably a confusion. E. R. Rugg, *The Descendants of John Rugg* (New York, 1911), p. 196, gives the names correctly, but dates the marriage erroneously in 1853 and describes Newton as "a lawyer of Northboro, Mass."

[11] *Addresses before the Members of the Bar of Worcester County*, p. 206.

sorrow the intelligence of the death of Benjamin F. Newton, Esq., late
District Attorney for the Middle District.

Resolved, That his fidelity and ability in the discharge of official duties,
his legal attainments, and his honorable and manly bearing, gave promise
of professional usefulness and eminence of no common order.

Resolved, That he was endeared to the members of this Bar by his
kindness of heart, his uniform courtesy, and his genuine simplicity of
character, while the cheerful energy with which he persevered in duty,
resisting the wasting progress of a fatal disease, and the calmness with
which he awaited death, commanded our highest respect.[12]

Emily Dickinson, at home in Amherst, must have seen in *The
Springfield Republican* for March 26 the brief announcement of
Newton's death, three sentences which spoke chiefly of an unex-
pired insurance policy.[13] She was not prepared for the blow. Only
a week before he had written her a letter hinting his true condition
so gently that she had not understood, a letter, now like a message
from Eternity, full of confidence in her extraordinary powers and
of earnest hope for her future. As the shadow of her loss darkened
the coming April days, she brooded over the unruly ways of death,
but there was no word in her lexicon to solve that mystery. Earth
could not answer, and after ten months she wrote to the Rev. Mr.
Hale to know if her friend were indeed in Heaven.

III

Leonard Humphrey, for whom so much has been claimed, died
on November 30, 1850; Newton twenty-eight months later. In
sketching her early life for Higginson, in the passage already quoted,
Emily spoke first of a friend who taught her immortality and second of her tutor, in terms that indicated that both men had died,
one shortly after the other. If we assume that Emily was thinking
of the actual sequence of their deaths, then Humphrey would be the
friend and Newton the tutor. But the language of her letter to Hale
so strongly associates Newton with lessons in immortality that it is

---

[12] *The Worcester Palladium,* March 30, 1853.

[13] She may not have seen it at once. Her letter to Austin of March 27 (*Letters,* p. 109;
there mistakenly dated March 28) is full of fun and high spirits; it is not the kind of letter
that she could have written immediately after hearing of a dear friend's death. Compare
the striking change of tone in the two letters that follow (April 16 and May 17), particularly in the latter.

not easy to accept any such conclusion. I suggest for what it may
be worth a different reading. As Emily, in 1862, recalled the events
of twelve years before, she probably thought first of her *parting*
with Newton, a separation made doubly poignant to her by his
death three years later. "When he went from us," she had written,
"it was as an elder brother, loved indeed very much, and mourned
and remembered." Then hardly a twelvemonth after Newton's
departure came the shock of Humphrey's sudden death, a shock
felt by the whole community; and Emily, who "always loved her
teachers," shared the general sorrow. But her own deep personal
grief, the parting so heartrending in its finality, stood foremost in
her recollection, so that when she wrote to Higginson, years later,
the chronology she followed was not the public one of death, but
the private calendar of her losses. This led her to speak first, and
as though he had died first, of the friend who taught her immortality (Newton), and then to add that her tutor (Humphrey) died
"soon after," meaning soon after that friend's departure. This explanation will, I think, commend itself the more it is pondered.

There remain two other passages in the letters to Higginson
which have been taken as references to Humphrey. These must
next be scanned.

My dying tutor told me that he would like to live till I had been a
poet, but Death was much of mob as I could master then. (June 7,
1862).

My earliest friend wrote me the week before he died, "If I live, I
will go to Amherst; if I die, I certainly will." (1876).[14]

It will save argument to assume, as Miss Pollitt and Miss Taggard
have assumed, that these two passages refer to a single person, at
once tutor and friend. The question, then, is whether they refer to
Humphrey or to Newton. To answer it we must examine in some
detail the circumstances leading up to the deaths of each.

Humphrey was never a man of robust health, but since his grad-
uation from Amherst in 1846 he had survived two years as principal
of Amherst Academy, a year of study at Andover, and four terms as
a tutor in Amherst College without a breakdown. When he left
Amherst on November 20, 1850, to spend the short interval between

[14] *Letters,* pp. 274 and 301.

the fall and winter terms with his parents, he had no reason to suppose that he would not return. According to an obituary notice he "died very suddenly . . . after an illness of ten hours. . . . He left town on Wednesday of last week, in his usual health. . . ." This account is confirmed by the historian of the college: "suddenly, in the midst of health and activity, he fell in the street—his heart had ceased to beat—'he was not, for God took him'."[15]

Newton, on the other hand, died of a lingering illness and had long known that he was dying. His obituary notice makes it clear that he was active to the end and was busily engaged in winding up his affairs.

He was out on Wednesday, the day previous to his decease, and called on several persons to whom he was indebted. He wished to settle his accounts now, he said, as he did not anticipate a much longer continuance of his life. He spoke calmly of his death; and seemed anxious that this event, so solemn to him, should cause no one any loss or trouble. He died peacefully, calmly, and hopefully at the early age of 32 years.[16]

With these facts in mind let us consider the passage in which Emily speaks of her "earliest friend" and his promise to go to Amherst. Humphrey left Amherst ten days before his death, in his usual health, and expecting as a matter of course shortly to return. According to his niece's recollection, he was "understood to be engaged" to a girl in Amherst who was certainly not Emily Dickinson. Why, then, should he have written to Emily at all within three days of his leaving town, and if he did write, what point could an expression of determination to go to Amherst alive or dead have had as coming from a man who lived there? But substitute Newton for Humphrey and all is clear. He had been away from Amherst for more than three years and was doubtful whether he would live to go there again. What more natural than that, as death closed in on him, he should express a wistful longing to see his friends once more? And finally, as the letter to Hale makes plain, he was in regular correspondence with Emily.

No long argument will be needed to show that the other passage

---

[15] *The Hampshire and Franklin Express,* Dec. 6, 1850; quoted by Taggard, *op. cit.,* p. 81. W. S. Tyler, *History of Amherst College* (Springfield, Mass., 1873), p. 339.
[16] *The Worcester Daily Spy,* March 25, 1853.

quoted is also an allusion to Newton. If Emily had used only the word "tutor," she might have meant Humphrey, but "my dying tutor told me" cannot have referred to a man who was not "dying" until he fell in the street unconscious only a few hours before his death. Newton, however, in deliberately taking leave of this world, would not have neglected to write a letter of farewell to the ardent little friend in Amherst with whom he had earnestly and tenderly spoken of books and nature and things unseen.

"My earliest friend wrote me the week before he died. . . ." "My dying tutor told me. . . ." Are not these equivalent statements, and is it not reasonably sure that both refer to a single momentous letter, the last that Newton ever wrote her? If so, that letter was one of the most decisive in shaping her destiny that Emily ever received, since it confirmed her secret intention of becoming a poet and gave her at the same time her first high moment of recognition. She never forgot that supreme clarification and concentration of her forces. When, much later, the all-powerful Colonel Higginson praised her verses, she thanked him with feeling but remarked: "Your letter gave no drunkenness, because I tasted rum before. Domingo comes but once. . . ."

Ben Newton, therefore, rather than Leonard Humphrey, should be recognized as Emily Dickinson's "earliest friend," the "preceptor" whose strength and grace of intellect stirred her to eager response; but not to the total exclusion of other friends. From her eleventh to her twentieth year Humphrey was a member of the close-knit college community, a fraternity mate of her brother Austin, and presumably a sharer in the picnics and parties, the Shakespeare readings and "Poetry of Motion" meetings of the brilliant group of young people with whom Emily then freely moved. There was an interval, after Newton had gone to Worcester, when she may have looked to the young college tutor for advice. This would explain her inclusion of him in the list of men who contributed to her education. But Humphrey's place is with the lexicon mentioned in the same passage. He was a mechanical accessory, a dim presence beside Newton and the "one more" and Higginson. Only three times in the published correspondence does Emily allude to him by name.[17]

---

[17] *Letters*, pp. 20, 40, and 44.

We have, in 1846, her enthusiastic approval of his appointment as principal of the Academy, and several years later her mention of his having called on her in company with Mary Warner. Finally there is her letter to Abiah on his death, which, because so much has been made of it, deserves a moment's attention.

. . . the hour of evening is sad—it was once my study hour—my master has gone to rest, and the open leaf of the book, and the scholar at school *alone,* make the tears come, and I cannot brush them away; I would not if I could, for they are the only tribute I can pay the departed Humphrey.

You have stood by the grave before . . . but I have never laid my friends there, and forgot that they too must die; this is my first affliction, and indeed 'tis hard to bear it.[18]

Emily is sincere, I think, but in the manner of the very young. If her schoolmaster's death is her "first affliction," it is because she has dutifully labored to make the grief of the village her very own. In life and fact, Emily's relation to her admired young teacher was not closer than Milton's to Edward King; her girlish letter shows her trying with all her might to weep for the local Lycidas. "The departed Humphrey"!

IV

So far, we have been tracing the history of Emily Dickinson's friendship with Newton, and in lesser measure with Humphrey, without reference to her poetry. But we have now reached a point from which certain of her lyrics on the theme of deprivation and loss may have taken flight. Though we cannot hope to demonstrate that this ground affords the only possible basis for these poems, yet as one possible basis, and that the earliest suggested by the events of her life, it deserves careful consideration. Like the first rapture of recognition, the first intensity of sorrow can never be quite equalled a second time.

Her later letters make it evident that Emily was profoundly shaken by successive bereavements that occurred in her family and the circle of her intimate friends. Among the losses that touched her most nearly were those of her aunt Lavinia Norcross (1860),

[18] Emily Dickinson's niece, in *The Life and Letters* (Boston, 1924), omitted this letter as of no "intrinsic importance." This ill-advised attempt to suppress an already published document resulted, of course, in placing a thoroughly misleading emphasis upon it.

Frazer Stearns (killed in action, 1862), Loring Norcross (1863), her father (1874), Samuel Bowles (1878), Dr. Holland (1881), Charles Wadsworth and her mother (1882), her nephew Gilbert (1883), Judge Lord (1884), and Helen Hunt Jackson (1885). This is by no means an exhaustive list, nor were the dead equally dear to her. Frazer Stearns, for example, was more her brother's friend than her own, and Judge Lord her father's. The grief she felt at the deaths of her aunt and uncle Norcross and of Dr. Holland was mingled with tender solicitude for those still more closely affected than herself. But the deaths of her father, and Bowles, and Wadsworth rocked her universe. These deeply personal losses, however, came relatively late in life. Long before they befell her she had known bereavement and the struggle to master the bitter fact of death.

Some memorial poems which can be dated in the early sixties were in all likelihood written with one or another of her "lost" in mind. "When I was small, a woman died" (IV, xxxiii)[19] may well have been a tribute to Frazer Stearns, whose mother had died in 1855; "This was in the white of the year" (IV, cvi), sent to her Norcross cousins in 1865, probably alludes to the death of their father (in January) and of their mother (in April). There are also other poems assignable to this period which refer to no specific loss, but which imply a background of personal sorrow, "that old nail in my breast" of which Emily spoke in a letter of 1863. "They say that 'time assuages'" (IV, lxxxv) was composed before 1866; "Safe in their alabaster chambers" (IV, iv) about 1861. These poems are among the few that can be dated by external evidence. Presumably they were not the only ones written at this time and in the same vein.

Several statements from Emily's letters supply a partial clue to the emotional history implied in the poems of this period, though they do not fully explain it. In March, 1853, on hearing that her brother has been trying his hand at poetry, she wrote gayly to warn him off what she even then considered her particular province:

And Austin is a poet, Austin writes a psalm. . . . Now Brother Pegasus, I'll tell you what it is. I've been in the habit *myself* of writing some few

[19] References are to *Poems*, Centenary Edition; the large and small Roman numerals indicate section and poem.

things, and it rather appears to me that you're getting away my patent, so you'd better be somewhat careful or I'll call the police.[20]

But in 1862, speaking of this same year and of her dying tutor's wish to live to see her a poet, she added: "Death was much of mob as I could master then." Clearly her first poetic activity was interrupted by the death of the man who had fostered it. She did not altogether stop writing, for there are at least twenty poems that can be assigned to the period from 1853 to 1860.[21] But her words seem to mean that she was struggling to grasp the significance of events rather than to express them. When after a time of bewilderment she resumed writing in earnest, in the winter of 1861-1862, it was to afford relief from the keenest suffering of her life. She had then, as her statement to Higginson shows, almost forgotten her earlier efforts or else was unwilling to acknowledge them.

I made no verse, but one or two, until this winter, Sir. I had a terror since September, I could tell to none, and so I sing, as the boy does of the burying ground, because I am afraid.[22]

To understand the state of mind which, in the spring of 1862, colored all her memories and threw her previous experiences of deprivation and the death of friends into high relief, we must attempt to trace at least in part what had happened in the nine years' interval between 1853 and the date of her letter to Higginson.

Shortly after Newton's death Emily had found the "one more" who more than took the place of her first preceptor, the man of whom she was later to speak as "my dearest earthly friend." The details of their relationship are still shrouded in mystery and need not concern us here. But in the spring of 1862 Emily was facing a separation from this friend, a separation which both he and she supposed would be final so far as this life was concerned. He had removed to a distant city. An intimation of his intended departure had, I assume, reached her the previous September, overwhelming her with dread. Once before she had gone through such a parting, and it had been followed by the death of the man whom she held

[20] *Letters*, pp. 109-110.
[21] See "A Chronological Grouping of Some of Emily Dickinson's Poems," by the present writer, *The Colophon*, Part 16 [1934].
[22] *Letters*, p. 273.

dear. Now the inexorable nexus of circumstance seemed to be coiling back upon itself and displaying a similar pattern, even more huge and hopeless to conceive than before. Is it any wonder that her life at such a moment should have appeared to Emily one monstrous fact of loss and God himself "an eclipse"? But she had now means to keep her head above disaster. "I sing, as the boy does of the burying ground, because I am afraid."

Here are all the elements needed to supply the background for one of her best known poems, "My life closed twice before its close" (I, xcvi). I do not know when this poem was written. There were other occasions when Emily had a double grief to mourn. But every word is comprehensible if read as an expression of her mood in the spring of 1862. She had then known the anguish of two momentous partings, one with Newton, who had died, and one still more recent and painful with Newton's successor, who she believed was going away to die. The tender concern that she had felt to know if her first friend were in Heaven, the sharp torment of apprehension and realization of a second and greater loss—these two facts lay side by side in her consciousness like two figures on a tomb. Was she not discriminating one from the other with a fine inward perception when she wrote the concluding lines?

> Parting is all we know of heaven,
> And all we need of hell.

In another and even better known lyric she returned to the same theme, but with a difference. This time she speaks of two bereavements by death, and of a third loss which may or may not be of the same kind.

> I never lost as much but twice,
> And that was in the sod.[23]

The ambiguity occurs in the second line, which may be read: "And that [also] was in the sod," or: "And that was in the sod, [this is not]." If we accept the second reading, then Newton's death may be one of the two losses mentioned in the first line, and the parting with her dearest earthly friend the loss which was not "in the sod."[24]

[23] *Poems* (IV, xl), p. 174.
[24] Miss Pollitt, *op. cit.*, p. 297, suggests that this poem may have been written after Wadsworth's death. But by 1882 the roll of Emily's "lost" was not confined to three.

What other name would Emily have joined with Newton's? I can only suggest Humphrey's, whose memory was linked in time with the days when she had known her earliest friend and whose death she had in her inexperience of grief called an affliction. But now in the light reflected upon the past by her supreme disaster every previous loss was magnified and accentuated. Newton, who taught her immortality, had ventured too near; Humphrey, who might have taken Newton's place, had died; and now the "one more," not content that she be his scholar, had "left the land," expecting never to return. Was it a conspiracy of "the redoubtable God"? Or would God relent?

> Burglar, banker, father,
> I am poor once more!

sighed Emily—and wrote to Colonel Higginson, whom she did not know, to ask if he would become her instructor. And once more the banker member of her Trinity saw to it that her draft was honored.

The Conscious Self in Emily Dickinson's Poetry
Charles R. Anderson

THERE ARE a number of poems by Emily Dickinson exploring the nature of the mind and the consciousness that have a special interest beyond their intrinsic worth. Her purpose in them was not to write philosophical poetry but to identify and define the Self, the "Single Hound" that attends the soul, as a point of view for comprehending experience and an instrument for controlling her art. In a verse-epigram written late in life she set down succinctly her attitude towards pure intellectuality:

> The Mind lives on the Heart
> Like any Parasite–
> If that is full of Meat
> The Mind is fat.
>
> But if the Heart omit
> Emaciate the Wit–
> The Aliment of it
> So absolute. (1355)[1]

The very poem which warns against the barrenness of aphorism is itself aphoristic, almost a verse-game in its gnomic form and the ingenuity of its quintuple play of suspended rhymes echoing from "Heart." She knew the limitations of this genre, yet her ebullient wit continued to release specimens for short flights throughout her life, increasingly in later years as the substantiality of the objective world faded. With a flick of the wrist one can easily catch a hundred of these butterflies in his net, the only question being whether such

[1] The texts of all poems quoted in this article are taken from *The Poems of Emily Dickinson* (Cambridge, Mass., 1955), 3 vols., edited by Thomas H. Johnson and published by the Harvard University Press. The figures in parentheses following each poem refer to the system of numbering there adopted. For poems with more than one version or with variants, I have felt free to choose the reading that seemed best to me, since there is no way to determine what her final choice would have been. (The versions printed first and in larger type by the editor of the Harvard Edition have no real priority but are simply "the earliest fair copy"— see *Poems*, I, lxi.)

Acknowledgement is hereby made to the following for permission to quote: Mrs. M. T. Bingham and Harper & Bros., the Harvard University Press, and Little Brown & Co.

fragile creatures deserve to be mounted even in a complete cabinet of her beauties.

Her precision of thought and her passion for economy in language made all of her utterance tend towards the epigrammatic. The precocious wordplay of her earliest letters had developed by maturity into a style of extraordinary sharpness and surprise. The danger of such a skill is that it leads to the sententious, and the letters of her last years are often that or downright cryptic. In part this may be because they are more nearly detached pieces of "conversation" than letters, as her withdrawal increased and writing became her chief medium of communication; they would probably be readily comprehensible if the modern reader knew the context. But it is also partly because the aphoristic habit finally became a mannerism indulged in for its own sake. At the height of her powers she could compose whole letters in a sequence of epigrams that fascinates by its sustained brilliance, as in the correspondence with her more intellectual friends such as Bowles, Holland, and Higginson.

More interesting to the student of her poetry are the scattered *pensées* pertinent to her great themes, as in the following cluster culled from the letters, her conversation, and some late jottings on slips of manuscript:

A finite life . . . is that peculiar garment that were it optional with us we might decline to wear.

Two things I have lost with Childhood–. . . But is that all I have lost–memory drapes her Lips. . . . Did we not find as we lost we should make but a threadbare exhibition after a few years.

There are those who are shallow intentionally and only profound by accident.

How do most people live without any thoughts. There are many people in the world (you must have noticed them in the street) How do they live. How do they get strength to put on their clothes in the morning.

It is essential to the sanity of mankind that each one should think the other crazy.

To live is so startling, it leaves but little room for other occupations.

So few that live–have life–it seems of quick importance–not one of those—escape by Death. . . . How extraordinary that Life's large Popu-

lation contain so few of power to us–and those–a vivid species–who
leave no mode–like Tyrian Dye.
It is delicate that each Mind is itself, like a distinct Bird–
The Mind is so near itself–it cannot see, distinctly–and I have none to
ask [in a letter requesting criticism of her poems].
I could not weigh myself–Myself–My size felt small–to me–
No dreaming can compare with reality, for Reality itself is a dream from
which but a portion of Mankind have yet waked and part of us is a not
familiar Peninsula–[2]

But Emily Dickinson was no aspirant Pascal, and it would do violence to her distinction as a poet to claim for her the status of a great
thinker.

The real value of these prose aphorisms is to lead into an examination of her aphoristic verse. It is noteworthy that the most memorable of those above are the ones made concrete by metaphor or
simile. So one should discriminate between her occasional attempts
to make poetry out of the wrong materials—the only evidence in
support of the charge that has been made against her of a "fatal
facility for rhyming"—[3] and her real successes in writing a poetry
of ideas, where the thought draws its proper "Aliment" from feeling
and is vividly imaged in things. Most of them, good and bad, take
the form of definitions, as though her Lexicon[4] were inadequate and
she had to compile her own in order to restore words to their true
meanings. Sometimes she slipped into the pitfall of the professional
lexicographer, by defining abstractions exclusively in terms of other
abstractions:

> Expectation– is Contentment–
> Gain– Satiety–
> But Satiety– Conviction
> Of Necessity

[2] The texts of all letters quoted in this article are taken from *The Letters of Emily
Dickinson* (Cambridge, Mass., 1958), 3 vols., edited by Thomas H. Johnson and published
by the Harvard University Press; similarly for the Prose Fragments (PF) printed at the end
of the *Letters*, pp. 911-929. The citations for the above cluster of quotations (in which
paragraph indications are omitted) are as follows: 385, PF 117 and PF 71, PF 113, 342a,
PF 87, 381, 275, 457, 260, 261, PF 2. Hereafter these figures, referring to the Harvard
Edition, are given in parentheses following the quotations.

[3] See Thornton Wilder, "Emily Dickinson," *Atlantic Monthly*, CXC, 43-48 (Nov., 1952).

[4] Webster's *American Dictionary of the English Language* in the enlarged edition of
1847, used occasionally in this article for definitions that differ from modern usage, is cited
simply as her "Lexicon." Referring to the period just prior to her poetic career, she said to
T. W. Higginson: "for several years, my Lexicon–was my only companion" (261).

Of an Austere trait in Pleasure–
Good, without alarm
Is a too established Fortune–
Danger– deepens Sum– (807)

Out of twenty-seven words two-thirds are abstract nouns and adjectives and the rest mere connective tissue, with nothing concrete from the external world as ballast. Dr. Johnson might have admired the ingenuity of her juggled Latinities, but even he would not have mistaken this for a poem. She wrought better than this.

Such an elusive concept as "truth," for example, was central to a poetry like hers founded on the exact conformity of words to thoughts and things. She knew it could never be snared in dictionary definitions, her Webster failing in spite of thirteen attempts, but the poet might be able to image it in action and so reveal some of its attributes. In a letter she once used a domestic figure to weave a number of its qualities into one shining fabric: "truth like Ancestor's Brocades can stand alone" (368). It is rich with gold and silver threads, it is traditional though always a bit old-fashioned to young minds, it can stand alone in the wardrobe but it can also be worn. Again, in a poem written a decade earlier, she turned the conventional idea of eternal verities into a daring conceit:

Truth– is as old as God–
His Twin identity
And will endure as long as He
A Co-Eternity–

And perish on the Day
Himself is borne away
From Mansion of the Universe
A lifeless Deity. (836)

The shock image of the corpse of God gives new life to the identification of truth with all that is meant by existence, both temporal and spatial. It is only a metaphor, to be sure, meaning that neither can die. But this gains new emphasis from its negative counterpart: if truth *were* extinguished all that would remain would be the vast death of the solar systems, the desolate "Mansion" it once inhabited.

Returning from such cosmic flights, she illuminated a homelier aspect of truth for her mercurial sister-in-law next door by enclosing in a letter this remarkable quatrain defining its opposite:

> Candor– my tepid friend–
> Come not to play with me–
> The Myrrhs, and Mochas, of the Mind
> Are it's iniquity– (1537)

This was presumably in reprimand for some overture or retreat on the part of her friend, because it had been couched in terms whose meaning could not be depended on. Emily Dickinson had no use for such "play." The figures she employs are scented exotics from Arabia, one Biblical the other modern, "The Myrrhs and Mochas of the Mind," a new and memorable phrase for the flowers of rhetoric. Remembering her penchant for punning, one is tempted to add that the tongue guilty of such language cannot be cleansed by all the perfumes of Araby. False words are "iniquity," both in the theological sense of wickedness and in the Latin root sense of being "unequal" to the meaning they intend to convey. For a poet the latter is indeed original sin.

Along with truth vital power was the essential value to her, whether for creative purposes or simply for living. "So few that live have life," she had written to a friend, "so few of power." Besides being a recurrent point of reference in her writings, vitality is the main theme of several interesting poems. The contrast between conventional people who fear intoxication and those who drink deep produced a strong new simile for the hackneyed wine of life:

> Between the form of Life and Life
> The difference is as big
> As Liquor at the Lip between
> And Liquor in the Jug
> The latter– excellent to keep–
> But for extatic need
> The corkless is superior–
> I know for I have tried. (1101)

The profusion of rums, juleps, and other symbols of inebriation in her poems is even more striking by reason of their being incorporated within strict hymn meters, which preserve some flavor of the village piety against which their meaning is set in ironic tension. The boast here that she has drunk freely from the jug is her shock tactic for expressing the need to break with orthodoxy, not only the forms of behavior and thought but the conventions of contemporary poetry, if she were to achieve vitality.

The same contrast between small and great capacity for life is made in another pair of images, similar to the limited "little Circuit" of routine lives she had once set against the "new Circumference" of heavenly ecstasy. This time she substitutes for the latter, which she had repeatedly declared unattainable, a fine new metaphor for the slow expansion of the artist:

> Except the smaller size
> No Lives are Round–
> These– hurry to a Sphere–
> And show– and end–
>
> The Larger– slower grow–
> And later hang–
> The Summers of Hesperides
> Are long– (1067)

The first stanza, with its dismissal of ordinary careers that "hurry to a Sphere" then show and end, anticipates the justification by a modern novelist for his exclusive concern with extraordinary lives because conventional ones are round like an egg with no story in them.[5] But her real stroke comes in the figure for herself as a poet, one of the Hesperides, a rare use of Greek mythology in her writings. These maidens, like the Sirens, were possessed of the gift of song, and since they are immortals their "Summers . . . are long" in their enchanted garden on the borders of the western sea. Anthropologists today hold that the delayed process of maturing in man is one of his distinguishing traits, closely related to his unique capacity for creating. She herself was nearly thirty before her poetic career got under way, and this poem was sent in a letter (316) to her chosen literary adviser as a mildly satirical commentary on the slowness of her own development. "Hesperides" also calls to mind the golden apples, the most celebrated fruit guarded by the singing maidens, once given by Earth to the queen of the gods as a symbol of fruitfulness for her marriage. "Grow" and "hang" in the second stanza

[5] Robert Penn Warren in *At Heaven's Gate* (New York, 1943).

justify the equation of this gift with the larger lives that expand slowly to produce their golden fruit. And some discarded lines in another version suggest an identification between a species of New England apples, probably called Hesperides locally, that mature late ("far after Frost") and her own poems. For they are disparagingly praised as "Hugest of Core" though presenting an "awkward Rind," a parody of Higginson's opinion of her productions as both remarkable and grotesque.

Most of the poems on vitality seem to have at least an indirect connection with her creative powers. This dual application to life and art is made explicit in the following aphoristic verses:

> To be alive– is Power–
> Existence– in itself–
> Without a further function–
> Omnipotence– Enough–
>
> To be alive– and Will!
> 'Tis able as a God–
> The Maker– of Ourselves– be what–
> Such being Finitude! (677)

Mere existence is unlimited power, but if in addition one can "Will" he can be a "Maker" like God. This elaborates the paradox she sent in a letter to Higginson: "I thought that being a Poem one's self precluded the writing Poems, but perceive the Mistake" (413). With vital energy and discipline one can both live and be an artist.

The decline of that power was for her the greatest of disasters. As much as she admired Browning, she would never have subscribed to the sentiment voiced in "Rabbi Ben Ezra": grow old along with me, the best is yet to be. Her portrait of old age, on the contrary, is devastating:

> The harm of Years is on him–
> The infamy of Time–
> Depose him like a Fashion
> And give Dominion room.
>
> Forget his Morning Forces–
> The Glory of Decay
> Is a denuded Pageant
> Beside Vitality. (1280)

For the injury that time inflicts she chooses the legal term for no-
torious disgrace, "infamy," since there is no way to keep it from being published abroad. All the euphemisms for old age are brought
under fire—the wise elder who is perhaps quaintly old-fashioned, the
angelic countenance of serenity, the halo of white hair. Instead her
aged man is "deposed" from his mortal power like something obso-
lete to make room for "Dominion." For the former her Lexicon
emphasized the meaning "to dethrone," for the latter a meaning lost
to modern usage, Dominions being, like Thrones and Powers, one
of the orders of angels to which he must now be translated. Such
is the "Glory of Decay," the juxtaposed words making this the shock
line of the poem, for aging is viewed here from the standpoint of
this world. Picking up the figure of a discarded "Fashion" from
the first stanza, the conclusion strips away the last shred of glamor.
In comparison with "Vitality," the spectacle presented by the old is a
"denuded Pageant." There is none of the compassionate humor of
Holmes's "Last Leaf" in this poem. Loss of vital power to her was
tragic.

For the poet, the ebbing of life is of little moment compared to the
ebbing of the *élan vital*. The process sets in long before death, and
in spite of its imperceptible progress the creative artist is almost
neurotically alert to any warning signals. This fascinated apprehension resulted in two remarkable poems, the first of which renders
the workings of atrophy with scientific detachment:

> Crumbling is not an instant's Act
> A fundamental pause
> Delapidation's processes
> Are organized Decays.
>
> 'Tis first a Cobweb on the Soul
> A Cuticle of Dust
> A borer in the Axis
> An Elemental Rust—
>
> Ruin is formal— Devils work
> Consecutive and slow—
> Fail in an instant, no man did
> Slipping— is Crashe's law. (997)

The mode of atrophy is described with sufficient precision in a pair of enclosing phrases, first as "organized Decays." In a healthy organism change is always at work, involving a perfect balance between waste and repair, but when this is upset by an excess of waste the process is called atrophic change. Its progress is "consecutive and slow," just as methodical as the processes that build living tissue, but it results in the gradual decay of vital functioning and with old age it paralyzes the entire body.

The second phrase carries the same scientific meaning but adds a note of controlled horror: "Ruin is formal." It follows a rigidly prescribed order, just as in the great ceremonial occasions of life, but this is "Devils work" that leads to death. With this leap into theology the poem frees itself from anatomical limitations, showing that atrophy was only her metaphor. Satan does not contend with God for man's body but for the spirit that animates it. Her analytic purpose has been that of a poet, not a scientist, all along. Even the central stanza, drawing most explicitly from the language of science, makes no attempt at exact description of cellular atrophy. Instead, it throws up a shower of images drawn from botany and chemistry as well as anatomy to illustrate the effect on vitality of any kind of "Delapidation." It is like the decay of metals through oxidation or the brown blight on growing things, though even more "Elemental." It is the worm in the main stem of a plant or of the spinal column. One's first awareness is of the epidermis hardening to a "Cuticle," or more terrifyingly of a "Cobweb on the Soul," a film settling over the source of creativeness. The poem ends with the same emphasis it began with. The process itself is not "an instant's Act," it is insidious, a creeping paralysis, a crash without a sound. Such is the inexorable law of atrophy, the formulation of which she attributes to Professor "Crashe," by analogy with other great discoveries in science like Ohm's law and Boyle's. Perhaps the pun is too farfetched, but it brings the poem to an ingenious conclusion.

Since the dedicated artist has staked all on the power to create, it is understandable that he should be hypersensitive to its waning and even occasionally give way to irrational fears that it has vanished irrecoverably. But Emily Dickinson's reaction to the terror at such frustration is remarkably different from the "romantic agony" of the

preceding generation.[6] Among the fragmentary notations that have
come down with her manuscripts, one reads: "The consciousness of
subsiding power is too startling to be admitted by men." And another: "Tis a dangerous moment for any one when the meaning goes
out of things and Life stands straight–and punctual–and yet no
signal comes. Yet such moments are. If we survive them they expand us, if we do not, but that is Death, whose if is everlasting."[7]
It is only in this context that the full meaning emerges from an
extraordinary but otherwise obscure poem:

> I've dropped my Brain– My Soul is numb–
> The Veins that used to run
> Stop palsied– 'tis Paralysis
> Done perfecter in stone.
>
> Vitality is Carved and cool.
> My nerve in Marble lies–
> A Breathing Woman
> Yesterday– Endowed with **Paradise.**
>
> Not dumb– I had a sort that moved–
> A Sense that smote and stirred–
> Instincts for Dance– a caper part–
> An Aptitude for Bird–
>
> Who wrought Carrara in me
> And chiselled all my tune
> Were it a Witchcraft– were it Death–
> I've still a chance to strain
>
> To Being, somewhere– Motion– Breath–
> Though Centuries beyond,
> And every limit a Decade–
> I'll shiver, satisfied. (1046)[8]

This poem was written near the end of 1865, her last great creative
year. Between 1859 and 1865 she had composed more than a thousand poems. After that, for the twenty remaining years of life, her

[6] See Mario Praz, *The Romantic Agony* (New York, 1933), for a broad treatment of
this theme, and Edward Davidson, *Poe: A Critical Study* (Cambridge, Mass., 1957), p. 45,
for a specific application of it to an American predecessor.

[7] These quotations are from PF 108 and PF 49, *Letters,* pp. 927 and 919.

[8] In line 4 my reading of the MS is "in," where the Harvard Edition reads "on."

productivity fell off to one-fifth that average.[9] At this turning point she may well have feared that the power to create had died in her, a fate far worse than physical death.

The opening line is a sufficient clue that what follows is all metaphorical. The narrator who says sensationally "I've dropped my Brain" is not describing her literal death, but imaging the final stage of that process of spiritual atrophy which began, in the preceding poem, with a "Cobweb on the Soul." The language of the first stanza spells out the sequence from numbness to palsy to paralysis. In the second this condition of death-in-life is replaced by the imagery of burial as she feels her "Vitality," the veins and nerves of a "Breathing Woman," carved into a marble effigy. Yet just yesterday she had been not only alive but "Endowed with Paradise." The next two stanzas make clear the meaning of this as the capacity to achieve immortality through art. All the phrasing relates to creative power. Her sensibility had responded to the experience of life ("smote and stirred"), she had wit ("a caper part"), capacity for motion and flight ("Instincts for Dance" and "Aptitude for Bird"), but chiefly articulateness ("not dumb").

This cue word for the poet, whose vital power has now atrophied, is picked up again in the climactic lines of the poem: "Who wrought Carrara in me/And chiselled all my *tune?*" Her song has been frozen into the epitaph on the tombstone of a dead poet. Such loss of creativity is more like "Witchcraft" than death. In her prose aphorism she had said of such moments, "If we survive them they expand us, if we do not, but that is Death." The poem does not decide between the actuality of this artistic death and the apprehensive fear of it, both being put conditionally ("Were it . . . were it"), and the conclusion remains somewhat baffling. The best interpretation seems to be that she still has a chance to live again "somewhere," even if her career as a poet is over—"Being," "Motion," and "Breath" in the final stanza echoing the language of artistic vitality in the central part. Since this may only come "Centuries beyond," the reference may be to immortality, but more likely to the immortality of her poems already created. To be alive and have the power to will, she had said in a previously quoted poem, is to be a "Maker"

[9] This graph of her productivity is taken from the "Tabulation of Poems Year by Year," Appendix 3, *Poems*, III, 1200-1201. Though the datings of poems in this edition are admittedly tentative, the overall pattern is presumably reliable.

like God. The loss of this creative vitality now causes her to ex-
claim extravagantly, "I've dropped my Brain." But since it has come
after a certain degree of achievement, the hope that she may live
again vicariously through her art makes her conclude, cryptically,
"I'll shiver, satisfied."

A number of Emily Dickinson's aphoristic verses are concerned
with keeping a proper balance between mind and heart. One of the
chief human defenses against the reality perceived is "hope," compensating for the inadequacy of experience by a faith that all will be
set right. She made several efforts to take its measure, the most
interesting of which follows:

> Hope is a strange invention–
> A Patent of the Heart–
> In unremitting action
> Yet never wearing out–
>
> Of this electric Adjunct
> Not anything is known
> But it's unique momentum
> Embellish all we own– (1392)

Hope does not exist in the nature of things but is a contrivance of
the heart to circumvent reality. To recapture the unity and significance of the scientific imagery running through this poem, one must
remember the state of technological development at the period when
it was written, 1877.

Man's visionary hope of inventing a perpetual motion machine
had been given new impetus by the marvels of recent experiments
in electricity, though the mystery still surrounding that substance is
reflected in her Lexicon's definition: "The subtile agent called the
electric fluid, . . . although we know very little of its nature." Further,
the believers in Galvanism were making fantastic claims about the
power of a newly invented electrical apparatus to restore the *élan
vital.* But by the same period scientists had fully established the
principle of the conservation of energy, which denied the possibility
of perpetual motion, and the medical profession was becoming con-
vinced of the limitations of electrotherapeutics. By skilfully merging the dreams of cultists with the findings of contemporary science,
she forged her definition of hope. It is just such a "strange inven-

tion" as those laying claim to perpetual motion, an "electric Adjunct" patented by the heart. Nothing is really known about it, but its "unique momentum," it is believed, will restore our lives. Yet how much of this pseudoscience can the reason accept? That she intended the unfavorable connotation of "embellish" in the last line, meaning the factitious improvement of appearances, seems indicated by her substitution of "inebriate" in a variant version. The heart, through hope, merely intoxicates the mind.

If her rational part did not trust the heart as a guide, she was also aware of the limitations of the mind as a dependable instrument. It is at best a "flickering identity," she once said. Thinking is not even a continuous process, subject to control, and capable of being worked out into systems. "A Thought went up my mind today–/ That I have had before," one poem began, but she confessed that she did not have the art to say why it came a second time, where it went, "Nor definitely, what it was" (701). Again, she admitted the lack of sequence in her powers of reasoning:

> I felt a Cleaving in my Mind–
> As if my Brain had split–
> I tried to match it– Seam by Seam–
> But could not make them fit.
>
> The thought behind, I tried to join
> Unto the thought before–
> But Sequence ravelled out of reach
> Like Balls– upon a Floor. (937)

Yet she persisted in trying to define all aspects of the human condition, whether emotions or ideas: Suspense, Wonder, Exhilaration, Renunciation, Expectation, Risk, Skepticism, and so on. Her aphorisms seeking to render them comprise some of the final flowers of her wit, but they tend to run off into fantasy or intellectual abstractions, both in prose and in verse.

Emily Dickinson was willing to admit that there are no final answers to the great traditional questions that continue to exercise poets and theologians: What are beauty, truth, goodness, love? And she was content to accept as part of a cosmic process beyond comprehension those questions that were coming more and more to vex modern philosophers and scientists: What is the nature of reality and of the consciousness? In her best poetry, unlike many of her contemporaries, she turned away from the pursuit of absolutes to an exploration of the existential self, something quite different from the subjective lyricism of an earlier generation. "It is delicate that each Mind is itself, like a Distinct Bird," she had written to Higginson (457). She never pretended she could penetrate another self:

> His mind of man, a secret makes
> I meet him with a start
> He carries a circumference
> In which I have no part. . . . (1663)

She was content to let others remain a mystery. The poet's awareness of self is his only reality. Yet she was aware, also, that the mind can never fully comprehend itself. In the darkness of a little bone box scarcely eight inches long subtle processes are going on, such as memory and dream, which will forever remain obscure. But she had confidence in the poet's powers, not to analyze the mind or to arrive at ultimate truths, but to illuminate endlessly the interior life.

The self-behind-the-self is her theme in an unusually interesting group of poems. The fact that she uses "soul," "mind," and "consciousness" almost interchangeably in these explorations should not be charged against her as a sign of confusion, nor should it be allowed to confuse the reader. This proliferation of terms simply reflects the transitional period in which she was writing, when the concerns of theology, philosophy, and psychology with the interior life of man were merging in a larger synthesis for many western thinkers. In her poetry, at least, soul and mind and consciousness all clearly stand for the same concept of the inner self, man's unseen essence. To explore this self requires fortitude, the bedrock principle of Existentialism. For it means not only renouncing the comforts of a gregarious world for the "polar privacy," as she once phrased it, of a "soul admitted to itself." This she achieved with ease. It also means leaving the security of time as well as place. Alone with itself the mind still cannot escape the ghosts of its own past:

> Remembrance has a Rear and Front–
> 'Tis something like a House–

It has a Garret also
For Refuse and the Mouse.

Besides the deepest Cellar
That ever Mason laid–
Look to it by it's Fathoms
Ourselves be not pursued– (1182)

Memory awake, as she described it elsewhere, is hell enough, for it
brings the cureless disease of remorse, rummaging in the rag-bag of
its "Garret." But its "Cellar," the unplumbed depths of the sub-
conscious, harbors terrors that made her conclude the first draft of
this poem as a prayer:

Leave me not ever there alone
Oh thou Almighty God!

Even if one seeks refuge in the present there is no peace, for he
is pursued by the ghost of his own identity:

One need not be a Chamber– to be Haunted–
One need not be a House–
The Brain– has Corridors surpassing
Corporeal Place–

Far safer of a Midnight– meeting
External Ghost–
Than an Interior– Confronting–
That Whiter Host.

Far safer, through an Abbey– gallop–
The Stones a'chase–
Than Moonless– One's A'self encounter–
In lonesome place.

Ourself– behind Ourself– Concealed–
Should startle– most–
Assassin– hid in our Apartment–
Be Horror's least–

The Body– carries a Revolver–
He bolts the Door–
O'erlooking a Superior Spectre–
More near– (670)

The horror here is veneered with the humor of pseudo-Gothic. The structure is cleverly made up of alternate pairs of contrasting lines, so that a consecutive reading of the first halves of the stanzas describes an actual haunted house, while the last halves echo this with the haunted house of the mind. The former constitute a parody of the outmoded tales of terror: the ghostly chamber, the midnight meeting, the horsed spectre galloping through an old abbey. Earlier parodists of the Gothic novel, like Monk Lewis, had mocked the supernatural with ingenious rationalizations; and so in the end her ghost figure is replaced by a flesh and blood assassin, against which the corporeal narrator seeks protection with revolver and bolted door. But the real horror is enhanced rather than diminished by this. For it has resided throughout in the ghost of the self, which prompts her finest images: the "Corridors" of the brain, the interior "Whiter Host," and the "Moonless . . . lonesome place" of the mind's encounter with itself. At the very point where the Gothic "Ghost" gives way to the mystery-thriller "Assassin," stanza four, she inverts her structure and places the internal "Superior Spectre" first. This unexpected shift gives emphasis to her most effective phrase for the haunted mind, "Ourself behind Ourself," the true theme of her poem. Objective fears of real assassins are "Horror's least." It is even "Far safer," she has reiterated, to confront supernatural ghosts than to encounter the hidden self. This shadowy terror has been there all along ("A Spectre–infinite–accompanying," as a variant line reads), but the ego has remained unafraid because unaware. When it suddenly looms from behind the conscious self it "startles most."

Nor is there any escape from "That awful stranger Consciousness" by contemplating the future, Emily Dickinson concludes in another poem on the same theme. Fortunately "Beliefs are Bandaged," for the sober mind would be turned to madness just as much by a vision of heaven as by fear of the grave, if either were fully realized (1323). The letters are filled with similar comments. When we "look within," she wrote, it is "so wild a place we are soon dismayed" (860). Again, "Had we the first intimation of the Definition of Life, the calmest of us would be Lunatics!" (492). And more explicitly: "Could we see all we hope, or hear the whole we fear told tranquil, like another tale, there would be madness near" (388). The precariousness of reason, especially for those who live deeply and intensely, is a constant theme. From the beginning of her poetic career she was well aware of herself as one set apart from the normal. As early as 1859 she wrote to a friend: "Insanity to the sane seems so unnecessary—but I am only one, and they are 'four and forty,' which little affair of numbers leaves me impotent" (209). Three years later she put the same idea into verse: "Much Madness is divinest Sense– . . . Much Sense–the starkest Madness," but demur from the majority and you will be chained as dangerous (435). The poet's traditional role of being "insane," and his consequent alienation from society, was one she readily assumed. But the reality behind this popular notion, the psychic pressures that in greater or less degree compel the poet to utterance, is another matter. Unless the tensions are brought under control the result may be psychosis instead of art. It has long been felt that in Dickinson's case the struggle was particularly acute, "so painful that it might have wrecked a weaker mind," as a recent interpreter has summed it up; but she won the battle and preserved her sanity "by the transformation into art of all phases of her inner experience during the time of crisis."[10] Tracing the possible causes of this crisis and her progress from near breakdown to final recovery must be left to the biographer. The critic can only be concerned with its transformation into poems.

The sequence on the recurrent problem of the self-behind-the-self contains some interesting if less successful poems (642, 683, 777, 1116, 1181, 1695). In them she went on to explore the need for integrating the separate selves, bringing the haunted mind under the mastery of the pragmatic mind without denying it, translating emotion into terms of mind in order to make possible the controls of art. Only then is the discovery of selfhood possible, the greatest treasure man can hope for. It will give him the capacity for solitude, to stand "Everywhere alone/As a Church," but this is a lone grey rock like the existential promontory of Wallace Stevens. It is all there is to build on, either in the experience of living or the experiment of dying. On the occasion of Higginson's second visit to Amherst she remarked: "there is always one thing to be grateful for– that one is one's self & not somebody else."[11] In the best of her poems on the interior self it is made memorable in a novel image:

[10] See Theodora Ward, "Ourself behind Ourself," *Harvard Library Bulletin*, X, 7 (Winter, 1956).
[11] Quoted in the note to letter No. 405.

This Consciousness that is aware
Of Neighbors and the Sun
Will be the one aware of Death
And that itself alone

Is traversing the interval
Experience between
And most profound experiment
Appointed unto Men–

How adequate unto itself
Its properties shall be
Itself unto itself and none
Shall make discovery.

Adventure most unto itself
The Soul condemned to be–
Attended by a single Hound
It's own identity. (822)

The soul is of necessity its own sovereign, she had said elsewhere, and so must stand in awe of itself. "How adequate unto itself," whether it will achieve self-realization or self-destruction, is the dilemma that gives tension to the present poem. "Condemned" suggests that it is being pursued by a bloodhound, but "Attended" suggests the faithful dog that offers companionship on the lonely journey. Instead of the ghost or shadow so often used to image one's awareness of his own "identity," she employs the concrete figure of the "single Hound." "Consciousness," her inclusive term for the soul so attended, is then ready to set out on its great private "Adventure," the experience of life and the experiment of death. Also, if one is a poet he is equally equipped to re-create this adventure in words.

Emily Dickinson's verse aphorisms analyzing the mind, the consciousness, the self, are not the measure of her real achievement in poetry, but they are a clue to the mastery that made it possible. The leap of ecstasy, the plunge into despair, these motions of the heart up and down furnished the themes for her great poems on the interior life. Out of her confrontation of the grave as Janus-faced, trapped perpetually between doubt and belief in another world beyond, she made her grand gestures of hail and farewell to the life of the spirit, the death of the body.[12] But always thrusting itself between was the conscious mind, the flickering identity of self that gives meaning to the bafflingly familiar pilgrimage from cradle to grave by questioning, discriminating, defining. This is what saves her from the sentimentalism of adopting either extreme as her whole view, ecstasy and belief or doubt and despair. Instead, she created her poems out of the tensions that issue from the clash of such powerful opposites.

The self, aware and in control, contains them all. Her absolute loyalty to mind was the instrument by which she achieved this balance, maneuvering her vision into focus, her emotions into forms. And she rarely lost sight of the fact that it was merely a disciplinary technique, not in itself a source or subject for poetry. Her best poems present their themes in the full context of intellect and feeling, not concerned with exploiting either as such but with rendering the experiences that fuse them both. An eminent critic has put this succinctly: "Unlike her contemporaries, she never succumbed to her ideas, to easy solutions, to private desires . . .; like Donne, she *perceives abstraction and thinks sensation.*" And he makes this the basis for a high claim to distinction, that she was probably the only Anglo-American poet of her century who achieved a fusion of sensibility and thought, attaining "a mastery over experience by facing its utmost implications."[13] A final verse aphorism—written coevally with the one that introduced this paper and forming a companion piece to it—takes this very fusion as its theme and makes it another image for the all-inclusive self:

> The Heart is the Capital of the Mind–
> The Mind is a single State–
> The Heart and the Mind together make
> A single Continent–
>
> One– is the Population–
> Numerous enough–
> This ecstatic Nation
> Seek– it is Yourself. (1354)

[12] The major poems on these themes, and on nature and art, are the subject of the present writer's forthcoming book *Stairway of Surprise: The Achievement of Emily Dickinson.*

[13] See Allen Tate, "Emily Dickinson," in *The Man of Letters in the Modern World* (New York, 1955), pp. 217-226.

"Compound Manner": Emily Dickinson and The Metaphysical Poets

Judith Banzer Farr

THE HABIT OF EMILY DICKINSON'S MIND led her, like George Herbert, to construct a "Double Estate" in which this world was "furnished with the Infinite," in which God was her "Old Neighbor," and death, agony, and grace were fleshly companions. The discipline that wrought many of her poems was the metaphysical one of a "Compound Vision" by which the eternal is argued from the transient, the foreign explained by the familiar, and fact illumined by mystery. She could speak of "Infinite March," of Calvary as another Amherst, of the "Diagram — of Rapture" because she practiced the metaphysical awareness of the unity of experience. Reared in the sternly religious society of the Connecticut Valley and in the rigorous atmosphere of the Dickinson household, she learned early to meditate upon essentials: mortality, the temporal presence of God, man's relationship with God and with creation. The acute sensibility that prompted the remark of the girl of twenty-one: "I think of the grave very often" shaped the witty double consciousness of the mature poet who saw, like Vaughan, "through all this fleshly dress/Bright shootes of everlastingnesse." Sharing the prime concerns of the seventeenth century, Emily Dickinson felt also its passionate interest in the microcosm of the self whose "polar privacy" was peopled with thoughts and emotions which supplied the data of existence and the stuff of art. Since that self was poised between scepticism and faith, desire and renunciation, optimism and despair, the artist, like Donne, sought release in a poetry of paradox, argument, and unifying conceits: "Much Madness is divinest Sense—"; "I cannot live with You—/It would be Life—"; "[A Pine is] Just a Sea—with a Stem." The Dickinson poems are the record of an imagination which kept "fundamental" both in substance and technique, recreating experience as it conceived it in terms of multiple connections and infinite semblances, often conveying its highly personal and analytic vision in the arresting manner of the metaphysical.

In comparing the matter and style of Emily Dickinson's verse with that of Donne or Herbert, one finds parallels which do not seem accidental. They suggest that her perspective was tempered and her craft confirmed from contact with the tradition of seventeenth-century poetry in England.

Almost certainly, Emily's reading was the cause of contact. She had easy access to metaphysical poetry in books owned by herself or her family and in periodicals which quoted or discussed it at length. What seem to be her pencil-markings of several poems argue close attention to their vision and technique. Emily Dickinson's poetry, however, creates a related idiom which is the crucial argument for her knowledge of Donne or Herbert; and this argument should be sifted first.

I

It is not difficult to find similarities between the insights and techniques of John Donne and Emily. Like her, he relished the divided joys of earth and spirit. Like hers, his poetry attempts, with frequent success, to fuse them. She refrained from professing Christ because it was "hard for [her] to give up the world"; he hesitated to take Holy Orders because he delighted in the pleasures of the questioning intellect and of the senses. Both enjoyed their disbelief for the aesthetic stimulus it supplied. Donne advised "doubt wisely"; Emily never relinquished her "old Codicil of Doubt." Yet each addressed God familiarly with petulance, awe, and passion as a divine lover. His orthodoxy hard-won, a middle-aged Donne demanded of God both intellectual rest and emotional satisfaction:

> Divorce mee, 'untie, or breake that knot againe,
> Take mee to you, imprison mee, for I
> Except you' enthrall mee, never shall be free,
> Nor ever chast, except you ravish mee.

Emily's faith was heterodox, her attitude towards God highly ambivalent. He was the central Idea to question, to attack or embrace in verse. Yet at the same age and with the same thirst for definition, she begged to be "Immured in Heaven," to be "ravished" by Love's "Bondage," insisting that Deity "Tie the strings to [her] life" and show her Himself. This quest for God, for permanence, was the generative impulse of visions alike evolved by the "columnar self" as it scrutinized values which transcended change. The reality of spirit and the chemistry of physical dissolution, the ecstasy of love and the pain of betrayal, the beauty of the mysterious, and the glamour of hard fact became, for Donne and Emily, firm truths in a world of motion and coexisted "in Being's center." Highly conscious of the supreme activity of the soul, both believed that "the body in his booke"; that

> The Music in the Violin
> Does not emerge alone
> But Arm in Arm with Touch, yet Touch
> Alone—is not a Tune—
> The Spirit lurks within the Flesh
> Like Tides within the Sea
> That make the Water live, estranged
> What would the Either be?

Therefore, they explained their sense of the communion of mystic with material in language drawn from both worlds. Donne compared love's increase with "new taxes" or spoke of Change as "the nursery/Of music," while Emily wrote of "the Grave's Repeal" and pronounced Doom "the House without the Door—." This locative language worked within poems of a subtle, all-encompassing framework; poems like mental theaters in which the scene, a garden or bedroom, a tomb or Gethsemane, was presented vividly and in which an aspect of the poet was chief actor, inviting us to transcend the limits of our experience and imagine "The Habit of a Foreign Sky" or the way in which Christ, a young woman, or the poet himself died. The persuasiveness of that invitation is apparent in dynamic first lines like "I'll tell thee now (deare Love) what thou shalt doe" or "I'll tell you how the Sun rose—." They are lines which convey a brilliant colloquial voice inflecting many moods, asserting the self that is its subject. This keen personal consciousness which analyzed its every awareness and most sharply, its sense of God, love, and death chose similar expression in the work of both poets. The most crucial techniques of Donne and Emily Dickinson are akin: the use of Anglo-Saxon and Latinate words as double wit-nesses of one truth in one phrase; the abortion of regular metrics to assist the immediacy of the speaking voice; the development of a poem according to the thesis of its opening line or by the elaboration of a radiant conceit like that of "The Flea" or of "He put the Belt around my life"; the use of religious phraseology to express profane love as in "The Funerall" or "There came a day at summer's full"; a fondness for paradoxical arguments like the following:

> Thou canst not every day give mee they heart,
> If thou canst give it, then thou never gavest it;
> Love riddles are, that though thy heart depart
> It stayes at home, and thou with losing savest it.

> A Death blow is a Life blow to Some
> Who till they died, did not alive become—
> Who had they lived, had died but when
> They died, Vitality begun.

Donne, who required the honest, original force of words like "itchy" and "snorted" in his most elegant poems, would have understood Emily's use of the provincialism "heft" to describe the solemn tenor of church music. An extraordinary number of poems like "The Legacie" or "I heard a Fly buzz—when I died—" demonstrate the delight each took in probing the sensation of death in shockingly intimate accents. Both crowded their lines with verbal excitement, as if in excess of athletic apprehension: "let/Mee travel, sojourne, snatch, plot, have, forget"; " 'Tis this invites, appals, endows,/ Flits, glimmers, proves, dissolves." Both enjoyed a pun and the poetry of each occasionally displays the unconciliating quality of the overly ingenious metaphysical wit:

> She guilded us: But you are gold, and Shee;
>   Us she inform'd but transubstantiates you;
> Soft dispositions which ductile bee,
>   Elixarlike, she makes not cleane, but new.

> Enchantment's Perihelion
> Mistaken oft has been
> For the Authentic orbit
> Of it's Anterior Sun.

Yet their central relationship is one which ordered these incidental ones: the participation in what Louis L. Martz in his study,

The Poetry of Meditation (Yale University Press, 1954) has defined as the "meditative" vision. Donne, practicing its three-fold mode of divine communion and Emily, moved by her theocratic environment to the constant contemplation of Essence, shared a conviction of the oneness of being. This produced in their poetry the continual creation of an explorative and unifying self. Eccentric imagery, syntax, metrics, the denomination of her freckled person as "Empress of Calvary," her shrewd colloquies with God, a bee, or the spirit of a word, demonstrate in Emily's verse the same sense of the drama of the "I" with which his meditative exercises informed the poetry of Donne.

George Herbert's verse functions within this vision also, and with him, Emily claims a distinct relationship. Herbert asserts, like Emily, that "There's newer—nearer Crucifixion" than the Biblical one and contemplates his intimacy with his divine lover in the virile assents of the speaking voice. He, too, expresses his confidence in the unity of being by describing the transcendent in material conceits of orderliness and neat symmetry.

The Temple, like Emily's lyrics, abounds in homely images of safe enclosure. For Herbert, Heaven is a "manour," furnished with "glorious household-stuffe"; the Trinity is a "statelie cabinet"; the soul, "a poor cabinet of bone" with rooms and a latchkey; Man is a "house" whose thoughts are walls and earth is his "cupboard of food" or, as his sepulchre, "God's ebony box." Emily used enclosure images similarly to capture an exquisitely-felt tension between body and spirit. In her "Ablative Estate," the soul has cellars and caverns which it roves or tries to shatter; the mind is a planked cell and gives banquets; the brain is furnished with mighty rooms and windy chambers wherein funerals, rejoicings, and visions occur; Heaven is the "house of supposition"; the sky is an "Astral Hall," swept by housewives like Herbert's Reason. Both poets devise poems in which enclosure is violated by the "marauding Hand" of God or a keen emotion; thus, Herbert's "Confession" or Emily's "The Soul should always stand ajar": poems which reverse the conceit of the opened door as Herbert attempts to shut out "cunning" grief, and Emily to let in "accomplished" Heaven. Herbert describes his apprehension of the divine in terms of habitation: he "dwells" in prayer, in peace, in sacred music; equally, he invites

God in "The Banquet," "A Parodie," and "The Glimpse" to live in his soul's "brave . . . palace" as in the days when he "didst lodge with Lot." Emily, too, speaks of her communion with God as that of host with Visitor:

> The Soul that hath a Guest
> Doth seldom go abroad—
> Diviner Crowd at Home—
> Obliterate the need—
>
> And Courtesy forbid
> A Host's departure when
> Upon Himself be visiting
> The Emperor of Men—

Both poets compare the perfecting or sensitive development of a soul to the erection of a building: thus, "The World" or "The Props assist the House." Even as Herbert called his sacred verse his "best room," Emily described the departure of inspiration from her soul's "unfurnished Rooms," expressing her aesthetic mission by means of an architectural conceit:

> I dwell in Possibility—
> A fairer House than Prose—
> More numerous of Windows—
> Superior—for Doors—
>
> Of Chambers as the Cedars—
> Impregnable of Eye—
> And for an Everlasting Roof
> The Gambrels of the Sky—
>
> Of Visitors—the fairest—
> For Occupation—This—
> The spreading wide my narrow Hands
> To gather Paradise—

Enclosure imagery functions here, as in Herbert's poems, to create a sense of freedom and union. Possibility, both the lively receptiveness of the poetic mind and Poetry itself, is as reliable as a house. It is fairer than the insular home of Prose because its many apertures withhold the cursory glance, admitting supreme callers and thoughts divinely positive as sun's rays. Like the house of man's soul, it is firm because it lacks limits.

The reflective practices which put Herbert forever in the divine presence and Emily's habit of strolling with Eternity prompted the signal similar movement in the work of both poets: one by which, ardently or childishly, they asked God's lasting interview, requiring him to yield their vision fullness:

> Come, Lord, my head doth burn, my heart is sick,
>   While Thou dost ever, ever stay;
> Thy long deferrings wound me to the quick,
>   My spirit gaspeth night and day.
>   O, show Thyself to me,
>   Or take me up to Thee!

> At least—to pray—is left—is left—
> Oh Jesus—in the Air—
> I know not which thy chamber is—
> I'm knocking—everywhere—

> Thou settest Earthquake in the South—
> And Maelstrom in the Sea—
> Say, Jesus Christ of Nazareth—
> Hast thou no Arm for Me?

The tradition that lives in Herbert's Sidneyesque, in Emily's urgent, tones is that which disposed their use of empiric conceit, their description of Shame as a wine or a pink shawl, their building of poems around Biblical theses, their discussions with Death or Passion, their domestication of mystery and soberly playful references to the "handkerchief" of Christ's "grave clothes" or to the "fashions —of the Cross—." It is the custom of seeing "Comparatively," of fitting all experience, sublime or ordinary, into one plane and finding it the haunted "Ground Floor" of a familiar Infinite. Emily Dickinson's exotic symbols: Cashmere, Domingo, Vera Cruz, "fairer —for the farness—/And for the foreignhood," merged in her awareness with the homely beauty of the Pelham hills to make a mental Eden round which Eternity swept "like a Sea." While Herbert praised Sunday as a

> day most calm, most bright,
> The fruit of this, the next world's bud,
> Th' indorsement of supreme delight,
> Writ by a friend; and with His bloud

she could rhapsodize the "General Rose" which those beneath her window augured and speak of a June when all corn will be cut, for which "Our Lord—thought no/Extravagance/To pay—a Cross—." Like Herbert, she found it an "Estate perpetual" to "entertain" her own sensations, discovering that Grief, like his Affliction, had "size"; like him, she used techniques which emphasized a personal and cohesive vision: forthright syntax and economical metaphor; litany-like exclamation and meters derived from hymns; the binding melody of the tercet and, in poems like "Publication—is the Auction/Of the Mind of Man," the framework of thesis, deliberation, directive that shapes his lyrics.

Emily's kinship with the metaphysical poets is remarkable. One suspects that it developed not simply through a creativity led by instinct and by Puritan and Transcendental forces to elect a meditative mode, but from a familiarity with that mode in the work of Donne, Marvell, and the rest. Her letters and poems provide slim support for this conclusion. She writes once of Vaughan to T. W. Higginson in 1880, spelling his name "Vaughn" and misquoting his line "My days, which are best but dull and hoary" as "My Days that are at best but dim and hoary." Emily spelled casually, as did her associates: a certain engaging cotton farmer was spoken of on three occasions in the 1863 *Springfield Republican* as Mr. "Vaughan," "Vaughn," and "Vaughne." Her substitution of "dim" for "dull" was perhaps due to a recollection of "glimmering" in the poem's next line. Her mistake argues an acquaintance with "They are all gone into the world of light!" But this is her sole allusion to Vaughan, although the following poem, with its interesting implication in the word "enables," suggests that, by 1863,[1] she knew his verse, as she did Thomas Browne's prose, intimately:

> Strong draughts of Their Refreshing Minds
> To drink—enables Mine
> Through Desert or the Wilderness
> As bore it Sealed Wine

[1] If we accept Thomas H. Johnson's dating in his *Poems of Emily Dickinson* (Cambridge, Mass., 1955), II, 545.

I am grateful to Charles R. Green of the Jones Library, Amherst, for advice and for access to Dickinson material; to William A. Jackson of the Houghton Library, Harvard, for permission to use Harvard's Dickinson collection; and to Mrs. Alfred Leete Hampson for allowing me to see Dickinson books still at Evergreens.

To go elastic—Or as One
The Camel's trait—attained
How powerful the Stimulus
Of an Hermetic Mind

That she tasted Herbert's "Sealed Wine" is deduced from her tran-
scription of the middle stanzas of "Mattens."[2] Her poem "I've
heard an Organ talk sometimes" suggests that she knew the basic
meditative tradition as it appeared in the devotional mysticism of
St. Bernard of Clairvaux. Describing her wordless rapture at hearing church music, she says that she had "risen up," afterwards, and
"gone away/A more Bernardine Girl—." She makes no reference
to Donne; none to Marvell, whose equations of the soul with a
garden resemble hers; none to Crashaw, Cowley, or King, some
of whose insights and conceits are like her own.

II

It is highly likely, however, that Emily read metaphysical verse
in her favorite newspapers and magazines and in books which she
owned or borrowed. She would have done so because this poetry
was available; because she read omnivorously; because critics, poets,
and friends she admired praised it.

Samuel Bowles was a friend of the Dickinsons and a frequent
correspondent of Emily's. His newspaper, the *Springfield Republican*, evinced the active spirit and wide tastes of its editor, becoming
"a sovereign authority in Amherst" and "next in importance to the
Bible in determining the mental climate of Emily Dickinson's
formative years."[3] Emily's letters indicated its importance to her
not only as a link with the busy world of politics and friends' lives
but as a literary guide. In the "vital times" when Bowles "bore the
Republican," aided by his associate editor, Emily's friend Dr. Holland, the paper reviewed reissued classics like Jeremy Taylor's *Holy
Living and Dying* or rebuked new volumes like *Dramatis Personae*.
It carried critical articles by Frank B. Sanborn, Emerson's biographer, which ranged from scathing accounts of the recent numbers
of the *Atlantic Monthly* and estimations of the poems of Whitman

    [2] See *Bolts of Melody*, ed. Millicent Todd Bingham, with Mabel Loomis Todd (New
York, 1945), p. 125.
    [3] Van Wyck Brooks, *New England: Indian Summer* (New York, 1940), p. 317;
George F. Whicher, *This Was a Poet* (New York, 1938), p. 170.

and Joaquin Miller to affectionate praise of Spenser's *Shepherd's Calendar,* Marlowe's plays, and Drayton's sonnets. Alongside lines from *Beppo,* advertising Hostetter's Stomach Bitters, were printed selections from Francis Bacon and *Paradise Lost.* On May 20, 1863, an extract from the *Providence Journal* anticipated Emily's decision that "Bees are Black, with Gilt Surcingles—/Bucaneers of Buzz": "A bee buzzed in at our window yesterday. He was dressed like a colonel of cavalry, in a dark suit, with yellow trimmings." The metaphysical school was not neglected. Marvell's "Bermudas" and Herbert's "Money" were reprinted at least three and four times respectively between 1858 and 1863, while "Dr. Donne's *Holy Sonnets* and the devotional poems of "holy Herbert" were applauded for their intent and reproved for "fantastic conceits" in 1863. In the same year, the following article appeared. It was probably written by Sanborn, who was then supplying critical articles to the Boston *Transcript* and *Traveller* as well as to the *Republican* and with whom Emily had corresponded in 1871, thanking him for literary advice. The article compliments Vaughan for the very economy that Bowles demanded of his reporters and that Higginson had required of his "Young Contributor."

(*The Springfield Daily Republican,* February 14, 1863)
BOOKS, AUTHORS, AND ART
Henry Vaughan and His Poems

We notice, in one of our exchanges, a poem entitled 'Dew and Frost,' credited to George Herbert. It is not, however, his, but was written by Henry Vaughan, and with additional verses forms the poem called in the collection of that author's works, 'LOVE AND DISCIPLINE.' It is sweet and suggestive; we give it entire, below. The mistake which attributed it to Herbert, had it occurred during the life time and within the notice of Vaughan, would have afforded him the greatest pleasure, as indicating a similarity between his own compositions and those of one whom he delighted to call his master. A few specimens of Vaughan's poetry may not be uninteresting to those of our readers who are not familiar with it. Amid the quaint conceits and profuse imagery which characterize his poetry, (though in a less degree than that of most authors of his age,) there sparkles the true radiance of genius. Here and there you find thoughts simply, strongly, tenderly expressed; a volume in a line; a nineteenth century essay in three words. And over all shines the hallowing lustre of a truly Christian spirit. As he himself says: "He that desires to excel in this kind of hagiography, or holy writing, must strive by all means for perfection and true holiness; that a door may be opened to him in heaven, and then he will be able to write with Hierotheus and holy Herbert, 'a true hymn.' "

Henry Vaughan was born A.D. 1621, and died A.D. 1695. The selections which follow are taken from a volume entitled 'SILEX SCINTILLA[N]S,' and published in London in 1655.

The article then quotes "Love and Discipline" and "The Evening-watch" in their entirety. They are followed by this comment on "Rules and Lessons" and an extract central to Emily Dickinson's creed:

'RULES AND LESSONS' is one of Vaughan's most characteristic poems. Though less pleasing in diction than some others, it is full of just and beautiful thought. We have space but for one verse:—

> Seek not the same steps with the crowd; stick thou
> To thy sure trot; a constant, humble mind
> Is both his own joy and his Maker's too;
> Let folly dust it on, or lag behind,—
> *A sweet self—privacy in a right soul*
> Outruns the earth, and lines the utmost pole.

The first six stanzas of "Cock-crowing" are quoted as exemplary of "Vaughan's sympathy with nature." The article then concludes with lines 25 to 50 of "The Seed growing secretly."

Emily Dickinson, who told the Hollands in a letter of autumn, 1853, that she "read in [the *Springfield Republican*] every night," probably saw this article. She might have been impressed with Vaughan's use of "Essential Oils" and she would have liked his lines "*A sweet self-privacy in a right soul*/Outruns the earth, and lines the utmost pole"; for she herself, in 1863, had commended the "solitary prowess/Of a Silent Life—" and written:

> Suffice Us—for a Crowd—
> Ourself—and Rectitude—
> And that Assembly—not far off
> From furthest Spirit—God—

It was the kernel of her life and art.

That frequent criticisms of metaphysical verse appeared in the *Republican* during Emily's most creative years is important. That they appeared under Bowles's aegis is also significant. He, like Emerson—himself a lover of Donne and Herbert—, was an occasional caller at Austin's villa, bringing books for Susan Dickinson and her "Sister" across the lawn. One of these was Charles A. Dana's *Household Book of Poetry,* published in 1860, and reviewed in 1864 by the *Republican.* In 1950, the book was presented to Harvard University by Gilbert Montague and is now preserved in Harvard's Houghton Library. A letter from Bowles, still in it, suggests that the volume was given to the Dickinsons shortly after its arrival in 1862 at the Boston publishers, Ticknor & Fields. The book contained a small selection of metaphysical verse. There were Marvell's "On A drop of Dew," "The Mower to the Glow-Worms," the "Horatian Ode," and "Bermudas." Herbert was represented by "The Call," "Complaining," "The Flower," and "Virtue." Of Vaughan, there were "Peace," "The Bee," "The Feast," the famous "They are all gone into the world of light!," and the important meditative poem, "Rules and Lessons." Crashaw's "On a Prayer Book Sent to Mrs. M. R.," his Italianate song "To thy Lover," and "Temperance: or the Cheap Physician" were included with scores of Herrick's lyrics including his "Litany to the Holy Spirit" and many of Carew's less "metaphysical" pieces. Emily, who was, as her letter demonstrates, a constant borrower of Sue's books, could have read these poems; but they would have been slender diet. Bowles's letter to Sue, however, had called the book the "complement to your collection of poets"; for the Dickinson libraries, both Austin's and Emily's, were replete with anthologies and volumes of verse.

One of the most interesting of these for our purposes is *The Sacred Poets of England and America,* edited by Rufus Griswold and published by D. Appleton & Co. in 1849. Like other books I shall discuss, it, too, was presented to Harvard in 1950 on the premise that it had been in the Dickinson family during Emily's lifetime. This last seems certain: it is inscribed to Susan by members of the Utica Female Academy, "Dec. 22, 1848." It contains a generous selection of metaphysical poetry. Donne is represented by Holy Sonnets I, VI, VII, and X, and by his hymns "To Christ at the Authors last going into Germany" and "To God, my God, in my sicknesse." Herbert's "The Collar," "The Quip," "Virtue,"

"Business," "Peace," and "Grace" appear, followed by Vaughan's "The Pursuite," "The World," "The Bee," "The Shepherds," "The Garland," "The Dwelling-place," "The Wreath," "Son-dayes," "The Retreate," "Childe-hood," "Peace," "Looking back," and "They are all gone into the world of light!" Marvell's "On a Drop of Dew" and "Bermudas" are printed, together with Crashaw's "The Martyr," "Dies Irae Dies Illa," and the "Full Chorus" from "In the Holy Nativity." There were Cowley's "The Garden" and "The Ecstasy" besides eight poems by William Drummond; several, including "The Anniversary" and "The Dirge," by Bishop King; many from Herrick's *Noble Numbers* and from Quarles's *Emblems* and several poems by Baxter and Habington. It is unthinkable that Emily, who was with difficulty kept from reading even Motherwell, overlooked this volume. Vaughan's poems are those which best convey the mystic insight she shared and the lines like "Eternity/In time" which she approximates. Donne's poems and sonnets, with the grand "death, thou shalt die," resemble many of hers in technique and in her affirmations that "Death [is] dead." Marvell's "On a Drop of Dew," with its delicate meditative structure, and Crashaw's "Full Chorus" would have appealed to her in substance and style, as would Cowley's "The Garden" or Herbert's "The Collar," which, like his "Love," her own poem " 'Unto me'? I do not know you" closely resembles.

But Emily did not require this volume to read Herbert. Her sister-in-law owned an 1857 edition of *The Temple*. Whether it was Susan's or Emily's is a nice question. The autograph signature on the flyleaf is "S. H. Dickinson." This suggests that it was signed by Sue shortly after her marriage in 1856, since her signature in the period of the seventies was "Mrs. Wm. A. Dickinson." In the latter fifties and early sixties, when she and Emily were reading *Aurora Leigh* and *Sordello,* her autograph on the flyleaves of those and other books bore the middle initial she had used as Susan Huntington Gilbert. Edward Dickinson, whose reading was "lonely and rigorous," may not have bought a Herbert for Emily; but, like Sue's Coventry Patmore, commended by Bowles, it doubtless crossed the lawn, remaining there, with Sue's copies of Theodore Parker's *Prayers* and Carlyle's essays, for the principal use of her sister-in-law. The Houghton Library catalogue describes the volume as "bearing pencil marks—probably by Emily." The conjecture is valid; for the markings in *The Temple,* as in other books I shall discuss, follow a pattern. This pattern is accompanied in other volumes by critical comments in what seems Emily's hand of the early sixties.[4] The major indication that the markings are Emily's is, in every case, what is marked or the nature of the comment. The hand that scored *The Temple* used the same light, single stroke to the right of the page as the one that scored the following passage in De Quincey's *Essays on the Poets:* "the literature of power builds nests in aerial altitudes of temples sacred from violation, or of forests inaccessible to fraud." Alongside the passage, in Emily's hand, is the note "View Mrs. Browning's *Essays on the Greek Poets.*" Throughout the Dickinson books are such markings, surmised to be Emily's, which are applied to passages that recall her poems. Thus, line 861 in "The Book and the Ring," "Art may tell a truth/Oblique-ly," resembles the notion conveyed in "Tell all the truth but tell it slant—"; while a line marked in Emerson's *Compensation,* "There is a deeper fact in the soul than compensation, to wit, its own na-ture," expresses Emily's belief in the value of the independent spirit. Whoever made these markings knew the mind of the poet as well as she herself. That they were made by Susan is unlikely: as Vin-nie Dickinson said, "to think" was Emily's job; Susan was a busy hostess to Austin's many friends; and those few of her books which she marked—*Palgrave's Treasury* (1877) for example—are under-lined or crossed in ink: a different system entirely. The marked passages in Herbert's *Temple* voice concepts crucial to Emily's creed. The following lines from "The Church-Porch," "A verse may finde him who a sermon flies,/And turn delight into a sacri-fice," assert Emily's conviction that a poet was the "Merchant—of the Heavenly Grace" whose creative activities were his form of worship; while others, like "Dare to look in thy chest; for 'tis thine own;/And tumble up and down what thou find'st there" declare the principle of self-analysis that supports all Emily's verse.

Edward Dickinson owned Robert Chambers's *Cyclopedia of English Literature,* in an edition published in 1847 by the Boston firm of Gould & Kendall. It contained metaphysical poems and

---

[4] This conclusion was reached after a comparison of the comments with specimens of Emily's writing given by Theodora Ward in the introductory chapter to Johnson's *Poems.* It is, of course, a layman's attempt to identify the writing chronologically.

criticisms of the poets. Sue Dickinson had an Edinburgh, 1844, edition of the same book. On its flyleaf, she records that it was purchased in 1856, before her marriage. It is possible that Emily received her volume after admiring Sue's. In Edward Dickinson's copy, the Vaughan section, like that of Crashaw, is well-thumbed and creased from right to left. It comprised "The Rainbow," "Timber," and "Rules and Lessons." The fourth stanza of the latter bears a thin line at right. The stanza alludes to Jacob wrestling with the Angel, a Biblical example of perseverance frequently cited by Emily in letters and in poems like "A little East of Jordan." The *Cyclopedia* also contained selections from Donne, pronounced—with some qualification—"real poetry, and . . . of a high order," including his "Valediction—forbidding mourning," "The Will," and "Satyre IV" from line 17b. "The Broken Heart," often compared with Emily's "My Life had stood—a Loaded Gun—" was criticized for its use of "mere conceit." Cowley's poems included "On the Death of Mr. Crashaw," "The Wish," "The Epicure," and others, along with two poems whose imagery is similar to Emily Dickinson's. In "Upon the shortness of Man's Life," human life is compared with an arrow; in "A Day! Help! Help! Another Day!", Emily had said, "my soul: What issues/Upon thine arrow hang!" Cowley's "Description of Heaven" contains the couplet, "Nothing is there To come, and nothing Past,/But an Eternal Now does always last"; Emily affirms "Forever is composed of Nows—/'Tis not a different Time." Crashaw, praised for his "mystical style of thought," was represented by "Wishes to a Supposed Mistress," "Music's Duel," "Temperance," and the "Hymn to the Name of Jesus," one of the finest examples of his peculiar meditative technique. Marvell's "The Nymph complaining," "The Garden," and his satire on Holland were included, together with Herbert's "Mattens," "The Pulley," and other poems. There were several selections from Wither, Davies, and Southwell.

The Dickinsons also owned a volume called *Hymns of the Ages,* subtitled "Selections from Wither, Crashaw, Southwell, Habington, and other Sources," published in Boston by Ticknor & Fields in 1861 and favorably reviewed by the *Republican* on December 7, 1864. As the book truthfully claimed, it contained "large selections" of the "tender and earnest numbers of Southwell and Crashaw and Habington, the gentle symphonies of Vaughan, the rugged verse of Donne . . . and the voluminous "Halleujah" of Wither, which touched with a poetic glow each object of daily life." The volume is neither autographed nor marked and carries no acquisition date. Emily Dickinson rarely autographed her own books: Martin Tupper's *Proverbial Philosophy* is one of the few which bear her own signature. Others, like *The Imitation of Christ* were marked "Emily Dickinson" by Sue or the giver. That this book is not autographed, unlike each of Sue's volumes, suggests that it may have been the poet's.

Selections and criticisms of metaphysical verse were available to Emily in magazines; in the Amherst College Library, of which Austin was trustee; in friends' libraries. She subscribed to the *Atlantic Monthly* and probably saw reviews of George Duyckinck's *Life of Herbert* in the June, 1859, issue and articles like E. P. Whipple's on John Donne and the "Minor Elizabethan Poets" in the July, 1868, issue. Copies of each issue are preserved with the Dickinson books. That Emily borrowed volumes from the college shelves is indicated by a letter, written in 1858, to the wife of Joseph Haven, professor of metaphysics at Amherst: "Have you . . . in [your] Library, either *Klosterheim* or the *Confessions of an Opium Eater* by De Quincey? I have sent to Northampton, but cannot get them there; and they are missing just now from the College Library." Unfortunately, the present Converse Library of Amherst College lacks check-out lists from Emily's time. But, through Austin, who was purchasing the library's books in the early sixties, she could have borrowed copies of *The British Poets* series of the works of Donne, Crashaw, and Davies, published in 1855 by Little, Brown & Co. and popularized by the *Republican*.

Emily's favorite authors praised and quoted metaphysical verse. This alone would have piqued the Dickinson curiosity. Higginson commended the "vital vigor" of Andrew Marvell's poems to his "Young Contributor." Emerson, in "The Oversoul," employed Emily's Dionysian conception of art to distinguish between the poetry of "accomplished talkers" like Pope and that of a "fervent mystic" like Herbert, "prophesying half insane under the infinitude of his thought." Browning invoked the "revered and magisterial Donne" in "The Two Poets of Croisic," and George Eliot quoted three stanzas of "The undertaking" and one of "The good-morrow" in Chapters xxxix and lxxxiii of *Middlemarch*.

Emily Dickinson's control of her inmost thoughts in lean, collo-quial, incandescent verse; her conviction that "Drama's Vitallest Expression is the Common Day" with its rare vibrations; her simul-taneous analysis of earth and eternity compose the "Compound Manner" that commits her to the metaphysical tradition. From the poets of this tradition she doubtless sought imaginative stimulus and an occasional technical lesson. Her genius and her poetry are unique, but her inner vision and unifying style link her with Donne, Marvell, Vaughan, and Herbert, poets who argued the community of all "that which God doth touch and own."

Emily Dickinson's "Further In Summer Than The Birds" and Nathaniel Hawthorne's "The Old Manse"

Sidney E. Lind

"FURTHER IN SUMMER THAN THE BIRDS" is generally considered to be one of Emily Dickinson's most difficult poems. Its extremely idiosyncratic diction and complete lack of punctuation intensify the obscurity of an ambiguous syntactical structure. As it stands, it is a speculative venture from beginning to end. The result is that we have a poem "difficult" in more than one sense, so difficult, in fact, that critics have been able to interpret it in various, even opposing, ways, while yet agreeing that it is an important or great poem.[1]

What is obviously required is a reading which will provide clarification. For such a task the ideal candidate would be one who has had the same experience as the poet and in addition possesses a poetic sensibility and the rhetorical resources to express complicated ideas. Were he to be a contemporary of Emily Dickinson in place as well as in time, he would bring to bear an authority beyond all challenge. Marvelously, there is such an interpreter, however unexpected his identity. Nathaniel Hawthorne, who died in 1864, about two years before the poem was written, has given us the most satisfactory reading of the poem.

I

In his essay "The Old Manse," which introduced his collection of tales *Mosses from an Old Manse* (1846), Hawthorne engagingly

[1] For the range of diversity of interpretation, see: R. P. Adams, "Pure Poetry: Emily Dickinson," *Tulane Studies in English*, VII, 150-151 (1957); Charles R. Anderson, *Emily Dickinson's Poetry: Stairway of Surprise* (New York, 1960), pp. 150-156; F. I. Carpenter, *Explicator*, VIII, Item 33 (1950); Richard Chase, *Emily Dickinson* (New York, 1951), pp. 171-172; R. H. and H. L. Elias, *Explicator*, XI, Item 5 (1952); Clark Griffith, *The Long Shadow: Emily Dickinson's Tragic Poetry* (Princeton, 1964), pp. 84-92; T. H. Johnson, *Emily Dickinson: An Interpretive Biography* (Cambridge, Mass., 1955), pp. 185-187; René Rapin, *Explicator*, XII, Item 24 (1954); Marshall Van Deusen, *Explicator*, XIII, Item 33 (1955); Yvor Winters, "Emily Dickinson and the Limits of Judgment," *In Defense of Reason* (New York, 1947), pp. 292-293.

presents a segment of autobiography.[2] He writes easily, with a light—even humorous—touch, as though he did not have a care in the world, rambling, as his fancy dictates, from his study to the Concord River, back to the house, and then out of doors again. When he comes to an account of an outing he took one beautiful summer afternoon with Ellery Channing, however, his tone becomes more introspective; like Wordsworth, he sees the constant interplay between material objects and their ideal state.[3] The sense of Nature, which earlier in the essay had been acknowledged almost formally, is now all-pervasive and leads him to his next ramble. This begins with the typical Romantic argument of the superiority of the country to the city, but very quickly changes from an almost commonplace statement to an increasingly personal and intensely felt reaction to the power of Nature, culminating in an ecstatic, mystical experience. Because no summary can accurately transmit the developing complexity of ideas as well as the sheer poetic quality of expression, the passage is given in full:

If ever my readers should decide to give up civilized life, cities, houses, and whatever moral or material enormities in addition to these the perverted ingenuity of our race has contrived, let it be in the early autumn. Then Nature will love him better than at any other season, and will take him to her bosom with a more motherly tenderness. I could scarcely endure the roof of the old house above me in those first autumnal days. How early in the summer, too, the prophecy of autumn comes! Earlier in some years than in others; sometimes even in the first weeks of July. There is no other feeling like what is caused by this faint, doubtful, yet real perception—if it be not rather a foreboding—of the year's decay, so blessedly sweet and sad in the same breath.

Did I say that there was no feeling like it? Ah, but there is a half-acknowledged melancholy like to this when we stand in the perfected vigor of our life and feel that Time has now given us all his flowers, and that the next work of his never idle fingers must be to steal them one by one away.

I have forgotten whether the song of the cricket be not as early a token of autumn's approach as any other,—that song which may be called an audible stillness; for though very loud and heard afar, yet

---

[2] Hawthorne moved into the Manse in July, 1842.

[3] *The Complete Works of Nathaniel Hawthorne, with Introductory Notes by George Parsons Lathrop*, Riverside Edition (Boston, 1883), II, 32. Hereinafter referred to as *Complete Works*.

the mind does not take note of it as a sound, so completely is its individual existence merged among the accompanying characteristics of the season. Alas for the pleasant summer time! In August the grass is still verdant on the hills and in the valleys; the foliage of the trees is as dense as ever, and as green; the flowers gleam forth in richer abundance along the margin of the river, and by the stone walls, and deep among the woods; the days, too, are as fervid now as they were a month ago; and yet in every breath of wind and in every beam of sunshine we hear the whispered farewell and behold the parting smile of a dear friend. There is a coolness amid all the heat, a mildness in the blazing noon. Not a breeze can stir but it thrills us with the breath of autumn. A pensive glory is seen in the far golden gleams, among the shadows of the trees. The flowers—even the brightest of them, and they are the most gorgeous of the year—have this gentle sadness wedded to their pomp, and typify the character of the delicious time each within itself. The brilliant cardinal flower has never seemed gay to me.[4]

The "prophecy" of autumn comes early for Hawthorne in these surroundings, sometimes as early as the first weeks of July, but certainly by August, heralded by the song of the cricket, an "audible stillness." Summer is at its full in the "blazing noon" of the August day, yet there is a "pensive glory" in the scene. The flowers, bursting in bloom, "typify the character of the delicious time," the "gentle sadness" which Hawthorne has epitomized as a "half-acknowledged melancholy" in the second paragraph.

And now, in a final, extended statement, Hawthorne breaks into a paean of religious ecstasy, casting off all reserve:

Still later in the season Nature's tenderness waxes stronger. It is impossible not to be fond of our mother now; for she is so fond of us! At other periods she does not make this impression on me, or only at rare intervals; but in those genial days of autumn, when she has perfected her harvests and accomplished every needful thing that was given her to do, then she overflows with a blessed superfluity of love. She has leisure to caress her children now. It is good to be alive at such times. Thank Heaven for breath—yes, for mere breath—when it is made up of a heavenly breeze like this! It comes with a real kiss upon our cheeks; it would linger fondly around us if it might; but, since it must be gone, it embraces us with its whole kindly heart and passes onward to embrace likewise the next thing that it meets. A blessing is flung

[4] *Complete Works,* II, 36-37. The reference to the cardinal flower in the last sentence has its antecedent description three pages earlier (p. 33):

abroad and scattered far and wide over the earth, to be gathered up by all who choose. I recline upon the still unwithered grass and whisper to myself, "O perfect! O beautiful world! O beneficent God!" And it is the promise of a blessed eternity; for our Creator would never have made such lovely days and have given us the deep hearts to enjoy them, above and beyond all thought, unless we were meant to be immortal. This sunshine is the golden pledge thereof. It beams through the gates of paradise and shows us the glimpses far inward.[5]

The source of Hawthorne's ecstasy is dual: the references to God, Creator, eternity, immortality, and paradise are Christian, but the ecstatic praise of Nature, "our mother," with her overflowing love for her children, is purely Romantic—even Transcendental— and utterly pagan.[6]

In the entire passage we see the unfolding of a complicated idea: in the fulness of summer, when not even one blade of grass reveals as yet the sear of autumn, we feel the change to come. As much as—if not more than—anything else, it is the song of the cricket which symbolizes the complex feeling of happiness infused with sadness. Yet there is nothing finally elegiac in this feeling: Nature and God in the recurring cycle of life promise immortality. Like the phrase "audible stillness," which Hawthorne explains in some detail, the second and third paragraphs take on characteristics of oxymoron, in which man's positive and perpetual relation to the totality of his existence is mystically affirmed, neither in spite of nor because of whatever sadness may be involved in such contemplation.

II

Such appears to be the meaning of this revealing sequence in "The Old Manse." The extent of its relevance to Emily Dickinson's poem may now be judged by an examination of her text:

> Further in Summer than the Birds
> Pathetic from the Grass
> A minor Nation celebrates
> It's unobtrusive Mass

[5] *Ibid.*, II, 38.

[6] Throughout the essay can be seen Hawthorne's rejection of the dogmatic religion symbolized by the Manse for the more "natural" religion symbolized by the out-of-doors.

No Ordinance be seen
So gradual the Grace
A pensive Custom it becomes
Enlarging Loneliness

Antiquest felt at Noon
When August burning low
Arise this spectral Canticle
Repose to typify

Remit as yet no Grace
No Furrow on the Glow
Yet a Druidic Difference
Enhances Nature now[7]

Emily Dickinson, like any other poet—and probably more than most—used her dictionary as she saw fit, selecting the most immediately appropriate definition from among a number given for any word. Nevertheless, a reading of her poem can be derived in its entirety from Hawthorne's passage. We must, however, allow for the compression of her ideas into sixty-four words as against the extension of Hawthorne's prose, with the consequent differentiation in emphasis of these ideas and of their tonal expression.

What is immediately clear is that throughout the poem the language of the liturgy has been used as metaphor to structure the progression of ideas.[8] Equally clear is that through such metaphor the poet wishes to transmit no more than the sense of an emotion, acquired from the solemnity of the occasion, which can be characterized as religious and mystical. Unless we accept the Christian symbols as metaphor only and not as the poet's belief, we shall find it difficult to explain her equally positive use of a pagan metaphor in the last two lines of the poem.

Apart from the spelling error of the first word in line 4 and the ecclesiastical borrowings, there are eight words which require special definition. These definitions, with the exception of the next-to-last, are approved, although not necessarily the most common, and all of them serve to clarify the poem:

[7] From *The Poems of Emily Dickinson*, ed. Thomas H. Johnson (Cambridge, Mass., 1955), II, 752.

[8] Line 3: celebrates; line 4: Mass; line 5: Ordinance; line 6: gradual, Grace; line 11: Canticle; line 13: Remit, Grace.

line 1. Further: to a greater extent
    2. Pathetic: affecting or moving the feelings
    7. pensive: expressing thoughtfulness or sadness
    9. Antiquest: [the poet's coinage, the superlative of *antique*: ancient]
    11. spectral: [synonymous with *ghostly*] spiritual
    13. Remit: slacken, abate
    15. Druidic: [proposed definition] prophetic
    16. Enhances: raises to a higher degree; intensifies; magnifies; raises the value of

Additionally, the following observations may be made:

1. Both authors are creatively inspired by the song of the cricket;[9]

2. Emily Dickinson uses two of Hawthorne's significant words (pensive, typify);[10]

3. The intense emotion comes at noon in August, and the descriptive and emotional aura is precisely the same in both texts: both authors are describing what is for them a state of grace; Hawthorne implicitly ("above and beyond all thought") and Dickinson explicitly;

4. The element of sadness (Hawthorne's "half-acknowledged melancholy"; Emily Dickinson's "Enlarging Loneliness") comes in the middle of both texts, in the poem precisely so, but by the end of both texts this element has been assimilated. In the poem the musical-mystical harbinger of autumn magnifies (Enhances) Nature in this most ancient of rituals within which man takes his natural place.

Both texts end with the same declaration: man is not alien in the scheme of things; to be alone is not to be isolated. There is an affirmative acceptance of an eternal verity. Hawthorne is explicit in his acceptance of the continuum of immortality, and if Emily Dickinson is explicit only in stating that this has always been Nature's

---

[9] Emily Dickinson entitled another version of this poem "My Cricket." See Charles R. Anderson, pp. 152-153; and T. H. Johnson, *Emily Dickinson*, p. 185.

[10] Each reader can decide for himself the relationship to the poem of other words found in Hawthorne's passage and in the essay generally. For example: antique (pp. 28, 31); antiquity (p. 27); grass (p. 37); and furrows (p. 22).

way, her statement is implicitly both a projection for the future and an acceptance.[11]

III

To go beyond this point in explication would be an imposition upon the reader's inalienable right to experience the poem finally on his own terms. But nagging questions persist: Is Hawthorne's text merely parallel, only a remarkable coincidence? Or did Emily Dickinson read Hawthorne's passage in "The Old Manse" and transform it to her poetic purpose? There is no specific evidence for such an assertion. We know that she read Hawthorne, as did her brother, that she could in a letter to him refer to Hepzibah and Clifford Pyncheon in a manner indicating close familiarity with *The House of the Seven Gables*.[12] All this beyond the reasonable assumption that Emily, the avid reader, would have read her fellow New Englander from cover to cover. If we do have a coincidence, then it strains the law of probability to the breaking point. It is easier to believe that Emily Dickinson read "The Old Manse," found in Hawthorne's passage confirmation of her own complex responses, and wrote her poetic version of the passage, thereby almost miraculously enhancing her own nature the more.

[11] Hawthorne's and Emily Dickinson's utterances invite comparison with Emerson's poem "Waldeinsamkeit" (1858).

[12] Jay Leyda, *The Years and Hours of Emily Dickinson* (New Haven, 1960), I, 223. In October, 1851, Austin Dickinson wrote to Susan Gilbert, who became his wife in 1856, listing *Mosses from an Old Manse* among other books "piled on my shelf & scattered over my table" (Leyda, I, 218).

"The Souls That Snow": Winter in the Poetry of Emily Dickinson

Ed Folsom

> The Seasons flit—I'm taught—
> Without the Snow's Tableau
> Winter, were lie—to me—
> Because I see—New Englandly—[1]

INVOLVED IN THE VERY ESSENCE of seeing "New Englandly" are the rotation—the "flitting"—of the seasons and especially the "Snow's Tableau" in winter. It would seem logical, on the basis of such a statement, to expect a great deal of winter imagery—cold, snowy Connecticut Valley imagery—in Emily Dickinson's poetry. Yet, except for a very few poems (i.e., 258, "There's a certain Slant of light, / Winter afternoons—"), winter imagery seems strangely absent. While poems concerning the other seasons abound, Thomas H. Johnson finds that she "devoted the fewest poems to winter."[2] In his article on Dickinson's late summer and autumn poems, Ernest Sandeen concurs, adding that "in view of her deep aversion to this season it is not surprising that she wrote very few winter poems . . . ."[3] And while several critics investigate Dickinson's seasonal-cycle imagery, no one goes much further than simply accepting the poet's "aversion" as a reason for winter's absence.[4]

---

[1] Poem number 285 in Thomas H. Johnson, ed., *The Poems of Emily Dickinson*, 3 vols. (Cambridge, Mass., 1955), I, 204. All future references to Dickinson's poems will be noted simply by the number of the poem, referring in each case to the Johnson edition. The title phrase, "Souls that snow," is from poem 927.

[2] Thomas H. Johnson, *Emily Dickinson: An Interpretive Biography* (New York, 1967), p. 185.

[3] Ernest Sandeen, "Delight Deferred by Retrospect: Emily Dickinson's Late-Summer Poems," *New England Quarterly*, XL (Dec., 1967), 485.

[4] Some of the most helpful commentary on seasonal imagery in Dickinson's work may be found in Charles R. Anderson, *Emily Dickinson's Poetry: Stairway of Surprise* (New York, 1960), where chapter 8 is on "Process" and is invaluable as a general source for Dickinson's use of the seasonal cycle; Albert J. Gelpi, *Emily Dickinson: The Mind of the Poet* (Cambridge, Mass., 1965), with incisive comments on seasonal imagery scattered throughout the book; Johnson's *Interpretive Biography*, with chapter IX, "Nature: The Haunted House," especially helpful; Sandeen's article on "Dickinson's Late Summer Poems," the first part of which is a succinct overview of her reactions to the various seasons; and William R. Sher-

Yet aversion hardly seems a viable reason for avoidance, especially for Dickinson, who consistently confronted adverse experience—pain, grief, death—and transmuted it into poetry. The fact persists as well that, living her whole life in Amherst, Dickinson could hardly ignore winter; the snowed-in village of nineteenth-century New England, while not always an idyllic scene, was at least a memorable one.

And, indeed, a more careful investigation of her poetry reveals some surprising facts concerning Dickinson's use of winter. Although Johnson, in his definitive edition of Dickinson's poetry, lists only four poems under "winter" in the subject index, no less than thirty of her poems directly mention winter, and nearly sixty mention snow, while many others contain imagery relating to winter, such as ice, frost, and freezing.[5] While these numbers are nowhere close to the pervasive references to summer (at least two hundred), they are nearly equal to the number of references to spring (around seventy)and greater than the references to autumn (about twenty-five). While it is true that some of her finest poetry focuses on spring, summer, and autumn, an overview of her entire poetic output is incomplete without a firm understanding of how winter is utilized and what meanings are associated with it. The "Snow's Tableau" *is* vital in Dickinson's poetry, and winter's shifting nuances reveal much of the nature of Dickinson's poetic stance, straddling American romanticism and realism, the transcendent reading of nature and the realistic rendering of it.

wood, *Circumference and Circumstance* (New York, 1968), with relevant statements distributed throughout the book.

[5] One of Johnson's winter listings in his subject index is incorrect; poem 1708 is listed but has nothing to do with winter; poem 1707 is a winter poem, though, and is probably the intended reference. As this essay demonstrates, a list of only four poems as "winter poems" is insufficient for formulating the meaning of winter in the poetry. Accordingly, I offer here a list of poems in which imagery relating to winter occurs, with the probable year of composition: *1851:* 2; *1858:* 6, 7, 20, 22, 36, 37, 45; *1859:* 58, 63, 64, 96, 99, 100, 104, 126, 131, 135, 136, 141; *1860:* 158, 178, 179, 180, 188, 191, 214; *1861:* 216, 221, 254, 258, 274, 275, 278, 281, 283, 285, 287; *1862:* 302, 311, 314, 325, 326, 335, 337, 341, 347, 366, 375, 386, 390, 403, 409, 411, 422, 442, 481, 495, 513, 519, 525, 532, 538, 561, 562, 577, 589, 591, 592, 619, 627, 640, 649; *1863:* 690, 709, 717, 736, 756, 759, 763, 768, 792, 804; *1864:* 846, 898, 912, 914, 927, 933, 942; *1865:* 968, 981, 995, 1014, 1025; *1866:* 1075, 1080, 1092; *1868:* 1115, 1121, 1133, 1135; *1869:* 1136; *1873:* 1252, 1259, 1276; *1874:* 1310, 1316; *1876:* 1361, 1381, 1388; *1877:* 1413, 1422; *1878:* 1444; *1880:* 1498, 1504; *1881:* 1519; *1883:* 1561, 1570, 1590; *1884:* 1628, 1635; *Undated:* 1649, 1664, 1669, 1670, 1695, 1696, 1707, 1756. Not all of these poems, of course, contain a developed statement on winter, but each one does contain at least one image relating to winter.

Winter for Dickinson is the season that forces reality, that strips all hope of transcendence. It is a season of death and a metaphor for death. While noon is always the zenith of transcendent hope in her poetry,[6] and summer the flourishing of life, it is on "Winter afternoons" that "a certain Slant of light" "oppresses" and gives "Heavenly Hurt":

> When it comes, the Landscape listens—
> Shadows—hold their breath—
> When it goes, 'tis like the Distance
> On the look of Death— (258)

Winter brings a chilling death, a cold immortality; it never offers transcendence to a life beyond this one, rather only threatens this life as it brushes death close by as a warning or, at some point, as a summons.

Basically, then, Dickinson wavered between a hope for an eternity of spring or summer, a new Eden, and a fear of an eternity of winter, a frozen grave. She attempted to create the eternal Paradise of unending summer in her poetry, but this warm Eden stubbornly remained only a construct of words, hopelessly displaced from reality. Winter thus served as a perpetual backdrop, an obdurate counterpoint to any transcendent hope. Only by ignoring winter, imagining it away, could a pure Eden result, as in poem 1056 where the winter solstice is obliterated:

> There is a Zone whose even Years
> No Solstice interrupt—
> Whose Sun constructs perpetual Noon
> Whose perfect Seasons wait—

In this zone the years are "even" because they are changeless; the cycle of the seasons is limited to summer following summer, culminating in an eternity of "Noon":

> Whose Summer set in Summer, till
> The Centuries of June
> The Centuries of August cease
> And consciousness—is Noon.

---

[6] Anderson, p. 155, and Sherwood, p. 132, offer this interpretation; see also letter 93 in Johnson, *Letters*, I, 210, where Dickinson refers to "the burning noon," in Thomas H. Johnson, ed., *The Letters of Emily Dickinson*, 3 vols. (Cambridge, Mass., 1958).

But it is seldom in her poetry that winter can be so blithely obliterated, even for an illusory moment; more commonly it hovers in the consciousness during all seasons, exercising its inexorable pull to the earth, away from transcendence, falling like the snow to cover or smother, and thus to keep earthly things on earth. An attempt to create a transcendent Paradise is therefore futile when winter shifts its frozen weight of reality upon man; then the imagined artistic eternity, the desire for eternal life outside the realm of shifting seasons, simply intensifies the cold reality which refuses to be "obviated" or "eased":

> Conjecturing a Climate
> Of unsuspended Suns—
> Adds poignancy to Winter—
> The Shivering Fancy turns
>
> To a fictitious Country
> To palliate a Cold—
> Not obviated of Degree
> Nor eased—of Latitude— (562)

As such a restraining force, winter is an undercurrent in the poetry, and only occasionally surfaces in an expansive, singular image; generally the winter imagery remains the bit of frost thrusting a mortal chill into hope. Perhaps that is why critics have felt that the winter imagery is nearly absent; actually it is pervasive, but subdued.

Often in the poetry, winter and death become concomitant conditions; the coming of one indicates the presence of the other.[7] The association appears in subtle ways, as in the vestments of the dead— "Uniforms of Snow" (125), "vest of snow" (58), "frocks of purest snow" (104)—as well as in more developed allusions; when death occurs in winter, the incident seems a redundancy:

> While simple–hearted neighbors
> Chat of the 'Early Dead'
> We—prone to periphrasis,
> Remark that birds have fled!

[7] Dickinson's letters emphasize how keenly aware she was of seasonal change; many letters describe the weather in detail and go on to draw meanings from it. The coming of winter seemed at times to correspond quite literally to human death; she writes in November, 1858: "I can't stay any longer in a world of death. Austin is ill of fever. I buried my garden last week—our man, Dick, lost a little girl through the scarlet fever. . . . Ah! democratic Death! Grasping the proudest zinnia from my purple garden—then deep to his bosom calling the serf's child!" (*Letters*, II, 341.)

Death is called "the everlasting snow" (158) and is referred to as "Bald, and Cold" (281). When the "Dial life" stops, the dead clock of mortality has a "pendulum of snow" (287); one "color of the Grave is white" and "You would not know it from the Drifts / In Winter—" (411). The hemlock, agent of death, "likes to stand / Upon a Marge of Snow— / It suits his own Austerity," for "The Hemlock's nature thrives—on cold—" (525). As the poet contemplates the "Austere Snow," its "chilly softness" blankets the newly dead (942). Winter's frost is continually associated with death; throughout the poetry, as Johnson notes, "frost destroys and is associated with winter. Frost is intentionally cruel . . . . He corresponds in the world of nature to the character of Death . . .";[8] thus, "The Frost of Death was on the Pane—" (1136). One of Dickinson's darkest poems is about the frost as "assassin," operating in an insouciant universe presided over by a cruel or unfeeling God who silently approves as

> Apparently with no surprise
> To any happy Flower
> The Frost beheads it at it's play—
> In accidental power— (1624)

Winter in these instances seems to be a blind process, a blind white force that freezes and kills life. Charles Anderson proposes that at times Dickinson is "haunted by the suspicion that at its center nature is only automatic process, without any meaning of a sort that the conscious mind can recognize."[9] This "automatic process" describes winter as it is used in the poems above.

But just as Dickinson never settled for the seasonal cycle as necessarily indicative of resurrection and immortality, so does she not view death as occurring only in winter; while winter suggests death, death does not operate, obviously, during one season only. Thus Dickinson employs winter imagery in another way; in her poetry, Death has its own winter, and the force of death can unleash winter's ravage in a body at any time of the year. Emphasizing how seriously she took this imagery, Dickinson employed it in a letter to Louise and Frances Norcross in speaking of the death of her mother:

---

8 Johnson, *Interpretive Biography*, p. 192.
9 Anderson, p. 158.

. . . [M]other's dying almost stunned my spirit . . . .
She slipped from our fingers like a flake, and is now
part of the drift called 'the infinite.'[10]

Dickinson employs a similar image in a poem about a man who
wants to die, but can only helplessly watch as his friends die instead,
"shifted like the Flakes / when Gusts reverse the Snow—" (759).
The dead, she says in poem 409, "dropped like Flakes." Death,
himself "the everlasting snow" (158), can render real winter relatively meaningless; external weather does not affect man as intensely
as internal weather:

> What care the Dead for Winter?
> Themselves as easy freeze—
> June noon—as January night— (592)

Death invades the body's summer of life, and the body, "warm—
at first—like Us—," slowly gives way to Death's encroaching winter:

> The Fingers grew too cold
> To ache—and like a Skater's Brook—
> It straightened—that was all—
> It crowded Cold to Cold— (519)

The "Climate of the Grave," Dickinson says elsewhere, is "A Power
of Renowned Cold" that, in order to overcome truly hearty people,
must inject ever colder winters into the body until warmth is finally
diminished:

> For some—an Ampler Zero—
> A Frost more needle keen
> Is necessary, to reduce
> The Ethiop within. (422)

When death occurs in summer, the internal winter undercuts any
hopeful meaning to be found in external weather:

> She was not warm, though summer shone
> Nor scrupulous of cold
> Though Rime by Rime, the steady Frost
> Upon her bosom piled— (804)

Fear and grief, like death, can bring a winter to the soul regardless of Nature's season; fear freezes internally, even in external sun:

---

[10] Johnson, *Letters*, III, 749–750.

When I feared—I recollect
Just the day it was—
Worlds were lying out to Sun—
Yet how Nature froze—

Icicles upon my soul
Prickled Blue and Cool— (768)

Nor is grief softened by springtime; daffodils delight only those who are in a spring-mood, who feel like being delighted, while lingering grief causes the soul to snow:

Absent places—an April Day—
Daffodils a-blow
Homesick curiosity
To the Souls that snow—

Drift may block within it
Deeper than without— (927)

And moments of winter suddenly materialize at other times of stress; when "some ghostly Fright" appears, it moves to the soul to "Caress her freezing hair" (512), and the snake is never encountered "Without a tighter breathing / And Zero at the Bone—" (986).

Winter, then, becomes an endurance test, a problem of persisting through adversity until the ease and warmth of spring return: "There's that long town of White—to cross— / Before the Blackbirds sing!" (221) Johnson feels that Dickinson's "observation of . . . the phenomena of the seasons is most lively when she sees them out-of-doors and in motion."[11] Her winter poems obviously are not as lively, for they occur generally in-doors and movement is frozen; shelter is sought as winter approaches and "We . . . fetch the Acres in" (1025). But this stasis has a power of its own; the iron grip of winter on life is a periodic testing of the will, a shrinking of hope that tests the soul's ability to find sustenance in stern reality; this is the "italic flavor" winter yields (1316). It is not surprising to find numerous references in the letters to the clinging to shelter in winter; the need for the warmth of the fire in the hearth is reminiscent of Hawthorne's work and carries much the same value. In early summer of 1858, she writes a letter recalling the past winter:

11 Johnson, *Interpretive Biography*, p. 192.

> . . . months of frost, and days of jingling bells,
> yet all the while this hand upon our fireside.[12]

This need for shelter, for warmth to cling to, in order to endure winter is reflected often in the poetry; Dickinson searches for the "snugly built" refuge that "must exclude the storm" (127). In recalling how she could have been the wife of a lost love, the poet tells of the inexorable thrust of winter as it tries to invade shelter, gain entry; to combat it, she offers comfort of companionship and fire:

> The Cold will force your tightest door
> Some February Day,
> But say my apron bring the sticks
> To make your cottage gay— (366)

In order to endure the gripping Winter, Dickinson considers various comforts that could help and settles on fire:

> Flowers—to keep the Eyes—from going awkward—
> When it snows—
> A bird—if they prefer—
> Though Winter fire—sing clear as Plover— (495)

And a housewife in poem 589 pulls the rocking chair "closer to the fire" one winter, checks "if Blinds be fast," and is so comforted that she can say, defiantly, "How pleasanter . . ./ The sleet—than May . . ." (589). Always the doors are hooked, the blinds pulled, to keep the persistent winter out, and only those who can avoid exposure are safe, as is the apple in the following poem, one of several poems that emphasize the cold isolation of the season by failing to mention human life:

> Like Brooms of Steel
> The Snow and Wind
> Had swept the Winter Street—
> The House was hooked
> The Sun sent out
> Faint Deputies of Heat—
>
> . . . .
> The Apple in the cellar snug
> Was all the one that played. (1252)

---

[12] Johnson, *Letters,* II, 335. See also related letters in I, 268, and II, 353.

The desolation, the absence of man, adds power to the image of the "Brooms of Steel," as if life itself had been swept away. It is a haunting poem; we do not know who is within the hooked house, but whoever (if anyone) is there is not "playing," is instead soberly contemplating the void left by the storm.

Even into safe shelter, winter and death can creep; shelter protects, but is no ultimate guarantee of inviolability; Death, "the postpone-less Creature," "gains the door" and, randomly choosing his victim, "Dresses each House in Crape, and Icicle— / And Carries one—out of it—to God—" (390). In another poem, the story of a shipwreck in which forty men were killed is later to be told to children; the winter seems to vibrate in sympathy to the mass death, and porten-tously nudges the shelter: "How will they tell the Story— / When Winter shake the Door—" (619). In one memorable winter poem, the poet "scanned my little life" and culled from it all of her valu-able memories, letting the dross "blow away." She then puts her valuable, lasting memories in a barn for safe-keeping. But winter invades the shelter, and, once again, a God who allows such things to happen is indicted, and man is forced to become a cynical realist:

> I went one winter morning
> And lo—my priceless Hay
> Was not upon the 'Scaffold'—
>
> Was not upon the 'Beam'—
> And from a thriving Farmer—
> A Cynic, I became. (178)

If one is *without* shelter, though, exposure in the winter is cer-tainly fatal. There are virtually no poems in which man comes into direct contact with ice, snow, frost, or cold and survives. The images of death in snow are powerful and poignant, capturing the cold's grip on life, then portraying life slipping helplessly away, as in the simile for "the Hour of Lead":

> This is the Hour of Lead—
> Remembered, if outlived,
> As Freezing persons, recollect the Snow—
> First—Chill—then Stupor—then the letting go— (341)

Elsewhere, "The Beggar Lad," helplessly exposed to the sleet and "bitter Wind" of winter, "dies early" while "It's Somewhat in the

Cold" (717), and the "Two Travellers perishing in Snow" fare no better, even as they try to strengthen each other with thoughts of heaven; the exposure to the elements of cold is too long:

> And then the cheer too solemn grew
> For language, and the wind
> Long steps across the features took . . . . (933)

And, in a metaphor equating winter with life, Dickinson contrasts men who face the harsh winter with the birds that instinctively flee to the warmth of the South:

> The Southern Custom—of the Bird—
> That ere the Frosts are due—
> Accepts a better Latitude—
> We are the Birds—that stay.

These birds—men—are beggars who helplessly confront the elements; they are "The shiverers around Farmer's doors" who have no warm shelter and thus finally accept death as a comfort, as a kind of last-resort shelter to insulate them from the cold:

> . . . till pitying Snows
> Persuade our Feathers Home . . . . (335)

So winter brings a trial of the will, forces men indoors to the life-giving hearth-fires in order to survive, and destroys those who face the elements. Again, it is significant that in her most expansive descriptions of winter, Dickinson portrays no human life; the scene is relentlessly one of desolation; snow is no place to frolic in Dickinson's poetic world. Thus, as we saw, the "Brooms of Steel" had swept the deserted winter streets (1252). In one of her most developed descriptions of a winter snowstorm, this same desolation is captured as snow quietly, faintly, softly, but effectively covers all, creating a smooth, white, dead stasis:

> It sifts from Leaden Sieves—
> It powders all the Wood.
> It fills with Alabaster Wool
> The Wrinkles of the Road—
>
> It makes an Even Face
> Of Mountain, and of Plain—
> Unbroken Forehead from the East
> Unto the East again—

Moving as if dimly conscious ("It reaches to the Fence— / It wraps it Rail by Rail"), the ubiquitous snow covers everything with its white veil, including the shelter, which is now devoid of life ("A Summer's empty Room"), and the stubble of the gathered crop, the memory of the past summer and its harvest obliterated except for the "Acres of Joints, where Harvests were," jutting in the snow. It brings beauty as well as desolation, then leaves in the same ghostly quiet in which it came (recalling poem 274, where the "only ghost I ever saw . . . stepped like flakes of snow"):

> It Ruffles Wrists of Posts
> As Ankles of a Queen—
> Then stills it's Artisans—like Ghosts—
> Denying they have been— (311)

In a later version of the poem, the quiet terror of the storm is further emphasized by the revised ending:

> It traverses—yet halts—
> Disperses while it stays
> Then curls itself in Capricorn
> Denying that it was—

As it enters the winter solstice, the storm evaporates into a denial of its own existence, a non-being abnegating responsibility (like an indifferent God) for the desolation. Here, with no implication of a rebirth, we find the ultimate nightmare of the seasonal cycle, halting abruptly in midwinter, leaving a blanket of snow. It is in winter that "The Sky is low—the Clouds are mean" with "A Travelling Flake of Snow," when "A narrow Wind complains all Day" (1075): Nature, too, has her bad moods, her undignified periods of "meanness," and they occur, in Dickinson's poetry, in winter.

The reaction to this terror of winter, with its concomitant threats of death, grief, fear, and desolation, is consistently one of gritting the teeth, of trying to keep the mind on the spring at winter's end, and asking or praying for strength to bear the winter through, to complete another cycle; the hope is that the season's turning will be a symbol for ever-renewing life instead of a halting pendulum of time signalling the end of the cycle for the individual. There is always a hovering threat that the year's temporary freezing could unexpectedly become permanent death, that winter might be a finality instead of a phase. Thus, as winter approaches—"A little this side of snow"—the poet prays: "Grant me, Oh Lord, a sunny mind— / The windy will to bear!" (131) She must continually remind herself that "It will be Summer—eventually / . . . / Tho' drifted deep, in Parian— / The Village lies—today—" (347). The crocus, protected by its winter shelter of soil, is a hopeful emblem for Dickinson, although the hope must be kept secret, must be whispered, for it is audacious to tempt or to defy winter:

> You and I the secret
> Of the Crocus know—
> Let us chant it softly—
> "*There* is no more snow!" (22)

The crocus, herald of spring, teaches the lesson that during the winter we must be cautious, seek shelter, be passively subservient: "The Crocus—till she rises / The Vassal of the snow" (7).

So one must will the mind, the imagination, to create an internal summer or spring, a hope, to offset the encroachment of the external cold: "Hope" is the thing that can keep "so many warm" even in "the chillest land" (254). This imagined internal summer of hope can warm in winter, then, just as effectively as the internal winter of death can freeze in summer:

> Not a Sleet could bite me—
> Not a frost could cool—
> Hope it was that kept me warm—
> Not Merino shawl— (768)

The imaginative construct is vital, for while winter rages outside, the mind can live on, protected inside; man can attempt in this way to "abolish Frost," for the imagination is powerful: "If Seasons perish or prevail / Is optional with Us—" (1014). Thought and hope can endure in adversity, and flowers can be planted in the internal soil of the imagination; Dickinson sums it up in a two-line poem:

> Winter under cultivation
> Is as arable as Spring. (1707)

There is, however, an irony involved even in this internal culti-vation. Man must never lose touch with reality, Dickinson warns, blithely living in imagined Paradises, oblivious to the real coldness outside; otherwise he becomes lost in the maze of fancy, and is

unable to cope with harsh actualities. The inordinate longing for
summer in winter can lead to destructive despair when one is
forced by circumstance to face winter again. To endure, man needs
a cynical mind, a mind wary of the realities around him; as long
as he is alive, he cannot obliterate the disagreeable actuality:

> How happy I was if I could forget
> To remember how sad I am
> Would be an easy adversity
> But the recollecting of Bloom
> Keeps making November difficult
> Till I who was almost bold
> Lose my way like a little Child
> And perish of the cold. (898)

Man must gather nourishment and carefully prepare shelter for the
winter, gather strength for any trying actuality, rather than fool-
ishly try to escape by transcendence; destruction crouches in wait
for those who refuse to adapt to change, to the cycles of nature.
Dickinson tells of the pause after summer when "My sentence had
begun," and she realizes the difficulty of adapting, of leaving the
Paradise of warmth and bloom for the trials of winter; she also
realizes the consequences of failure to adapt:

> To winter to remove
> With winter to abide
> Go manacle your icicle
> Against your tropic Bride. (1756)

The failure to adapt, to seek shelter, to strengthen oneself for trial,
brings death, and even death's winter can be a comforting relief
for someone whose fitness to endure the real winter is lacking:
"Some, too fragile for winter winds / The thoughtful grave en-
closes—" (141).

Dickinson suggests that instead of trying to obliterate winter—
hardship, reality—with constructs of the imagination, man should
keep his hand "upon the fireside," maintain but not be engulfed
by a hope or memory of summer or spring, of happiness, and
remain aware of and retain a certain respect for the power of the
frost. The awareness of the contrast of seasons, of emotions, is
valuable, sobering, and keeps man in touch with reality; it reminds
him of the fact that no single mood, vision, experience, or season is

isolated and eternal, that life is a process of change—a "Wonderful Rotation" (6)—and that happiness is heightened by knowledge of grief, warmth by an awareness of coldness. That is why "Winter is good," for yielding "Italic flavor" "To Intellects inebriate / With summer . . ." (1316). Dickinson also states this belief in a poem less often quoted; as she watches a light snowstorm that brings, pleasantly, "Snow that never drifts," "transient, fragrant snow," she feels a certain disappointment, as if winter were not exercising its full terror, thus not teaching man, testing him, challenging him, offering contrast:

> Were every storm so spice
> The Value could not be—
> We buy with contrast—Pang is good
> As near as memory— (1133)

For those who do endure, reward comes; the cycle passes beyond the hardships of harsh winter and brings resurrection. The frigid terror of winter teaches by contrast of the warmth to come. Dickinson notes that as "Water, is taught by thirst," so "Birds, by the Snow" (135). As the crocus is resurrected, many men share in the new birth, but inevitably for some the cycle has come to a halt, and winter yields no spring; in the moment of transition from winter to spring, Dickinson finds that "New children play upon the green— / New Weary sleep below—" (99). But, for those who have adapted, who have endured, new life "unexpected come[s]" like "Arctic creatures, dimly stirred— / By Tropic Hint" (513). Birds replace snow: "The Robins stand as thick today / As flakes of snow stood yesterday" (64). And as "Winter instantly becomes / An infinite Alas," spring delivers "The Proclamation of the Suns / That sepulture is o'er." (1519)

Winter, the "Finland of the Year" (1696), is pervasive, then, in Dickinson's poetry. Its existence is often subdued as it serves as a chilling backdrop or undercurrent to other themes and poems of other seasons. But its importance in Dickinson's canon is surely greater than critical opinion has, until now, given it. Poems which employ winter imagery are distributed throughout Dickinson's work and are not limited to a certain phase or certain years (see footnote 5). The imagery is consistent in tone but varied in implication and use. Winter is seldom used as a positive or optimistic image beyond the "Italic flavor" it offers, although there are minor exceptions: counting "snow flakes" leads to a happy "jig" (36); a ballet is described on "wheels of snow" (326); the "sunset in the snow" is purely intimate (1504); and there is a kind of perverse joy in "stroking the frost" of an imagined dead lover (577).

Winter, though, is generally associated with more than just death; it is a harsh reality, a test of endurance of the darker hours of life. Another writer raised on New England winters, Henry Adams, encapsulizes the meaning of winter for Dickinson as he recalls his own young reactions to the seasons in Massachusetts: "Winter was always the effort to live; summer was tropical license."[13] The associations for both seasons apply as well to Dickinson, who was "Inebriate of Air" (214) in summers and struggling to endure the winters. Winter for Dickinson is the obdurate force of reality, hovering behind any leap to transcendence, any ultimate affirmation of spiritual reality, diminishing ecstatic hope with its cold memories; in winter, "Peace is a fiction of our faith" (912). The Amherst cold winter with its "Tableau of Snow" was the season, finally, that forced realism on a mind searching the cycle of the seasons for a sign of a transcendental realm of "perfect seasons" (1056):

> The Winters are so short—
> I'm hardly justified
> In sending all the Birds away—
> And moving into Pod—
> Myself—for scarcely settled—
> The Phebes have begun—
> And then—it's time to strike my tent—
> And open House—again—
>
> It's mostly interruptions—
> My summer—is despoiled—
> Because there was a Winter—once—
> And all the Cattle—starved—
> And so there was a Deluge—
> And swept the World away—
> But Ararat's Legend—now—
> And no one credits Noah— (403)

Here the role of winter is seen in its full terror: the persistent

13 Henry Adams, *The Education of Henry Adams* (New York, 1946), p. 9.

threatening undercurrent of fear, the need for enclosure in shelter, the cold force of trying reality, and the mythic association with ultimate destruction. The "Grief of Cold" (561)—winter and the recollection of winter, even a destructive winter long past—hovering incongruously in summer, promising to return sometime in the cycle, or to return in the form of death at any moment, finally prevented Dickinson's discernment of a transcendent goodness in the natural cycle. Winter, for Emily Dickinson, was a primary source of her realism.

The Latin Imprint on Emily Dickinson's Poetry: Theory and Practice

Lois A. Cuddy

> "Put it in Latin—left of my school—
> Seems it dont shriek so—under rule."[1]
> c. 1862   *Emily Dickinson*

THE INFLUENCE of Emily Dickinson's classical education on the style and content of her poetry is only now being explored in criticism.[2] Concerning that issue, I have suggested in a paper published in *Comparative Literature Studies* that the Stoddard and Andrews Latin textbook used by Dickinson in her student days at Amherst Academy be considered an important source for her style and voice.[3] That article contends that Dickinson's forms—the functional metres, capitalization, and internal punctuation—are integrally linked to Latin quantitative metrics and caesurae. The present study expands on that theory of influence by revealing how Dickinson's "scrambled" syntax and grammatical "idiosyncrasies" may also derive from the rules in her Latin textbook.[4] In fact, her

---

[1] *The Poems of Emily Dickinson*, ed. Thomas H. Johnson, 3 vols. (Cambridge, Mass., 1955), poem 426. All lines and poem numbers are taken from this edition. Although Dickinson's obvious reference in poem 426 was to putting "Dead" into Latin in order to make the word more bearable and comprehensible, her meaning was of course more complex than the surface subject of the poem. Her indirection in revealing aesthetic purpose may perhaps be explained by another of her lines, "Tell all the Truth but tell it slant," poem 1129. I suggest that Dickinson is likely "slanting" the truth in poem 426 by speaking of her poetic techniques and style in the guise of another subject.

[2] See Nancy McClaran, "Dickinson's 'Of Death I Try to Think Like This,'" *The Explicator*, XXXV (Winter, 1976), 18–19, for the Virgilian allusion in that poem.

[3] Lois A. Cuddy, "The Influence of Latin Poetics on Emily Dickinson's Style," *Comparative Literature Studies*, XIII (Sept., 1976), 214–229.

[4] Solomon Stoddard and Ethan Allen Andrews, *A Grammar of the Latin Language; for the Use of Schools and Colleges* (Boston, 1843). Hereafter cited in the text of the paper as *S&A*. Dickinson's acquaintance with this textbook is verified by Jack L. Capps, *Emily Dickinson's Reading, 1836–1886* (Cambridge, Mass., 1966); and by one of the poet's letters, *The Letters of Emily Dickinson*, ed. Thomas H. Johnson and Theodora Ward (Cambridge, Mass., 1958), ltr. 92, p. 208. For further documentation regarding the poet's knowledge of and interest in Latin, see Jay Leyda, *The Years and Hours of Emily Dickinson* (New Haven, Conn., 1960), I; Thomas H. Johnson, *Emily Dickinson: An Interpretive Biography* (New York, 1967); Richard B. Sewall, *The Life of Emily Dickinson* (New York, 1974), II; and Cuddy, n.3 above.

literal application of Latin language principles to English poetics accounts for many of the unconventional qualities in her work.

Thus, if we follow Dickinson's advice and approach her work with Latin rules in mind—if we, in fact, "put it in Latin"—apparent technical errors in her poems no longer "shriek" but assume a new dimension of aesthetic integrity and creativity. To support this point of view, this paper will examine the Dickinsonian syntactical and grammatical elements, those presumed aberrations and errors which become both correct and appropriate when considered by the rules of the Latin textbook's Appendix.[5]

Much interest has centered on the Dickinson syntax, which often defies categorization within the traditional English sentence order of subject, verb, and object or predicate nominative. Yet Dickinson's strange inversions are actually conventional if approached from a Latin orientation. She continually follows a Latin structure in which it is common practice to end a sentence or clause with the verb. And a predicate nominative may logically be inserted between the subject and verb, as in Dickinson's poem 790 which begins: "Nature— the Gentlest Mother is." Numerous examples of similar syntactical performances may be noted, such as in poem 24, "There is a morn by men unseen"; poem 63, "If pain for peace prepares"; and poem 1581, "How Life's reverberation / It's Explanation found."[6] In poem 584, line thirteen reads: "Nor what consoled it, I could trace—." Dickinson ends with her verb, in the usual Latin style, while the direct object noun clause ("what consoled it") precedes both subject and verb. The purpose for exercising such freedom with the word order in the above line is to preserve the iambic metre and to rhyme "trace" with "Peace."[7] Yet, more than imagination granted this poet such stylistic range. The justification for this practice of reversing the natural order of words in English comes directly from the Latin language rules in her basic grammar book.

[5] The Stoddard and Andrews Appendix immediately follows the chapter on Prosody which figures significantly in my previous paper on Dickinson's metrical and punctuational forms. (See n.3.)

[6] Spatial limitations necessarily restrict the number of examples that can be offered for each rule discussed in this paper. Therefore, I have attempted to range over the poet's whole writing career in selecting samples from different periods to show that the Latin influence was intrinsic to her style of writing and thinking, rather than a transitory interest.

[7] See Johnson, *Biography*, Chapter 4, for a discussion of the different types of rhymes in Dickinson's poems.

The Stoddard and Andrews textbook clearly delineates such syntactical structures. The first exemplary lines used in the chapter on
"Prosody"—which is essential in explicating Dickinson's metrics,
versification, and internal dashes—will clarify the relationship between Latin and Dickinsonian word order: "Conscia mens recti
famae mendacia ridet"—Ovid (*S&A*, p. 259). A literal translation in
English would sound like this: "Alert mind [of] right fame at lies
laughs," or, conforming to English syntactical principles: "An alert
mind of respectable fame laughs at lies."[8] Another example from the
first page of the Prosody chapter illustrates both syntax and omission,
which will be discussed later: "De nihiio nihil, in nihilum nil posse
reverti"—Persius (p. 259). Literally, this line says: "From nothing
nothing, into nothing nothing can be turned," or, to say it clearly
in English: "Nothing [is derived] from nothing [just as] nothing
can be turned into nothing." Thus, when Dickinson reverses the
syntax and deletes words, she is using the Latin textbook as her
guide in recreating poetry modeled after some of the greatest writers
in Western history—the poets of the Latin Golden Age. She was
indeed in good company.

What seems to be poetic license in altering syntax for rhyming or
metrical purposes, then, is simply a functional appropriation of
Latin language principles. And if that were not enough justification
for her deviation from conventional English word order, one of the
Latin rules of syntax suggests further, almost unlimited, freedom
to this poet. An important "Figure of Syntax" in the Stoddard Appendix is defined as follows: "*Hyperbaton* is a transgression of the
usual order of words or clauses" (*S&A*, p. 300). This rule covers
several related stylistic practices: (1) "inversion of the order of two
words" (*Anastrophe*); (2) "reversing the natural order of the sense"
(*Hysteron proteron*); (3) "interchange of constructions" (*Hypallage*); (4) "confused position of words" (*Synchysis*); and (5) in-
sertion in a sentence of a word or words which interrupt the natural
connection (*Parenthesis*). Let us examine Dickinson's reliance on
these concepts for her own work.

The first principle of *Hyperbaton* is *Anastrophe*, which can be il-
lustrated by the last line in poem 1468: "Rekindled by some action

---

[8] Adrienne Williams, Classics Dept., Brown University, has translated the Latin lines
quoted in this paper.

quaint." The last two words are reversed, according to English usage, but follow precisely the Latin rule. The following example illustrates several other elements of *Hyperbaton*:

> From Cocoon forth a Butterfly
> As Lady from her Door
> Emerged—a Summer Afternoon—(poem 354)

Here is an obvious "transgression" of English syntax in which the words might be reversed to read: "A Butterfly [came] forth from [a] Cocoon, As [in the same way that a] Lady emerged from her Door [on] a Summer Afternoon—." Or, if we assign temporal significance to the word "As," then the lines could have the following meaning: "As [a] Lady Emerged from her Door [on] a Summer Afternoon, a Butterfly [came] [emerged] forth from [a] Cocoon." The only defense for destroying the beauty of the poem by such rephrasing is to make the point that the complexity of construction enforces an ambiguity that might seem to be poetic awkwardness or ineptness but is actually a sophisticated use of the Latin rule. Besides reversing the word order for understanding, the reader also must determine whether "Emerged" refers to both the Lady and the Butterfly and whether "As" refers to style and/or time of action. Through "constructional interchange" (*Hypallage*) and the "confused position of words" (*Synchysis*), Dickinson has compressed several meanings into a very few words—just by their "strange" placement. As for the fifth part of *Hyperbaton*, her constant insertions between dashes are often perfect examples of *Parenthesis*. Dickinson's syntactical reversals adhere to the common Latin language principles and even to the deviations which are always appropriate within the wide parameters of Latin structures.

Another related figure of syntax found in the Latin textbook's Appendix and throughout Dickinson's poetry is *Ellipsis*, defined as "the omission of some word or words in a sentence" (*S&A*, p. 298). Dickinson's poems offer infinite possibilities for translating this rule into English verse. Poem 354 (above) is one illustration, as are the following lines: "On a Columnar Self—/How ample to rely" (poem 789). Obviously the subject and verb "it is" should be inserted in the second line for sense in English, so our minds automatically reverse the word order and almost simultaneously supply those words. One of the initial difficulties in reading Dickinson's poems is that the mind must make such necessary conceptual adjustments before meaning can be apprehended.

Another aspect of *Ellipsis* is this poet's frequent omission of the auxiliary verbs, as in the line "Before it [can] see the Sun" (poem 1255); or in the first line of poem 516: "Beauty—be not caused—It Is" ("Beauty [can] not be caused—It Is").[9] Both *Hyperbaton* (reversal of word order) and *Ellipsis* (omission) are evident in the first line of poem 89: "Some things that fly there [may] be." In the line "So be her's the error" (poem 1124), word order and omission are related to *Hysteron* ("reversing the natural order of the sense") and to *Synchysis* ("a confused position of words"). The early critical inclination to assume that Dickinson's techniques were unconscious or unintentional expressions of an aesthetically undisciplined mind is especially interesting in light of the following lines: "Tell Her, I only said—the Syntax—And left the Verb and the Pronoun—out: (poem 494, version II). This poet knew precisely what she was doing—and why.

The last figure of syntax to be discussed has profound ramifications for Dickinson's grammatical practices, often interpreted as errors attributed to the poet's limited education, carelessness, or metrical priorities. Her application of the following Latin rule to English grammatical structure, however, redefines this poet's aesthetic sophistication and intentions: "*Enallage* is a change of words, or a substitution of one gender, number, case, person, tense, mood, or voice of the same word for another" (*S&A*, p. 299).

The "change of words" or "use of one part of speech for another" is called *Antimeria* in the Stoddard textbook (p. 300), and Dickinson's poems are rich in examples of this principle. She began as early as 1854 to use adjectives for nouns, as in the line "In a serener Bright" (poem 5). In poem 372, both *Parenthesis* and substitution of an adjective for a noun are found: "The last—a scanty Num-

---

[9] The omission of auxiliary verbs leads to some confusion about the poet's intentions regarding the use of indicative and subjunctive moods. This is actually not an irrelevant point, for Dickinson's use of the Latin subjunctive rules for her own thematic and emotional purposes is quite remarkable. Although that subject requires a more extensive study than the necessary limits of this paper allow, the point of subjunctive significance must at least be proposed as a point for future exploration. Dickinson's awareness of this language concept is indicated by one of Johnson's notations in *Poems*, III, p. 966: the word "subjunctive" is in the worksheet draft (Bingham 98–4B–12) of poem 1396 but was changed to "mechanic," then to "confiding" in the fair copy.

ber—/'Twould scarcely fill a Two—." Adverbs are used for nouns in "I lingered with Before" (poem 609), "An Everywhere of Silver" (poem 884), and "skirts the Acres of Perhaps" (poem 696). Nouns are used for verbs, "I'll mis sum them" (poem 877) and for adjectives in "Muslin souls . . . Broadcloth Hearts" (poem 278) and "A Quartz contentment" (poem 341). In one poem (poem 341), a verb is substituted for a noun: "Of Ground, or Air, or Ought." Later, in "We talk in *careless*—and in *toss*" (poem 663), we find both an adjective and a verb used as nouns.

Throughout her work Dickinson employs adjectives and adverbs in a most intriguing way. She often uses the same word to modify a noun and verb simultaneously: "Until the tender Carpenter/Perpetual nail it down" (poem 1123). "Perpetual" modifies both "Carpenter" and "nail" to expand the significance of all the words' inherent meanings. This poet also continually uses adjectival for adverbial forms, depending on the metrical (and thematic) requirements for the line: "Recited fluent—here" (poem 313); "The Heaven —unexpected come" (poem 513); and "frequent" for "frequently" in poems 576 and 939. Yet, in the latter poem, she uses "equally," according to conventional grammatical usage, and indicates in many other instances that she is well aware of the correct English form: "So notelessly—are made!" (poem 278); "Had God willed differently" (poem 588); "And simultaneously, a Soul/Escaped" (poem 948). Poem 104 combines *Enallage* (use of an adjective for an adverb), *Hyperbaton* (inverted word order), and *Epizeuxis* (repetition of words for emphasis—*S&A*, p. 302) in the first lines of each stanza: "Where I have lost, I softer tread"; "Whom I have lost, I pious[ly] guard"; "When I have lost, you'll know by this"; and "Why, I have lost, the people know." Of course, "pious" could be modifying either "I" or "guard"—or both—since her flights of grammatical fancy provide for such emotional and thematic compression.

Yet, if uncertainty remains about the reasons for her misspelling or misuing adverbs, poems like 106 should clarify Dickinson's purposeful reliance on both Latin and English rules, depending on her need:

> The Daisy follows soft the Sun—
> And when his golden walk is done—
> Sits shily at his feet—

In line three the adverb "shily" modifies the verb "Sits" and follows English spelling rules for adverbs. The word "soft" in line one, however, probably should be "softly" to modify the verb "follows." As it stands here, "soft" describes the Daisy and the Sun as well as the movement, which now becomes a reticent, humble action to reinforce the "shiness" in line three. Such free application of a rule like *Enallage* is effective in allowing the poet to maintain metrical consistency in this iambic poem and in combining description with feeling and action. Multiple realms of experience can be united in one image created by the single word "soft."

The substitution of one form of a word for another abounds in Dickinson's verses. Her freedom with verb number, for example, pervades the work: "His Name—remain" (poem 307), "A Duchess were too common" (poem 333), and "My Bond—have just begun" (poem 400). She uses "Justify" instead of "Justifies" (poem 698), "Assert" for "Asserts" and "connect" for "connects" (poem 515), and so on. It is the practice of this rule which jars the reader's sensibilities in the lines used as an epigraph to this paper: "Put it in Latin—left of my school—/Seems it dont shriek so—under rule." Within the Latin structures, "it dont" is no longer disquieting but grammatically and metrically appropriate as the poet substitutes first-person "do" for third person "it doesn't." And it is a perfectly acceptable omission to leave out the "o" (or apostrophe) in "dont." The sounds and metrical schemes of the verses seem to determine, at least to a considerable degree, her reliance on the creative latitude provided by this aspect of *Enallage*.

Then there is the substitution of one case for another. In "At you and I!" (poem 10) and "As I of He" (poem 885), Dickinson uses the nominative for the objective case and apparently does so for the rhyme scheme (I/employ and He/Me). Again, her knowledge of accepted English forms is surprisingly evident in other poems when it suits her purpose to be "conventional": "Away from Home are some and I" (poem 821) and "—to Him—and me" (poem 418).

Another frequent type of *Enallage* is exemplified in this poet's freedom with tenses. In the service of a rhyme scheme, Dickinson altered the correct English form when she rhymed "Is a soul 'forgot!' " with "shot!" (poem 8). For metrical purposes, "was chose" justifiably glares out of poem 356: "The Grace that I—was chose—

/To Me—surpassed the Crown." Lest intention be mistaken for indifference, the poet often reminds us that she is quite capable of proper English grammatical usage: "When once it has begun" (poem 565).

The conceptual and technical functions of *Enallage* in Dickinson's work are remarkable. The incorporation of other people with her own "self" is achieved by words like "Themself" in "Themself are all I have" (poem 1094) and "Between Ourself and Heaven" (poem 1043). There is a distinct sense of her own separation even in community. A more unreserved association with others, on the other hand, is expressed in lines like "We wonder it was not Ourselves" (poem 448), "Themselves as easy freeze" (poem 592), and "Between Ourselves and the Dead!" (poem 949). Clearly, her use of language principles is self-serving. To "put it in Latin" rules, then, is to redefine grammatical correctness in Dickinson's poems.

While *Ellipsis* is a "figure of syntax" referring to the omission of words, the Appendix also lists "figures of orthography and etymology" (*S&A*, p. 298) which relate to the omission (or addition) of letters or syllables. A letter or syllable taken from the beginning of a word—as in Dickinson's 'Twould, 'tis, 'twas, 't, 'twere—is called *Aphaeresis*. To delete a letter or syllable from the middle of a word (like Dickinson's e'en, dont, ne'er, shan't, e'er) is called *Syncope*. And *Apocope* is "the omission of the final letter or syllable of a word," like Dickinson's thro', o', or alway'. Whenever the metre or sound requires it, such omission may be made with perfect ease, with or without an apostrophe, according to Latin guidelines.

The "rhetorical figures" listed in the Stoddard Appendix also can be associated with the Dickinson style. For example, the following use of the word "Hay" has been noted as one of her distinctive stylistic traits: "The Grass so little has to do/I wish I were a Hay" (poem 333). According to Dickinson's Latin textbook, this would be an example of both *Metonymy* ("substituting the name of an object for that of another to which it has a certain relation"—a Hay for a blade of grass) and *Synecdoche* (putting "a genus for a species, . . . a whole for a part" and its contrary) (*S&A*, p. 301). Dickinson's "Bandaged" in poem 512 is a *trope* ("The turning of a *word* from its original and customary meaning"—*S&A*, p. 301). "Calvary" too is a *trope* when it expresses her emotional anguish. By including several meanings in the word "Calvary," this poet is employing the rhetorical figure called *Metalepsis* (the including of several *tropes* in one word—*S&A*, p. 301). Not only does Dickinson use *Hyperbole*, another term in the Stoddard text (p. 301), but she includes the word itself in her poetry: "This limitless Hyperbole/Each one of us shall be" (poem 1482).

In fact, the poet's concern for and familiarity with grammatical and prosodic terms become evident even in her poetic diction which comprises, among other terms, *conjugates, syllable, metre, transitive,* and *ablative.* The latter word is perhaps the most significant for our purposes since the ablative case is part of the Latin language, not English. According to the Stoddard text, "The ablative denotes *privation,* and many other relations." Dickinson uses the term in that sense in poem 1741: "That if it be, it be at best/An ablative estate." See also poem 1744.

When other words like *Augustan, Halcyon, Pinnace, Cato, Caesar,* and many more, all found in Dickinson's poetry and the Stoddard textbook, are added to the Latin words in her poems—from the Latin expressions in poem 3 to *Arcturus* and *Resurgam* in poem 70 to *ignis fatuus* in poem 1551—then Dickinson's interest in Latin and the language textbook cannot be denied or assigned to coincidence.[10] Despite the presumed "paucity of classical allusions in Dickinson's work,"[11] many other examples of diction and imagery derived from Latin and the Stoddard textbook attest to this poet's conceptual and referential language model.

A poet's latitude in going beyond restrictive language principles

---

[10] Sewall, *The Life of Emily Dickinson,* II, provides information which reinforces the view of Dickinson's interest in Latin. He notes that even her herbarium had "its carefully printed Latin name for each item" (p. 345). Pages 348–350 mention her classical education and the study of English "composition and orthography," which would have made her Latin textbook more comprehensible—and universal. (See *S&A,* p. 298, for "figures of orthography" and p. 81 of this paper for Dickinson's application of those rules.) A letter, sent from Amherst Academy to parents in 1827 and quoted in Sewall's superb biography, supports this paper's contention regarding Dickinson's awareness of Latin and English grammatical principles and their relations:

"There is both a Classical and English department. The learned languages will be taught in such a manner, as to make the study of text-books a study of interesting facts and sentiments, as well as of words and their grammatical relations. Instead of confinement to the dry details of agreement and government, there will be constant endeavours to excite interest, by adverting to ancient literature, politics, manners and customs." (p. 338)

[11] McClaran, "Dickinson's 'Of Death I Try to Think Like This,' " p. 19.

is stressed several times by Stoddard and Andrews. For example, they state that "the quantity of syllables is determined by certain established rules, or, in cases not included in the rules, by the *authority* of the poets" (*S&A,* p. 259). Again, "The last syllable of every verse . . . may be either long or short, at the option of the poet" (p. 279). With regard to the caesural pause, they note that "In several kinds of verse, its place is fixed; in others, it may fall in more than one place, and the choice is left to the poet" (p. 286). Throughout the chapter on Prosody Stoddard notes the exceptional practices of the major Latin poets, thereby giving permission for such freedom from the constraints of a language apparently controlled by constricting formalism. And, finally in the Appendix, within the list of *grammatical figures* which Stoddard defines as "certain deviations from the regular form and construction of words" (p. 298), Dickinson was again offered almost unlimited freedom for experimentation and intentional defiance of the "regular forms" of language and verse. However strange and idiosyncratic her constructions seem to be, every practice was sanctioned by the prestigious Stoddard and Andrews textbook.

There is considerable biographical precedent for Dickinson's iconoclastic traditionalism in poetry. While she believed in the principles of Christianity, she nevertheless remained a "free thinker" and refused to join any church. This individualism within societal boundaries can be applied to every aspect of her life. She lived within the walls of her home but let her imagination soar; insisted on taking the title of "Wife" but never married; remained within the confines of Christianity but allowed her questing mind to range over multiple possibilities of belief; and worked within the formal patterns of language yet applied the rules in her own way. Thus, consistent with her whole intellectual and emotional orientation, Emily Dickinson revolutionized poetic forms by using prosodic laws from the past for comfort and justification. And Stoddard and Andrews not only suggested but encouraged such paradoxical experimentation within convention.

To apply Latin rules to English is to gain entrance into a new and liberating dimension of English language and prosody; then to apply exceptions and deviations to the accepted Latin syntax and grammar is to move into an apparently unrestrained realm of creative freedom. Yet, as we have noted, it was not license which dictated Dickinson's innovations, for she never violated the rules. Instead, she conceived a new aesthetic theory formulated on the principle of fusing Latin with English, undoubtedly an intellectual and artistic achievement surpassing the praises of even her most ardent admirers.[12]

[12] I wish to thank Professors George Monteiro and David Hirsch, Brown University, for their time and suggestions.

Thirst and Starvation in Emily Dickinson's Poetry
Vivian R. Pollak

"EMILY DICKINSON I did like very much and do still," wrote her friend Joseph Lyman to his fiancée in 1858. "But she is rather morbid and unnatural."[1] Lyman, who lived with the Dickinsons during the winter of 1846, had formed a close platonic attachment with Emily at that time and continued to use her as his touchstone of a superior woman throughout his life. In singling out unnatural morbidity as the single defect in an otherwise flawless character, he was referring, I think, not merely to Dickinson's early and lifelong fascination with illness, with death, and with dying. He was suggesting also the absence of inner vitality, the emotional numbness which was the subject of many of her greatest poems and the enabling wound to her artistic bow. Her poetry was an attempt to keep herself alive by memorializing a range of feeling and experience threatened with extinction from without and within. The relationship between the "Death blow" aimed by God, nature, and human beings, and the "funeral" in the brain was one to which Dickinson addressed her sharpest creative intuitions. She explored this relationship with particular subtlety and sophistication through images of thirst and starvation.

Dickinson uses thirst and starvation metaphorically to represent a broad spectrum of needs: spiritual, emotional, and intellectual. The characteristic response of her deprived persona is to strive for self-sufficiency, for intellectual mastery, and for esthetic sublimation of the debilitating emotions occasioned by neglect or persecution. To this end, her starving-thirsting "I" cultivates a strategy of renunciation, a "Banquet of Abstemiousness," which is an attempt to deny the needs of the social self. However, the Dickinsonian persona cannot depend on the religious, social, and moral context which made the economy of compensation work for such Puritan poets as Anne Bradstreet and such transcendental philosophers as Emerson and Thoreau. Thus her persona also responds to deprivation imposed by

---

[1] *The Lyman Letters,* ed. Richard B. Sewall (Amherst, Mass., 1965), p. 65.

God, by nature, and by humans, involuntarily. The strategy of shrinking vital needs to the point where crumbs and drops suffice, if pushed to the limit, results in the extinction of appetite. What Dickinson portrays, in her most psychologically complex poems, is that loss of life-hunger causes the death of the self.

The "Death blow" in Dickinson's poetry is typically inflicted on a powerless, guiltless self. Her poetry incorporates a wide range of references to such deaths as crucifixion, drowning, hanging, suffocation, freezing, premature burial, shooting, stabbing, and guillotinage. Perhaps because of her deep religiosity, she excludes images of sudden, overt self-destruction from her poetic universe. She does not eliminate images of lingering, covert self-destruction, "Murder by degrees." The most thoroughly worked out of these images is the "I" whose response to privation imposed from without is abstinence to the very point of death, if not beyond. Starving and thirsting occur because of the parsimony of a stingy god; the inaccessibility of nature; and the failure of human love. Or starving and thirsting occur without identifiable cause. Starving and thirsting can also be the unconscious response of a self conditioned by deprivation. Striving desperately for self-reliance, the Dickinsonian persona finds itself unable to respond when

> Victory comes late—
> And is held low to freezing lips—
> Too rapt with frost
> To take it—
> How sweet it would have tasted—
> Just a Drop—
> Was God so economical?
> His Table's spread too high for Us—
> Unless We dine on tiptoe—
> Crumbs—fit such little mouths—
> Cherries—suit Robins—
> The Eagle's Golden Breakfast strangles—Them—
> God keep His Oath to Sparrows—
> Who of little Love—know how to starve—(690)[2]

---

[2] All references to Dickinson's poems are taken from *The Poems of Emily Dickinson*, ed. Thomas H. Johnson, 3 vols. (Cambridge, Mass., 1955). The parenthetical numbers refer to the chronological numbering in this work. Citations from Dickinson's letters are taken from *The Letters of Emily Dickinson*, ed. Thomas H. Johnson, 3 vols. (Cambridge, Mass., 1958). The letter "L" precedes such citations to differentiate letters from poems.

Thus death from thirst or starvation can represent extinction from without and from within, as in the poem just cited. It is the interface of murder and suicide.

While the backgrounds of Puritanism and transcendentalism have been fully explored in discussions of Dickinsonian renunciation, the importance of gender has not been sufficiently recognized. Throughout the nineteenth century, the compensatory ethic of "woman's sphere" incorporated the tensions of self-sacrifice and self-affirmation which Dickinson characterized as "The Battle fought between the Soul / And No Man."[3] The imagery of eating and drinking is especially appropriate to this theme, drawn as it is from woman's sphere. If the persona of her food and drink poems appears devoid of gender and history, her letters make it clear that the strategy of shrinking vital needs to the point where crumbs and drops must suffice developed as a defense against the sexual politics of Victorian America, especially as represented by the Dickinson family. Like her poems, her letters show that this defense was not fully adequate to the monumental task of negating the cultural and psychological tensions it was designed to contain. In 1859, writing to her friend Elizabeth Holland, whose husband was about to return from a lecture tour promoting his best-selling books, she commented, "Am told that fasting gives to food marvellous Aroma, but by birth a Bachelor, disavow Cuisine" (L204). Emily Dickinson was not by birth a bachelor, as even the most superficial reading of her poems and letters indicates.

As John Cody has remarked in a psychoanalytic discussion of oral imagery in *After Great Pain,* Dickinson's letters reveal her preoccupation with oral nourishment.[4] She refers to food and drink in approxi-

---

[3] Three recent works defining nineteenth-century American attitudes toward women are Nancy R. Cott, *The Bonds of Womanhood: "Woman's Sphere" in New England, 1780–1835* (New Haven, Conn., 1977); Ann Douglas, *The Feminization of American Culture* (New York, 1977); and Barbara Welter, *Dimity Convictions: The American Woman in the Nineteenth Century* (Athens, Ohio, 1976).

[4] (Cambridge, Mass., 1971). Cody believes that Dickinson suffered a total mental collapse just before the onset of her great creative period 1858–1862, and that this breakdown was due, in no small measure, to the inadequacies of Emily Norcross Dickinson as a mother during the poet's childhood. Cody sees in Dickinson the characteristics of the emotionally starved child, and has found her oral imagery especially compelling. He writes, "Her insatiable love needs and their frustration saturate the poetry and the letters, and one finds her forever deriving new images of emotional want and fulfillment from the basic metaphor of food and drink," p. 39. Unlike Cody, I believe that Dickinson's gradual withdrawal from the social world was primarily a political response to the extreme sex segregation of mid-century Victorian America, and that the psychodynamics of the Dickinson household represented cultural, rather than personal, disease.

mately three hundred letters, a ratio of almost one in three. Humans, animals, literary, historical and Biblical figures hunger, feed, drink, thirst, starve. Uninterested in housework, she took to cooking easily and naturally. In 1845, at the age of fourteen, she explained to her friend Abiah Root, "You asked me if I was attending school now. I am not. Mother thinks me not able to confine myself to school this term. She had rather I would exercise, and I can assure you I get plenty of that article by staying at home. I am going to learn to make bread to-morrow. So you may imagine me with my sleeves rolled up, mixing flour, milk, salaratus, etc., with a deal of grace" (L8). Fine cooking became her forte. Her father, so she told T. W. Higginson "*very* dreamily" in 1870, would have no bread but hers, "& people must have puddings" (L342a).

Emily Dickinson's letters tell another story as well. Her descriptions of herself stress her smallness, her frailty, her thinness. Especially during her teens and early twenties, the figure of the starved, stunted child, unable or unwilling to take on the plumpness of true womanhood, is essential to her self-characterization. She uses smallness to disguise and to suppress appetites Victorian America was attempting to refine out of "Woman's Sphere": especially anger and aggressive sexuality. In "The 'Scribbling Women' and Fanny Fern: Why Women Wrote," Ann Douglas describes the ruses resorted to by popular women writers during the 1840's and fifties, to obscure their effective competition with men.[5] Fearful of rendering themselves unfeminine in their own eyes and in the eyes of society, they insisted on their own passivity, helplessness, and weakness, while functioning effectively and aggressively in the literary market place. Hawthorne, writing to his publisher in 1855, protested, "America is now given over to a d—d mob of scribbling women, and I should have no chance of success while the public taste is occupied with their trash." Grace Greenwood, a member of the flowery sisterhood enraging Hawthorne, defined "true feminine genius" as "ever timid, doubtful, and clingingly dependent; a perpetual childhood." She concluded, "A true woman shrinks instinctively from greatness."[6]

---

[5] *American Quarterly*, XXIII (Spring, 1971), 3–24. Elaine Showalter's analysis of "feminine" literature in England, represented by such writers as the Brontë sisters, Elizabeth Barrett Browning, and George Eliot, whom Dickinson especially admired, advances the same sort of argument for the conflict between the vocation of the artist and the vocation of the true woman. See *A Literature of Their Own* (Princeton, N.J., 1977).

[6] The citations are from "The 'Scribbling Women' and Fanny Fern: Why Women Wrote."

The ethic of abstinence Dickinson came to employ grew out of cultural tensions she shared with the women of her generation. A paradigmatic letter of the early 1850's shows her withdrawing from confrontation with her father and brother by invoking the protection of smallness. Letter 45, to Austin, begins with an excited observation on the female usurpation of male prerogatives. At a time when Edward Dickinson was comparing Austin's letters home from Harvard Law School to Shakespeare's, and threatening to publish his correspondence because of its literary merit, his sister was replying,

I have just finished reading your letter which was brought in since church. *Mr.* Pierce [the postmaster] was not out today, the wife of this same man took upon her *his* duties, and brought the letter *herself* since we came in from church. I like it grandly—very—because it is so long, and also it's *so* funny—we have all been laughing till the old house rung again at your delineations of men, women, and things. I feel quite like retiring, in presence of one so grand, and casting my small lot among small birds, and fishes—you say you dont comprehend me, you want a simpler style. *Gratitude* indeed for all my fine philosophy! I strove to be exalted thinking I might reach *you* and while I pant and struggle and climb the nearest cloud, you walk out very leisurely in your slippers from Empyrean, and without the *slightest* notice request me to get down! As *simple* as you please, the *simplest* sort of simple—I'll be a little ninny—a little pussy catty, a little Red Riding Hood, I'll wear a Bee in my Bonnet, and a Rose bud in my hair, and what remains to do you shall be told hereafter.

Two years later, when Austin's letters are still the focus of family praise (there isn't a single description of family approval of *her* writing), she asks him, "Are you getting on well with 'the work,' and have you engaged the Harpers? Shall bring in a bill for my Lead Pencils, 17, in number, disbursed at times to you, as soon as the publishment" (L110). No Freudian eye is necessary to see that the humor, like her insistence on her smallness, disguises jealousy.

The autobiographical sources of Dickinson's starving-thirsting persona, and the culturally sanctioned, defensive denial of appetite, are evident by the time she had begun organizing her poetry into packets in 1858. The following cycle of deprivation, self-deprivation, and attempted self-sustenance emerges from her poems. The chronology is psychological and internal, and bears no significant relation to the probable order of composition. It does, however, bear a strong relationship to Dickinson's life experience, as my discussion of her letters has suggested.[7]

The Dickinsonian speaker, contrary to all expectations, has been deprived of ordinary "food." Her hunger absorbs all of her attention, and the value of food is inordinately inflated. When she finally approaches a full table, she finds it strongly distasteful. She watches others eat, unable to understand their savage appetites, while she makes do with her "crumbs." She is surprised and awed to discover that she has lost her appetite when invited to partake of the "feast," and concludes that while there may be something profoundly distasteful about the feast, there may also be something wrong with her. She expends a good deal of psychic energy insisting that anyone in her situation would make the same observations, but one of the satisfactions denied her is a steady sense that others are really responding as she does. Appetite which she identifies with both the desire to live and the imagination, always dies as soon as it is gratified, and satiation, even disgust, then sets in. The sensuous apprehension of reality depends, in her view, on distance and denial. Prudence and happiness consist in knowing that the feast is available but untouched. The highest gratification is the ecstasy of the realization that, at last, the feast is available, but wisdom consists in not eating, since eating will destroy the self. This, then, is the "Banquet of Abstemiousness."

In all, slightly more than 10 percent of Dickinson's poems employ images of food and drink, but because these poems are among her best, incorporating as they do the basic tensions of her experience, the qualitative impression exceeds numerical weight.[8] The chief interest

[7] For an intelligent justification of the virtues of viewing Dickinson's lyrics as "one long poem," see Robert Weisbuch, *Emily Dickinson's Poetry* (Chicago, 1975), pp. xi–xxv. He writes, "I choose to view Dickinson's lyrics as one long poem, to the same extent that Whitman's lyrics constitute a *Leaves of Grass*. It is a key tenet of romanticism, put forth by Emerson in the past century and by Yeats in ours, that a writer's work, in its totality, should constitute a biography of his consciousness. To treat such a 'life' critically, categories and subcategories may be necessary, but they had best be willing to destroy themselves by merging finally into a totality."

[8] David Luisi came to similar conclusions in "Some Aspects of Emily Dickinson's Food and Liquor Poems," *English Studies*, LI (Feb., 1971), 32–40. He established that "Among the poems of Emily Dickinson are an impressive number which deal directly or indirectly with food and liquor. Of the more than two hundred poems which employ this kind of imagery, approximately three quarters of them do so in a subordinate fashion. The remaining fifty or more poems, however, provide a sufficient number in which this imagery supplies the basic metaphors for her thoughts." Luisi concentrates primarily on the "spare richness" of this imagery, seeing in it the conjunction of both the Puritan and Epicurean strains of Dickinson's sensibility.

of these poems is the way in which they document the changes in the self wrought by deprivation; that is, the internalization of deprivation by the poetic persona. Thus the term "compensation," which critics such as Whicher, Gelpi, Sherwood, and Wilbur have employed, while of historical value, is misleading as a characterization of Dickinson's meaning, since it fails to take account of the vulnerability and threatened deterioration of the self.[9] "Compensation" implies, at least by omission, that the suffering soul remains constant while waiting for its ultimate reward. The Dickinsonian persona concentrates its energies on redefining the normal meaning of starvation and repletion, and in the process attempts to redefine and recreate the self.

Excluded from the feast, excluded from raw experience and especially from human love, the loss of appetite and the romantic aggrandizement of appetite confront her. Obsessively, she watches bees drink from flowers, cattle being led to pasture by boys, apples being harvested, birds dining off worms, dogs sucking the marrow out of bones, while she is starving silently and helplessly. Why is she starving? Why did God give a loaf to every bird, while she has only a crumb, why do gnats get more to "eat" than she does? These are the fixed parameters of her world, and she doesn't always question their genesis. She clings to the vestiges of hunger, to the gnawing pain within, as a vital sign. Hunger seems, *in extremis,* her only link with the living.

It becomes clear that, whatever interest Dickinson had in daily life in baking for her father and in winning prizes for her rye and Indian bread, in her poetry eating and drinking are symbolic, highly stylized acts. Solitary rituals concern her, not the actual or immediate sensuous properties of any particular kind of food or drink. The specific foods her poems record, cocoa, berries, dates, bread, are few. On the other hand, she describes "feeding" off of improbable substances such as her lexicon, hermetically sealed minds, and logarithms, observing

[9] George Frisbie Whicher, *This Was a Poet* (Ann Arbor, Mich., 1960); Albert Gelpi, *Emily Dickinson* (Cambridge, Mass., 1965); William R. Sherwood, *Circumference and Circumstance* (New York, 1968). The most extended study of Dickinsonian compensation is Richard Wilbur's essay, " 'Sumptuous Destitution' " in *Emily Dickinson: Three Views* (Amherst, Mass., 1960). Wilbur discusses the poet's "repeated assertion of the paradox that privation is more plentiful than plenty; that to renounce is to possess the more; that 'the Banquet of abstemiousness/Defaces that of wine.' " When he goes on to observe, "The frustration of appetite awakens or abets desire, and that the effect of intense desiring is to render any finite satisfaction disappointing," he anticipates some of my concerns.

wryly, " 'Twas a dry Wine" (728). She capitalizes on the capacity of
liquors to alter consciousness and to arouse sacramental associations.
Spices, stimulating and insubstantial, have a special fascination for
her.

Dickinson's food and drink images are not closely observed, detailed representations of actual sense properties. Food has no taste,
no texture, no color, no shape. What it has is size, which she manipu-
lates to great effect to symbolize status; and odor, which can be perceived from afar. The perception of these qualities does not depend
on ingestion. The poet is concerned with the acquiring of food and
the retention of it, and with its psychosocial effects on the communi-
cant, but implicitly her poems announce that she never gets close
enough to it to describe its immediate sensuous properties. The very
lack of elaboration of her imagery illustrates one form of abstemiousness, of the poet's distancing of the world.[10]

Let us examine more closely the concept of the Banquet of Abstemiousness, as set forth in a poem written about 1877, in the highly
compressed, antinarrative manner of Dickinson's late style:

> Who never wanted—maddest Joy
> Remains to him unknown—
> The Banquet of Abstemiousness
> Defaces that of Wine—
>
> Within it's reach, though yet ungrasped
> Desire's perfect Goal—
> No nearer—lest the Actual—
> Should disenthrall thy soul—(1430)

The setting is formal: a banquet for one. "Abstemiousness" serves as
food and drink, and is superior, in its ability to confer pleasure, to
wine. "Wine" represents anything rare and fine, implying the esthetic connoisseurship the poem endorses. The shocking negative
abstraction, "Abstemiousness," coming after a sequence which pre-

---

[10] This perspective enables her to describe any abstraction as food or drink. Success is
a nectar, best understood by dying soldiers who will never actually taste it (67). "Fame is a
fickle food," scorned by crows, coveted by men (1659). "The Consciousness of Thee" is
a "single Crumb" (815). "Impossibility" is like wine, "Possibility/Is flavorless," "Enchant-
ment" is an "ingredient" (838). "Victory comes late—/And is held low to freezing lips—"
(690). "Surprise is like a thrilling—pungent—/Upon a tasteless meat" (1306). Thoughts
are "signal esoteric sips/Of the communion Wine" (1452). "Grief is a Gourmand" (793).
"Hope is a subtle Glutton" (1547): "His is the Halcyon Table—/That never seats but
One—/And whatsoever is consumed/The same amount remain."

pares for the introduction of some actual food or drink, startles the reader into attending closely to what follows. The image itself brings the banquet tantalizingly near, then whisks it away. The images in the second stanza, where Desire, another abstraction, grasps like a hand, again brings the material world up close, yet distances it. The second stanza indicates that the banquet of life is to remain untouched, except by the imagination. This notion that anticipation is always superior to fulfillment, that fantasy is the only fulfillment, is the most limited aspect of Dickinson's ethic and one which her poetry as a whole, in its concern for preserving and gratifying the urgent thirsts and hungers of the instinctual self, refuses to accept.[11]

Having established a psychological law in this representative poem, which in effect posits an absolute cleavage between reality and imagination, Dickinson predictably violates the tenets of this rigid dualism in much of her poetry. The need for closure which her philosophy of renunciation attempts to satisfy is but one aspect of the unstable flow of experience. If one compares this paradigmatic poem to earlier formulations of the theme of renunciation, it is evident that this is a weak poetic statement. In the famous "Success," for example, written in 1859, and subsequently extorted from the poet for publication by Helen Hunt Jackson, Dickinson poises perfectly between the extremes of morbid cynicism and naive idealization. In that poem, published anonymously and attributed by reviewers to Emerson, intellectual clarity is balanced against agonized defeat. The poet does not assert the superiority of defeat to victory, as is sometimes supposed.[12] Rather, she juxtaposes the perception of victory to the experience of defeat, making perception and experience interdependent antagonists. And while Dickinson writes a good many poems asserting the inviolability of the soul and the educative value of suffering, she also recognizes that clarity of vision is not a necessary or even a probable consequence of exclusion:

[11] Other food and drink poems which affirm the central Dickinsonian paradox of possession through renunciation are "Who never lost, are unprepared" (73); "Water, is taught by thirst" (135); "To learn the Transport by the Pain" (167); "I taste a liquor never brewed" (214); "Exhiliration—is within" (383); "A Prison gets to be a friend" (652); "Deprived of other Banquet" (773); "God gave a Loaf to every Bird" (791); "The Luxury to apprehend" (815); "To disappear enhances" (1209); "Art thou the thing I wanted" (1282); "I took one Draught of Life" (1725).

[12] Wilbur, p. 40, asserts that "the more one ponders this poem the likelier it grows that Emily Dickinson is arguing the superiority of defeat to victory, of frustration to satisfaction, and of anguished comprehension to mere possession."

Undue Significance a starving man attaches
To Food—
Far off—He sighs—and therefore—Hopeless—
And therefore—good—

Partaken—it relieves—indeed—
But proves us
That Spices fly
In the Receipt—It was the Distance—
Was Savory—(439)

Both "Who never wanted—maddest Joy" and "Undue Significance" do, in fact, reflect some loss of the life-hunger which is the
inevitable consequence of the atrophy of the social self. Despite
Dickinson's intermittent adherence to a religion of art, this religion
must feed on the vitality of ordinary human appetitiveness. Thus her
philosophy of renunciation receives its strongest poetic embodiment
when the starving-thirsting "I" is still capable of imagining what
freedom and amplitude might mean. Such a poem as the following,
for example, invokes self-restraint only in response to an inflexible
economics of scarcity:

God gave a Loaf to every Bird—
But just a Crumb—to Me—
I dare not eat it—tho' I starve—
My poignant luxury—

To own it—touch it—
Prove the feat—that made the Pellet mine—
Too happy—for my Sparrow's chance—
For Ampler Coveting—

It might be Famine—all around—
I could not miss an Ear—
Such Plenty smiles upon my Board—
My Garner shows so fair—

I wonder how the Rich—may feel—
An Indiaman—An Earl—
I deem that I—with but a Crumb—
Am Sovreign of them all—(791)

Dickinson's fullest poetic statement of the relationship between
external deprivation and internal inhibition is poem 579, "I had been
hungry, all the Years." It was written in 1862, before her own seclu-

sion had hardened into an unalterable mannerism, at a time when her hopes for love and literary recognition were still very much alive. The narrative structure provided by the journey allows her to incorporate the entire cycle of deprivation, self-deprivation, and self-sustenance. The poem records the death of the social self. After years of unsatisfied hunger, the speaker's "Noon" has come "to dine." The wonderful ambiguity of the phrase perfectly identifies her own effort with the cooperation of external circumstance. The moment she has been enlarging through anticipation, her moment of fulfillment, is before her. She had imagined this chance often enough, as she stared through windows into opulent houses where people were "eating" as a matter of course, knowing that she could not even hope for such abundant happiness. Trembling with eagerness, she draws the table close to her and merely touches the strange wine. Having anticipated some ultimate communion, her reaction startles her:

> I did not know the ample Bread—
> 'Twas so unlike the Crumb
> The Birds and I, had often shared
> In Nature's—Dining Room—
>
> The Plenty hurt me—'Twas so new—
> Myself felt ill—and odd—
> As Berry—of a Mountain Bush—
> Transplanted—to the Road—
>
> Nor was I hungry—so I found
> That Hunger—was a way
> Of Persons outside Windows—
> The Entering—takes away—

In the past she has successfully shared "crumbs" with birds, and it is possible to read the poem as contrasting this overwhelming "ample Bread" with her accustomed spare, yet life-sustaining ration. But the poem goes further. Since the crumbs always left her hungry and frustrated, exiled from human society and reduced to the company of birds, the really significant event is the loss of appetite she experiences when the opportunity to merge intellectual anticipation and sensuous realization occurs. The self has been so completely defined by its starvation that food threatens to destroy it. The speaker cannot, in the end, conceive of the relaxation of restrictions as enabling growth and change. Thus she resists food in order to survive. A berry transplanted from a mountain bush to the public highway dies. Eating crumbs in nature's dining room is better than not eating at all. But the loss in human relatedness is awesome.

The paralyzing consequences of prolonged emotional starvation are subjected to further scrutiny in poem 612, where the low comedy analogy with the gnat controls the poet's despair. Here, the attempt to renounce natural hunger is thwarted, as is the ability to gratify instinctual urges.

> It would have starved a Gnat—
> To live so small as I—
> And yet I was a living Child—
> With Food's necessity
>
> Upon me—like a Claw—
> I could no more remove
> Than I could coax a Leech away—
> Or make a Dragon—move—

This hunger surprises her, as the single unavoidable confirmation that she is alive. Her hunger symbolizes her vitality, but it also serves to emphasize her powerlessness. The gnat has "The privilege to fly / And seek a Dinner" for himself: "How mightier He—than I—". She is totally dependent on mysterious forces beyond her control to supply her wants and enlarge her existence. The gnat can be forthrightly aggressive and acquisitive: she can only wait. Furthermore, the gnat can kill himself on the imprisoning window pane, ensuring the cessation of all consciousness. As a human being, she recognizes that, even after contriving her own death, she might have to "begin—again." In context, this suggestion of life after death is not comforting. The life that would begin again, she implies, would be a life so small, so constricted by want, that she would continue to envy gnats.

In her poetry as in her life, Emily Dickinson pursued a strategy of containing hungers, in response to externally imposed deprivation, beneath which the pressures of a volcanic self continually threatened to erupt. This strategy, as she recognized when her poetic vision was most comprehensive, became an active agent in the death of the psychosocial self. Like the paralyzed speaker in "It would have starved a Gnat," she was unable either to extinguish such inevitable hungers as the desire for literary recognition and for sexual gratification, or to renounce them. As late as 1881, she jotted down the poignant lines, "Let me not thirst with this Hock at my Lip / nor beg, with Domains in my Pocket—" (1772). Thomas Johnson describes them as "the rough draft of lines on a scrap of paper in an envelope containing messages which in their final draft presumably were sent to Judge Lord." Striving to accept celibate obscurity, she wrote each of nearly eighteen hundred poems as though it were her last, and as though she were encapsulating a final vision. However, just as she could not accept the death of love and fame for herself, or the postponement of such rewards until eternity, neither could she wish such a fate on others. The desire to nurse the dying back to life with "food and drink" is everywhere recorded in her poems and letters.

What is not recorded is a single instance where this effort is unquestionably rewarded. Ranging from occasional verse to Samuel Bowles ("Would you like summer? Taste of ours. / Spices? Buy here! / Ill! We have berries, for the parching!") to private, confessional threnodies ("I am ashamed—I hide— / What right have I— to be a Bride— / So late a Dowerless Girl—"), these efforts are at best inconclusive.[13] Poem 773, "Deprived of other Banquet, / I entertained Myself—", is representative of these unconsummated transactions, with its "Berry" reserved for charity. The offering is made to an unrepresented other whose response is unknown. Even the manic exuberance of "Doubt Me! My Dim Companion!" results in a conditional phrasing when Dickinson attempts to describe herself as food offered to her lover (275).

None of these efforts yields a single poem in which the poet's summer is unmistakably tasted. Despite the fact that, from 1875–1882 Emily Dickinson was nursing her stroke-ridden mother with obvious fidelity; despite her Indian summer romance with the widowed Judge Lord; despite the lowering of gingerbread for children; despite the incessant exchanges of food and wine with the women of Amherst; none of these efforts yields a single poem where the offering of self as woman or as poet is accepted.

Inevitably, the starved self does not have the emotional or the practical resources to function effectively as a nurturer. The following poems, "A Dying Tiger—moaned for Drink—," and "I bring an unaccustomed wine," will serve as examples. The first is a brilliant

---

13 Poems 691 and 473.

vision of the frustration of generous nurturing impulses in a dream-like setting charged with anxious sexuality. The second attempts to revivify moribund humanity, and fails. Verbal echoes of a distant religious tradition of charity cannot be reattached to present human sympathy. In both poems, the imaginative distance between Emily Dickinson and her persona has collapsed. The hardness of response she describes, the legacy of conflict, is unquestionably hers.

> A Dying Tiger—moaned for Drink—
> I hunted all the Sand—
> I caught the Dripping of a Rock
> And bore it in my Hand—
>
> His Mighty Balls—in death were thick—
> But searching—I could see
> A Vision on the Retina
> Of Water—and of me—
>
> 'Twas not my blame—who sped too slow—
> 'Twas not his blame—who died
> While I was reaching him—
> But 'twas—the fact that He was dead—(566)

The tiger, a potent threatening masculine symbol, has been rendered harmless because he is dying. The speaker carries the life-giving water in her bare hands, and the very sparseness of the wasteland makes this an elemental meeting. There are no cups or glasses. She has to offer herself, her hand, in offering the "dripping" of the rock. She arrives too late, the tiger is dead by the time she has returned to him, yet he arouses vague feelings of guilt in her. His last sight was "Of Water—and of me—" and she is haunted by his unfulfilled longing. Tiger and speaker are leagues away from parlor niceties. The last stanza attempts, somewhat lamely, to shift the blame away from the tiger and the tardy nurse "who sped too slow" onto an impersonal universe: "the fact that He was dead." The hardness of response, here, is a denial of feeling, a this-has-nothing-to-do with me statement. Yet the guilt is there, despite the denial. If there were no guilt, there would be no poem.

Wine functions as a potential medicine in "I bring an unaccustomed wine," just as water was a medicine in the preceding poem, but again, the speaker is neither Jane Eyre ministering to a blinded Rochester, nor Florence Nightingale:

I bring an unaccustomed wine
To lips long parching
Next to mine,
And summon them to drink;

Crackling with fever, they Essay,
I turn my brimming eyes away,
And come next hour to look.

The hands still hug the tardy glass—
The lips I w'd have cooled, alas—
Are so superfluous Cold—

I w'd as soon attempt to warm
The bosoms where the frost has lain
Ages beneath the mould—

Some other thirsty there may be
To whom this w'd have pointed me
Had it remained to speak—

And so I always bear the cup
If, haply, mine may be the drop
Some pilgrim thirst to slake—

If, haply, any say to me
"Unto the little, unto me,"
When I at last awake. (132)

At the beginning of the poem two figures, nurse and patient, are
dying of thirst. This thirst is a compound of physical need and love-
lessness. Both people are unused to "wine," let alone an ample supply
of water. The patient is feverish and physically ill, the nurse is nomi-
nally healthy. Each has been, in some measure, dehumanized by
thirst. Devoid of "Circumstances— / And a name" (382), they are
both merely "lips." As the poem progresses, the speaker loses the
ability to sympathize. At first her eyes are brimming with tears, but
she turns them away, and when she takes another look at the striving
lips an hour later, the patient is dead. Her tears were futile water. By
stanza four she is describing the dead patient as "this" and "it."
Cloaked with cheerfulness, hers is the frozen bosom of the automaton
do-gooder. She dies emotionally, while the patient dies physically.
Ironically, "its" spirit may have survived, while hers has been denied
the sense of useful relatedness.

What kind of regrets does this situation engender? The speaker is eager once again to absolve herself of all responsibility for the death. She does this by the comparison between the just dead corpse and "The bosoms where the frost has lain / Ages beneath the mould." In addition, she emphasizes her willingness to help by asserting that, if only the just dead corpse had remained to speak, it could have directed her to someone else in need of her ministering. This attempt to profit from misfortune, to bring good out of evil, becomes morally obnoxious when she goes on to explain that she intends to use a whole series of patients to ensure the welfare of her soul. She always tries to help dying people because, perhaps, her good deeds will be rewarded after her own death. Notice, however, that all she is able to describe is bearing the cup, and that the image of the cup of sympathy refused is the one the poem leaves us with, along with the eyes and lips and hands that never connect.

Dickinson's food and drink imagery, then, describes a cycle of deprivation, self-deprivation, and attempted self-sustenance. Typically, her persona is starving, unaccountably and unjustly, in a world of plenty. This prolonged exclusion causes her appetite to shrivel so that when the external restriction is removed, she no longer desires "food." She discovers that the only way she can sustain her desire to live and the vitality of her imagination is to welcome the absence of food and drink, symbolic of the desires of the social self. Inverting the normal meaning of starvation and repletion, she insists that the ideal constructs of her imagination are more vitalizing than any outer wine. However, although both her ability to be nourished and to nourish others has been impaired, she never fully renounces the thirsts and hungers of the social self.

While it is perhaps unnecessary to explain why the near contemporary of Emerson, Thoreau, Hawthorne, and Poe should have attempted to create an invulnerable artistic persona out of the ashes of a vulnerable human identity, Emily Dickinson's strategy of self-deprivation is best understood as a specifically female response, conditioned by American Victorian definitions of true womanhood. More isolated during her years of creativity than any of her literary contemporaries, "Homeless at home," she nevertheless emerges as the spokeswoman for a whole generation of nineteenth-century women. Her recoil from the world, her attempt to live in a separate sphere, and her obsessive fascination with the sexual and social power she could never attain was theirs. In *Literary Women,* Ellen Moers identifies "that vexed question of access to experience, the worst limitation, it is always assumed, that society has imposed upon the woman writer." She hastens to add that "It was by reading, of course, that women writers acquired the remarkable quantity and quality of information about workaday realities that they brought to literature."[14] Dickinson was alert to the compensatory function of art, to satisfy the thirsts and hungers of a deprived persona; but she was ever more insightful into the changes in the self wrought by exclusion. Struggling against the extremes of naive idealization and deadening cynicism, she would have understood the point of Joseph Lyman's comment, "Emily Dickinson I did like very much and do still. But she is rather morbid and unnatural." Virtually all of her critics have disagreed with this assessment, preferring instead to cast her in the role of a detached clinician of death. The starving-thirsting "I" of Emily Dickinson's poetry expresses its bitterness toward God, toward nature, and toward human society through the language of withdrawal. This language controls the impulses to murder and to create. "Renunciation," she tells us, "is a piercing Virtue" (745).

[14] (Garden City, N.Y., 1976).

Dickinson and Rich: Toward a Theory of
Female Poetic Influence

Betsy Erkkila

> Then all day long, with their hearts in agreement, they basked
> In each other's presence, embracing with love and forgetful of sorrow,
> And each received joy from the other and gave joy in return.
> Then smooth-coifed Hecate came and lovingly kissed
> The holy child of Demeter, and the queen from that time
> Served as Persephone's priestess and faithful companion.
> —"To Demeter," 7th century, B.C.[1]

To influence, or flow into, originally referred to an occult ethereal fluid, emanating from the stars, which had the power to alter one's character and destiny. Retaining some of the original sense of influence as power, studies of literary influence have focused on the power relations between men as the key to literary history and aesthetic value. "Poetic history," argues Harold Bloom, is "indistinguishable from poetic influence, since strong poets make that history by misreading one another, so as to clear imaginative space for themselves."[2] The paradigm that Bloom proposes is modeled on Freud's family romance and the power relationships between dominant and submissive that it encodes: he traces a series of hierarchical relationships among male poets, in which the poet as son struggles to master, surpass, or overthrow the power of his precursor-father. Pointing out the exclusively male nature of Bloom's model of literary history, several feminist critics have asked: "What if the poet is a woman?" Gilbert and Gubar, Joanne Feit Diehl, and Margaret Homans trace the unique anxieties and strategies that emerge when the poet is a woman attempting to

---

[1] *The Homeric Hymns*, trans. Thelma Sargent (New York: Norton, 1973), p. 13.
[2] *The Anxiety of Influence: A Theory of Poetry* (New York: Oxford Univ. Press, 1973), p. 5.

American Literature, Volume 56, Number 4, December 1984. Copyright © 1984 by the Duke University Press. CCC 0002-9831/84/$1.50

clear imaginative space for herself in the patriarchal tradition.[3] But while these studies have renewed and extended our readings of women poets, they have not significantly questioned the validity of the Bloomian model as a tool for understanding the female poetic tradition; nor have they considered the different kind of family romance that emerges when the poet and the precursor are both women. How useful is the Bloomian model when the poet attempts to define herself not in relation to her poetic fathers but in relation to her poetic mothers?

The question is important not only in the study of the female poetic tradition but in formulating the theoretic base of feminist scholarship. As Elaine Showalter says in her recent review essay: "Too often women's place in literary tradition is translated into the crude topography of hole and bulge, with Milton, Byron, or Emerson the bulging bogeys on one side and women's literature from Aphra Behn to Adrienne Rich a pocked moon surface of revisionary lacunae on the other."[4] By using the male-defined models of Freud and Bloom in the discussion of a female poetic tradition, feminist critics end by reinscribing the terms they seek to transform; women poets become "revisionary lacunae" rather than visionary avatars of their own self-created and self-creating tradition. If a woman's text is fathered, it is also, and perhaps primarily, mothered. While Gilbert and Gubar and Diehl point up the importance of the female precursor to the female writer, and while Homans examines the role Dickinson's identification with Eve played in the formation of her poetic identity, their primary focus is on the ways that women's writing is shaped by the male literary tradition. Beginning with Virginia Woolf's idea that "we think back through our mothers if we are women," other feminist critics, including Ellen Moers, Louise Bernikow, and Lillian Faderman have examined some of the patterns that char-

[3] Sandra M. Gilbert and Susan Gubar, *The Madwoman in the Attic: The Woman Writer and the Nineteenth-Century Literary Imagination* (New Haven: Yale Univ. Press, 1979); Margaret Homans, *Women Writers and Poetic Identity: Dorothy Words-worth, Emily Brontë, and Emily Dickinson* (Princeton: Princeton Univ. Press, 1980); Joanne Feit Diehl, *Dickinson and the Romantic Imagination* (Princeton: Princeton Univ. Press. 1981).

[4] "Feminist Criticism in the Wilderness," *Critical Inquiry*, 8 (1981), 204.

acterize the personal and literary relationships between women, but no one has applied these patterns to a theory of female influence.[5]

In the attempt to discover an approach to the female literary tradition that is based on female patterns of interaction, such psychoanalytic studies as Dorothy Dinnerstein's *The Mermaid and the Minotaur* and Nancy Chodorow's *The Reproduction of Mothering* provide suggestive models.[6] In a recent article, Elizabeth Abel makes use of Chodorow's object-relations theory of female development to study the fusion and differentiation that characterize female friendships in contemporary women's fiction; and she suggests that a similar dynamics might operate in the literary relations between women. She proposes what she calls a "triadic female pattern," in which "the relation to the male tradition reflects women's oedipal issues, the relation to the female tradition reflects the preoedipal."[7] However, as suggestive as the models of Chodorow and Abel are in developing a theory of female poetic influence, here again the problem lies in the Freudian categories of Oedipal and pre-Oedipal; whether referring to a Greek play or a psychological process, both terms reinscribe a male- rather than a female-centered model of development. As Marianne Hirsch says in a recent review of scholarship on mothers and dauthers, there is a "need to transform more radically the paradigms within which we think, to invent new theoretical frameworks that allow us, in our study of relationships between women, truly to go beyond patriarchal myths and perceptions."[8]

While no paradigm, no matter how radical, can entirely exclude male definitions or include the range of relationships that have shaped the female literary tradition, the mother-daughter myth of

[5] Virginia Woolf, *A Room of One's Own* (New York: Harcourt, Brace & World, 1929), p. 79. Ellen Moers' *Literary Women* (New York: Doubleday, 1976) includes an excellent discussion of the relationship between Emily Dickinson and Elizabeth Barrett Browning. For other discussions of the relationships between literary women, see Louise Bernikow, *Among Women* (New York: Crown, 1980), and Lillian Faderman, *Surpassing the Love of Men: Romantic Friendship and Love Between Women From the Renaissance to the Present* (New York: Morrow, 1981).

[6] *The Mermaid and the Minotaur: Sexual Arrangements and Human Malaise* (New York: Harper & Row, 1976); *The Reproduction of Mothering: Psychoanalysis and the Sociology of Gender* (Berkeley: Univ. of California Press, 1978).

[7] "(E)Merging Identities: The Dynamics of Female Friendship in Contemporary Fiction by Women," *Signs*, 6 (1981), 433–34.

[8] "Mothers and Daughters," *Signs*, 7 (1981), 221.

Demeter and Korê enacts a pattern of female union, separation, return, and renewal that more adequately suggests the particular configuration of female relationships than the Oedipal model of Freud and Chodorow, Bloom and Abel. Like Persephone in the Underworld, the female poet in the patriarchal world frequently experiences a sense of separation from her matrilineal heritage; she seeks release and renewal through reunion with her matrilineal sources. In response to their poetic mothers, American women poets often experience neither a Bloomian "anxiety of influence," nor what Gilbert and Gubar call an "anxiety of authorship"; rather, in returning to their poetic mothers, they experience a release from anxiety. By defining themselves in relation to rather than in reaction against each other, these women poets reverse the pattern of male relationships, summed up by Ralph Waldo Emerson: "Genius is always sufficiently the enemy of genius by over-influence."[9] In fact, the relationships between women poets suggest another paradigm of poetic history, inscribed by the myth of Demeter and Korê, enacted by the rites of Eleusis, and summed up by Adrienne Rich as "The drive/to connect. The dream of common language" ("Origins and History of Consciousness").[10] Reversing Emerson's competitive model and Bloom's anxiety-ridden model of male literary influence, American women poets have frequently invoked each other as part of what Amy Lowell calls "a strange, isolated little family . . . of singing sisters."[11] While the sense of kinship among women poets may manifest itself in textual similarities and borrowings, more often the bond between women poets becomes a source of personal identity, self-confirmation, and creative power. And this sense of herself and her power is particularly important for the woman poet. Unlike the female fiction writer, who can compose out of the social world and separate herself from her fictional characters, the female poet must become her own heroine; as a poet, she must place herself at the center of her poems and create out of a sense of her own identity and power. Thus, until recently, there have been many fewer women poets than women

---

[9] "The American Scholar," in *Selected Writings of Emerson*, ed. Donald McQuade (New York: Modern Library, 1981), p. 50.

[10] *The Dream of a Common Language: Poems 1974–1977* (New York: Norton, 1978), p. 7. Subsequent references to this volume will appear in the text.

[11] "The Sisters," in *The Complete Poetical Works of Amy Lowell* (Boston: Houghton Mifflin, 1955), pp. 459–60. Subsequent references to this volume will appear in the text.

novelists. While the female poet can experience her power to create with both body and pen as a double potency, she can also be split between the body and matrices of her woman self and the mind and power of her poet self. Amy Lowell explores this division in her poem "The Sisters":

> I wonder what it is that makes us do it,
> Singles us out to scribble down, man-wise,
> The fragments of ourselves. Why are we
> Already mother-creatures, double-bearing,
> With matrices in body and in brain? (p. 459)

For Lowell, as for other American women poets, it is through a return to her matrilineal sources, including Sappho, Elizabeth Barrett Browning, and Emily Dickinson, that she seeks to transform the matrices of body and mind into a unified sense of self and power.

While the family romance between women poets has some of the same ambivalence as the relationship between mothers and daughters, there is a primary sense of identification and mutuality between women poets that sets them apart from the more agonistic relationship between precursor and ephebe in the Bloomian model. This relationship of fusion that characterizes women poets may in part reflect the initial union and identification between biological mother and daughter. If, as Nancy Chodorow argues, the early identification of mother and daughter creates more relational capacities and more fluid ego boundaries among women, then the female poet's longing to merge with rather than swerve from her poetic mothers might reflect a particularly female pattern of literary influence. Out of this primal relation with the mother might also arise the sense of shared, sometimes unnamed and unnameable knowledge among women poets. Like the mother-daughter bond of Demeter and Korê, which gave rise to the Mysteries of Eleusis, the kinship among women poets is sometimes experienced as a secret, sacred, and witch-like bond of knowledge and power.

The relationship between Emily Dickinson and Adrienne Rich provides a suggestive model of the pattern of separation, return, and renewal that marks the dynamics of interaction among American women poets. Before she learned to mask her female experience in imitations of the male poets she read as an undergraduate, Rich kept private notebooks of poems imitating Dickinson and Edna St.

Vincent Millay: "I spent months, at sixteen," says Rich, "memorizing and writing imitations of Millay's sonnets; and in notebooks of that period I find what are obviously attempts to imitate Dickinson's metrics and verbal compression."[12] She was impressed not only by the language and meter of Dickinson's verse but by her precise notation of psychic states. Rich was also struck by the split between the power of the woman poet and the powerlessness of the legendary child-woman, a split she herself was beginning to feel between the potency of the girl who wrote poems and the passivity of the girl who played a more orthodox feminine role.

In her first volume of poems, *A Change of World* (1951), Rich wore a similar mask of passivity and containment—a mask that gained her immediate acceptance by the male literary establishment. But in their response to Rich, as in their response to Dickinson, the critics mistook the mask for the thing itself. In the foreword to *A Change of World*, W. H. Auden observed: "The poems a reader will encounter in this book are neatly and modestly dressed, speak quietly but do not mumble, respect their elders but are not cowed by them, and do not tell fibs: that, for a first volume is a good deal."[13] Responding to the volume as if it were the body of fifties' womanhood, Auden misperceived the nature of Rich, just as Thomas Higginson had misperceived Dickinson. He missed the fact that beneath the neat and modest dress of the poems lurked "storm warnings," "murmurings of missile-throwers," and an atmosphere of physical and psychological violence that endangered men, women, and the future of the world.

Only occasionally in these early poems—in the startling juxtapositions and child-like tone of "A View of the Terrace" or in the cosmic riddles of "What Ghosts Can Say" and "Purely Local"—do we find evidence of Rich's private apprenticeship to Dickinson. Whereas Dickinson's poems are imagistic, metaphysical, stylistically slant, Rich's poems, at this stage, are discursive, social, stylistically balanced. Unlike Dickinson's experimental form, Rich's craft is a sign of her formalist detachment from, rather than her engagement of, her own poetic resources. Eager to be sufficiently universal, and thus nonfemale, Rich imitated the style of her male

---

[12] Rich, in *On Lies, Secrets, and Silence: Selected Prose 1966–1978* (New York: Norton, 1979), p. 40. Subsequent references to this volume will appear in the text as *LSS*.

[13] *A Change of World* (New Haven: Yale Univ. Press, 1951), p. 11.

masters, who included Robert Frost, T. S. Eliot, William Butler
Yeats, and Wallace Stevens. She had not yet discovered her female
experience as a subject for poetry and a source of poetic power.
The weight of her feminine and feminist awareness was contained
and controlled by the craft of her formalist verse; and any conflict
she felt between woman and poet was projected through male
personae and the objective masks of female artist figures such as
Aunt Jennifer and "Mathilde in Normandy."

The masking evident in Rich's first volume of poems corresponds
with the masking that characterized her life in the early fifties.
Having married a Harvard professor in 1953, and given birth to
three sons in 1955, 1957, and 1959, Rich was split between the
role she was expected to play as a wife and mother and the script
she was trying to write for herself. After the publication of her
second book of poems *The Diamond Cutters* (1955), she stopped
writing poetry. Between 1955 and the publication of *Snapshots of
a Daughter-in-Law* in 1963, Rich struggled to unite the divided
energies of body and mind, woman and poet, relation and creation,
in order, as she said in a 1958 notebook, "to give birth to—a
recognizable, autonomous self, a creation in poetry and in life."[14]

Rich was aided in the process of giving birth to herself by a
renewed contact with Dickinson, whom she read in the late fifties
in Thomas Johnson's unbowdlerized edition of *The Complete
Poems* (1955). "More than any other poet," she says, "Emily
Dickinson seemed to tell me that the intense inner event, the
personal and psychological, was inseparable from the universal;
that there was a range of psychological poetry beyond mere self-
expression" (*LSS*, p. 168). In redeeming and validating female
psychic experience for universal purposes, Dickinson aided Rich
in the process of giving birth to herself as the source and subject
of her poetry. Rejecting her 1955 volume *The Diamond Cutters*
as "mere exercises for poems I hadn't written," in the late fifties
Rich was able, as she says, "to write, for the first time, directly
about experiencing myself as a woman" (*LSS*, pp. 42, 44).

Rich's experience as a woman is at the structural and thematic
center of her next volume of poems, *Snapshots of a Daughter-in-
Law*. While the poems have some of the contemporary tone of

---

[14] *Of Woman Born: Motherhood as Experience and Institution* (New York: Norton,
1976), p. 29.

Robert Lowell's *Life Studies* (1959), her focus, as the title suggests, is on a woman's way of seeing and ordering a world circumscribed by the laws of the fathers. Her words at the outset of *Snapshots*, "Now knowledge finds me out;/in all its risible untidiness," sum up the impulse behind the break with traditional poetic and social forms that took place in the eight years between *The Diamond Cutters* and *Snapshots*.[15] As knowledge found Rich out as a woman poet in fifties America, she began to retrieve Dickinson, along with such other women writers as Mary Wollstonecraft, Simone de Beauvoir, and Denise Levertov as part of a collective heritage; and in the process of retrieving a female literary heritage, she also gave birth to a new poetic voice.

Rich's new voice is most evident in the title poem, "Snapshots of a Daughter-in-Law," a poem in which the "ghost" of Dickinson is also evident. As Rich discovers a form commensurate with the "risible untidiness" of her knowledge as a woman—a daughter-in-law—defined and bound by the laws of the patriarchy, her style and vision begin to approximate the unfinished, fragmented quality of Dickinson's verse. For Rich, as for Dickinson, the fracture of image and syntax becomes not only a poetic strategy but an emblem of a female way of being and seeing in a world split by the polarities of masculine and feminine, mind and body, subject and object, transcendence and immanence. Through the precise, imagistic notation of female states of mind, Rich achieves some of the psychic intensity and range that she admired in Dickinson's verse.

In "Snapshots of a Daugher-in-Law," Dickinson's life and writing become part of Rich's critique of patriarchy, as she reflects on the ways female energies have been warped and thwarted by the rigidly defined codes that circumscribe female lives:

> Reading while waiting
> for the iron to heat,
> writing, *My Life had stood—a Loaded Gun—*
> in that Amherst pantry while the jellies boil and scum,
> or, more often,
> iron-eyed and beaked and purposed as a bird,
> dusting everything on the whatnot every day of life.
> (*Snapshots*, p. 22)

---

[15] "From Morning-Glory to Petersburg," in *Snapshots of a Daughter-in-Law: Poems 1954–1962* (New York: Norton, 1963), p. 12. Subsequent references to this volume will appear in the text.

The oppositions between reading/waiting, writing/pantry stress the conflict between creative energy and destructive confinement summed up in Dickinson's lines, "My Life had stood—a Loaded Gun—."[16] Sandwiched between the wall of her Amherst pantry and the boil and scum of jellies, Dickinson becomes for Rich an exemplar of all those women who, like herself, experience their potency as an instrument of destruction or as a form of daemonic possession.

As Rich's allusion to Dickinson in "Snapshots" might suggest, her renewed contact with Dickinson in the fifties was not free from the ambivalence daughters frequently experience in relation to their mothers in patriarchal society. "The materials are here for the deepest mutuality and the most painful estrangement," says Rich of the mother-daughter bond.[17] The image of Dickinson in "Snapshots," like the images of women throughout the volume, reflects a negative and destructive dimension of the mother from which the free-spirited daughter seeks to release herself. The liberation Rich conceives at the end of "Snapshots of a Daughter-in-Law" comes not from bonding with but from rising above women's lives:

> Her mind full to the wind, I see her plunge
> breasted and glancing through the currents,
> taking the light upon her
> at least as beautiful as any boy
> or helicopter,
>   poised, still coming,
> her fine blades making the air wince
>
> but her cargo
> no promise then:
> delivered
> palpable
> ours.
>
>   (*Snapshots*, pp. 24–25)

At least as beautiful as any boy or helicopter, Rich's new woman

---

[16] In "Vesuvius at Home: The Power of Emily Dickinson," Rich refers to "My Life had stood—a Loaded Gun—" as "the real 'onlie begetter' of my thoughts here about Dickinson; a poem I have mused over, repeated to myself, taken into myself over many years," *LSS*, p. 172. She used the image of "a loaded gun" a few years later in "Face to Face" to suggest the power of unexpressed energies in early American life: "burning under the bleached scalp; behind dry lips/a loaded gun"; in *Necessities of Life: Poems 1962–1965* (New York: Norton, 1966), p. 49.

[17] *Of Woman Born*, p. 226.

defines herself in relation not to her matrilineal heritage but to the
male-centered and technological values of the patriarchy. In fact,
Rich borrows the image of the helicopter from Simone de Beauvoir,
who also saw female biology as the source not of female power but
of female oppression.[18] But while Rich conceives of female liberation in traditional terms, the lines, images, and syntax of this final
passage are broken in ways that point toward a more experimental
use of language and form. Already the decomposition of language
has become part of the process of giving birth to an autonomous
female self—"a creation in poetry and in life."

"Snapshots of a Daughter-in-Law" sums up Rich's poetic vision
at this point: still inhabiting and inhabited by the kingdom of the
fathers, Rich, like Persephone in the Underworld, is cut off from
the power of her mothers. She dwells upon the female figure as a
victim rather than a creator; she emphasizes destructive rather than
creative female energies; she conceives of liberation as a breaking
away from rather than a bonding with women's lives; she projects
her imaginative release as the liberation of the male rather than
the ˙female part of herself; and she seeks liberation from rather
than transformation of the world. Only in her experimental use of
language and form does Rich begin to move back into the house
of her poetic mothers. But it is not until her next volume of poems,
Necessities of Life (1966), that this movement becomes part of a
self-conscious program.

The poems of *Necessities of Life* reverse the final vision of
"Snapshots of a Daughter-in-Law": the new theme of this volume
is survival or, as the title suggests, the necessities of life. In the
title poem, which opens the volume, Rich records a process of
rebirth that comes from repossessing herself and women's culture.
The future she imagines is inhabited by women in houses, waiting
breathlessly to tell their tales:

> I have invitations:
> a curl of mist steams upward
>
> from a field, visible as my breath,
> houses along a road stand waiting

---

[18] *Snapshots*, p. 64.

like old women knitting, breathless
to tell their tales.
                    (*Necessities of Life*, p. 10)[19]

This new emphasis on herself and women's lives as a source of
creation and transformation is the dominant note of *Necessities of
Life* and future volumes.

As Rich sought to achieve a unification and concentration of
energies in her life and in her art, she came to look upon Dickinson
not as a victim but as a survivor, whose discipline, seclusion, and
isolation made her a countervailing figure—a spirit-sister—in
Rich's struggle against the culture of domesticity represented by
her biological mother and her own motherhood. "Given her vocation," said Rich of Dickinson, "she was neither eccentric nor
quaint; she was determined to survive, to use her powers, to practice
necessary economies" (*LSS*, p. 160). It is as a figure of "necessary
economies" that Dickinson entered Rich's life and work during
the sixties and seventies. In Dickinson's choice for herself and her
art, Rich saw not only a model of female survival in patriarchal
culture; she also saw a figure of female poetic power, creating
herself and recreating the world through the power of language.

"I Am in Danger—Sir—," which appears at midpoint in *Necessities of Life*, underscores Dickinson's centrality to Rich's new
ethics and poetics. The title of the poem is taken from one of
Dickinson's letters to Higginson, who apparently suggested that
she regularize—or eliminate entirely—her rhyme and meter. She
replied: "You think my gait 'spasmodic'—I am in danger—Sir—
You think me 'uncontrolled'—I have no Tribunal."[20] Rich's title
capitalizes on the ambiguity of Dickinson's response. Her unorthodox metrics are a sign of the danger and risk of engaging her
poetic powers and pushing beyond the bounds of conventional
womanhood. But there is another kind of danger: both Dickinson's
life and her language are endangered by the patriarchal culture in
which she lives.

---

[19] *Necessities of Life* (New York: Norton, 1966). Subsequent references will appear
in the text.

[20] Letter to Thomas Higginson, 7 June 1862, #265 in *The Letters of Emily
Dickinson*, ed. Thomas Johnson and Theodora Ward (Cambridge: Harvard Univ. Press,
1958), II, 409.

Imitating some of Dickinson's "half-cracked" poetic strategies, including the dash, Rich attempts to cut through the moth-balled legend to discover who Dickinson is:

"Half-cracked" to Higginson, living,
afterward famous in garbled versions,
your hoard of dazzling scraps a battlefield,
now your old snood

mothballed at Harvard
and you in your variorum monument
equivocal to the end—
who are you?
                    (*Necessities*, p. 33)

In the course of the poem, Rich undertakes to answer this question; and in so doing, she works her way back beyond the "garbled versions" of the patriarchy to discover Dickinson as a model of artistic resourcefulness. Unlike her earlier allusion to "My Life had stood—a Loaded Gun—," here Rich sees Dickinson's life and art as an emblem of the creative rather than the destructive dimensions of female power:

Gardening the day-lily,
wiping the wine-glass stems,
your thought pulsed on behind
a forehead battered paper-thin,

you, woman, masculine
in single-mindedness,
for whom the word was more
than a symptom—

a condition of being.
                    (*Necessities*, p. 33)

Behind the publicly acceptable mask of domesticity, Rich sees pulsating the genius of the poet: whatever seemed battered in her demeanor, she suggests, was the product not of weakness, but of inward power thrusting itself against a hostile world in single-minded devotion to her art.

In describing the word as "a condition of being" for Dickinson, Rich suggests that it was in and through language that Dickinson realized herself and her creative power. Reversing the traditional view of Dickinson as a victim forced into seclusion and renunciation by a failed love affair, Rich presents Dickinson's lifestyle as the self-conscious choice of a woman artist who, in saying yes to her creative power, had to say no to the "spoiled language" of the patriarchy:

> the air buzzing with spoiled language
> sang in your ears
> of Perjury
>
> and in your half-cracked way you chose
> silence for entertainment,
> chose to have it out at last
> on your own premises.
>
> (*Necessities*, p. 33)

The perjury that sang in Dickinson's ears is the false witness of female lives embedded in patriarchal language and culture. Rather than perjure herself, suggests Rich, Dickinson chose withdrawal and silence as a means of surviving as a woman poet in nineteenth-century America. Rich repeats "half-cracked" at the end of the poem to stress the disjunction between the "cracked" image of Dickinson and the absolute sanity of her choice: her life and her poems only appear "cracked" in the spoiled and perjured context of the patriarchy. Rich's repetition of *chose* at the end of one line and at the beginning of another further underscores Dickinson's powerful will to survive. No longer dwelling on the image of Dickinson pinned between the boil and scum of jellies in her Amherst pantry, Rich underlines the connection between her decision to stay at home, her determination to have her own will, and her power to create herself and recreate the world, by yoking the three ideas in the final image of the poem: "on her own premises." Unlike the house in *Snapshots of a Daughter-in-Law*, here the house has become a locus not of destructive energies but of potency and necessary economies.

However, if Rich begins in *Necessities of Life* to explore the sources of female power, in this volume and in the 1969 *Leaflets* she continually projects her own poetic power as a masculine daemon or male lover who comes from outside to take possession of her. It was not until the late sixties and early seventies, in the poems of *The Will to Change* (1971) and *Diving into the Wreck* (1973), that Rich consistently located the sources of creative power within herself and within other female figures. During this time of personal and social upheaval, she came to see the reunification of the fractured elements of male and female as the means to achieve personal and political transformation. She enacts this process of reunification in the title poem of *Diving into the Wreck*, as she plunges into the sources of self and world to discover the buried treasure of "I am she: I am he."[21] Within the next few years, however, she moved away from the androgynous vision of *Diving into the Wreck* to the lesbian-feminist position she summed up in her speech to the Modern Language Association in 1976: "It is the lesbian in us who is creative," announced Rich, "for the dutiful daughter of the fathers in us is only a hack" (*LSS*, p. 201). As Rich embraced lesbian-feminism as personal life-style, poetic strategy, and political vision, her effort to reclaim Dickinson as a poetic mother became part of her broader effort to reclaim motherhood—the physical capacity for conception, gestation, transformation, and nurture—as an intellectual and creative force.

Of Woman Born: Motherhood as Experience and Institution, which is dedicated to Rich's grandmothers and which draws upon the life of her mother as a "continuing example of transformation and rebirth," appeared in 1976; in the same year, Rich published her major essay on Dickinson, "Vesuvius at Home: The Power of Emily Dickinson." In this essay, as in her study of motherhood, Rich engages in a quest to recover the mother as a source of transformation and rebirth. Like the rites of Eleusis, Rich's quest begins in Spring, with a return to the house of her poetic mother. Her return to Dickinson's house becomes the occasion for an extended meditation in which she seeks to reclaim Dickinson's life and work for herself and other women writers. By reading Dickinson in the context of women's culture, Rich seeks to overturn the popular legend: she lived not in hermetic seclusion, argues Rich, but in relation to a self-selected and primarily female network of personal and literary relationships; she was not the quaint and sentimental girl-child popularized by *The Belle of Amherst*, but a proud, unorthodox woman of powerful will; her poems were not

---

[21] *Diving into the Wreck: Poems 1971–1972* (New York: Norton, 1973), p. 24. For a discussion of Rich's female-centered vision in *Diving into the Wreck* see Rachel Blau Du Plessis, "The Critique of Consciousness and Myth in Levertov, Rich, and Rukeyser," *Feminist Studies*, 3 (1975), 199–221; Wendy Martin, "From Patriarchy to the Female Principle: A Chronological Reading of Adrienne Rich's Poems," in *Adrienne Rich's Poetry*, ed. Barbara Charlesworth Gelpi and Albert Gelpi (New York: Norton, 1975), pp. 175–89; and Laurence Goldstein, "The Evolution of Adrienne Rich," *Michigan Quarterly Review*, 15 (1976), 360–66.

sublimations of failed love but signs of her self-created and self-creating power of transformation; the male daemons of her poems were not reflections of male lovers but projections of her own poetic genius. Thus, in the process of repossessing Dickinson as a source and a foremother, Rich raised Dickinson criticism to a new level of discourse.[22]

As a figure of female power, Dickinson became part of the dream of a common language—the drive to connect word and thing, mind and body, daughter and mother, personal and political, past and present—that Rich invokes in *The Dream of a Common Language* (1978) and *A Wild Patience Has Taken Me This Far* (1981). In these volumes, Rich focuses on the theme of female power that she had begun to explore in her relationship with Dickinson. Just as her bond with Dickinson becomes a bond of mutuality and power, so Rich's new vision is centered not on an Emersonian concept of individual power but on an ethics and poetics of female bonding, based on the primal mother-daughter bond and summed up in the following lines from "Transcendental Etude":

> two women, eye to eye
> measuring each other's spirit, each other's
> limitless desire,
> a whole new poetry beginning here.
> *(Dream*, p. 76)

Retrieving the voice of the early poet who imitated Dickinson and Millay in her private journals, and who defined herself as a woman poet writing in a tradition of women poets, Rich draws upon female energies and female community as a source of personal, poetic, and social transformation. She projects female power no longer as

---

[22] Ellen Moers says that Rich's essay on Dickinson is the "single best critical essay we have"; see "A Poet's Feminist Prose," *New York Times Book Review*, 22 April 1979, p. 12. This essay, along with her 1971 essay "When We Dead Awaken: Writing as Re-Vision," has had a noticeable impact on recent studies of women writers, including Suzanne Juhasz's *Naked and Fiery Forms* (New York: Harper & Row, 1976), Gilbert and Gubar's *The Madwoman in the Attic*, Homans' *Women Writers and Poetic Identity*, Diehl's *Dickinson and the Romantic Imagination*, and Barbara Mossberg's *Emily Dickinson: When a Writer Is a Daughter* (Bloomington: Indiana Univ. Press, 1982). In fact, as Marilyn Farwell points out in "Adrienne Rich and An Organic Feminist Criticism," Rich has had a major impact on the philosophy and practice of feminist criticism, and yet her work is frequently not cited in review essays on feminist scholarship; see *College English*, 39 (1977), 191–203.

a masculine or androgynous figure but as an old crone, who composes out of the treasured fragments of women's lives.[23]

In her effort to re-member the scattered fragments of women's lives, Rich returns to Dickinson for what she calls her "third and final address" in *A Wild Patience Has Taken Me This Far*. Beginning with the lines, "Strangers are an endangered species," the section on Dickinson is part of Rich's more general meditation on her relationship to the history and landscape of New England in "The Spirit of Place." Returning once again to a theme of "I Am in Danger—Sir—," Rich presents Dickinson's life and legend as another instance of the ways "instantaneous violence   ambush   male/ dominion" endanger not only women's lives but women's past and history. In this final return to Dickinson's house, Rich finds neither frustrated energies nor female potency, but a legacy of violation. It is not Dickinson who inhabits her house, but the scholars and legends that have reinvented her according to the patterns of the times:

> In Emily Dickinson's house in Amherst
> cocktails are served   the scholars
> gather in celebration
> their pious or clinical legends
> festoon the walls like imitations
> of period patterns
>
> (*. . . and, as I feared, my "life" was made a "victim"*)
> (*Wild Patience*, p. 42)[24]

Under the description of the festivities of the cultists, Rich places in parenthesis a fragment from one of Dickinson's letters to Susan Gilbert, in which she complains of feeling victimized by the church leaders at an Amherst meeting: the parenthetical and italicized fragment underscores the fact that Dickinson's life is in danger of being extinguished by the imitations that festoon the wall. Even in her death, Dickinson has been a victim of pious or clinical academics, who paw her relics:

[23] For recent studies of Rich's female sources see Susan Friedman, " 'I go where I love': An Intertextual Study of H.D. and Adrienne Rich," *Signs*, 9 (1983), 228–45; and Wendy Martin, *An American Triptych: Anne Bradstreet, Emily Dickinson, Adrienne Rich* (Chapel Hill: Univ. of North Carolina Press, 1984), pp. 167–234.

[24] *A Wild Patience Has Taken Me This Far: Poems 1978–1981* (New York: Norton, 1981), p. 9. Subsequent references to this volume will appear in the text.

The remnants pawed   the relics
the cult assembled in the bedroom

and you   whose teeth were set on edge by churches
resist yor shrine
                    escape
                         are found
nowhere
              unless in words   (your own)
                         (*Wild Patience*, p. 42)

In her death, as in her life, Dickinson seeks to escape the patterns
of the time through the power of language—a language that, like
Rich's words on the page, decomposes and transforms traditional
patterns in the process of escaping them. It is in Dickinson's own
words that Rich finds the figure of the stranger/woman poet who
eludes the scholars as she eluded her Amherst contemporaries. Rich
incorporates the following passage from a letter Dickinson wrote
to Catherine Turner in 1859:

> *All we are strangers—dear—The world is not*
> *acquainted with us, because we are not acquainted*
> *with her. And Pilgrims!—Do you hesitate? and*
> *Soldiers oft—some of us victors, but those I do*
> *not see tonight owing to the smoke.—We are hungry,*
> *and thirsty, sometimes—We are barefoot—and cold—*
> (*Wild Patience*, p. 43)

Recognizing Dickinson's essential "strangeness," and thus her difference from herself, Rich resolves to cease her effort to decode
Dickinson's life and work in terms of her own lesbian-feminist
needs:

> This place is large enough for both of us
> the river-fog will do for privacy
> this is my third and last address to you
> (*Wild Patience*, p. 43)

After years of attempting to enter into Dickinson's mind through
her poems and letters, Rich comes to an almost mystic acceptance
of Dickinson as stranger. But while Rich refuses to endanger Dickinson's "strangeness" and integrity by appropriating her into the
words of another poem, she does suggest that, as female pilgrims
in an alien world, they will continue to be linked by a common
though unvoiced bond of knowledge and power. Recognizing the

patriarchal weight of language, Rich, like an Eleusinian hierophant, takes a vow of silence in her relationship with Dickinson—a vow that reflects her growing interest in silence as a means of suggesting unvoiced female experience.[25]

Making explicit the mother-daughter relationship that was implicit in her earlier addresses to Dickinson, Rich enacts the process of freeing Dickinson to be herself through a series of ritualistic images in which she addresses Dickinson first as daughter, then as sister, and finally as mother:

> with the hands of a daughter I would cover you
> from all intrusion   even my own
> saying   rest to your ghost
>
> with the hands of a sister I would leave your hands
> open or closed as they prefer to lie
> and ask no more of who or why or wherefore
>
> with the hands of a mother I would close the door
> on the rooms you've left behind
> and silently pick up my fallen work
>
> (*Wild Patience*, p. 43)

While Rich performs a kind of death ceremony, she also inscribes the legend of her relationship with Dickinson and the potency of the bond between them. Each of Rich's actions, linked by the recurring image of tenderly protective hands, suggests a different dimension of her relationship with Dickinson. As the daughter whose growth as a poet had been nurtured by Dickinson as mother, Rich resolves to protect her from future intrusions, including her own effort to erect her as a feminist shrine. As the sister, who had discovered in Dickinson's life and work a relation to her own condition as a woman poet in America, Rich resolves to accept Dickinson's strange integrity. No longer asking "who or why or wherefore," Rich turns away from the question, "who are you?" which she asked in "I Am in Danger—Sir—"; recognizing that in probing for the answers to these questions, she too had endangered Dickinson, Rich allows her to have it out on her *own* premises. And finally, as the mother who had given birth to new

---

[25] Joanne Feit Diehl examines Rich's use of silence as a strategy of female expression in "Cartographies of Silence: Rich's *Common Language* and the Woman Poet," *Feminist Studies*, 6 (1980), 530–46.

conceptions of Dickinson's life and work, Rich resolves to free
Dickinson to be herself.

Rich's use of a series of familial images in her final address to
Dickinson sums up the nature of the relationship between them.
Although the poem enacts a process of death and release, the house
setting and the familial images of daughter, sister, and mother
underscore the common premises and bonds of kinship that continue to link them; and the fluid, interchangeable roles of daughter,
sister, and mother suggest a process of transformation and rebirth.
Rather than overthrowing her parent in an attempt to give birth
to herself, according to the model of poetic history proposed by
Bloom, Rich projects an alternative model of relations among
women poets. The influence that passes between Dickinson and
Rich is double-bearing and empowering. Dickinson's life and art
flowed into Rich at various stages in her own poetic gestation,
empowering her to know, to understand, and to draw upon her
own creative energies. At the same time, in her several addresses
to Dickinson, Rich served as a kind of poetic mother, giving birth
to new conceptions of Dickinson's life and art; Rich sought not to
misconceive but to re-conceive Dickinson, and these reconceptions
led Rich not to reject Dickinson but to reclaim her as an influence
on herself and other women writers.

The role reversals in Rich's last address to Dickinson make clear
the double-bearing nature of their relationship. Rich does not seek
to overpower or destroy Dickinson to give birth to herself: she
becomes herself both daughter and mother, as Dickinson becomes
both mother and daughter, thus reintegrating the images of mother
and daughter that have frequently been split in the kingdom of
the fathers. As the mother-poet addressing her child-precursor, Rich
gives birth to Dickinson's self at the same time that, in taking up
her "fallen work," she gives birth to *her* self. The house within
which this double birth takes place is ultimately not Dickinson's
only, but the common world they both inhabit; and while Rich
works in a public space that is different from the privacy of Dickinson's rooms, the rooms she left behind remain part of a common
female edifice. Thus, there is a final sense in which Rich is mother
to Dickinson: as a woman poet who has cast her lot with those
who seek to reconstitute the world, Rich addresses Dickinson as
the child of the new creation in poetry and in life to which she,
as mother, will continue to give birth.

"Tender Pioneer": Emily Dickinson's Poems on The Life of Christ

Dorothy Huff Oberhaus

E MILY Dickinson's poems on the life of Jesus Christ, written from early to late in her canon, reflect a poetic concern spanning her entire creative life. When read together as a
group allowing each to illuminate the others, these meditations
on Jesus' birth, life, Crucifixion, and Resurrection form something like a nineteenth-century American Gospel.[1] By recreating
the Gospels, often with wit and American colloquial language,
Dickinson assumes the role of that "warbling, typic Teller" her
"supposed person" observes the Bible needs to "captivate" readers.[2] As "little 'John,'" her persona in one of many poems addressed to Jesus, she stresses the Gospels' contemporary relevance
and makes them freshly available to her "Sweet countrymen"
(497, 441). But while spoken "New Englandly" (285) and in her
unique voice, the deep structure of her Gospel poems places
them in the poetic tradition of Christian devotion, a tradition ex-
tending from the "Dream of the Rood" and *Pearl* poets, through
the medieval lyricists, Herbert, Vaughan, Crashaw, and Hopkins, to Eliot and Auden in our own day. The salient feature
uniting Christian poets in a single identifiable poetic mode is
their reverential attention to the life of Jesus Christ and their

---

[1] Charles R. Anderson, *Emily Dickinson's Poetry: Stairway of Surprise* (New York:
Holt, Rinehart & Winston, 1960), p. xiii, first posited that Dickinson's poems are best
read in thematic groups to allow each to illuminate the others.

[2] "Typic" is a variant word for "warbling" in Poem 1545, *The Poems of Emily
Dickinson*, ed. Thomas H. Johnson, 3 vols. (Cambridge: Harvard Univ. Press, 1955).
Hereafter poems are cited in parentheses in the text according to Johnson's numbering.
Letter 268, *The Letters of Emily Dickinson*, ed. Thomas H. Johnson and Theodora Ward,
3 vols. (Cambridge: Harvard Univ. Press, 1958). Hereafter letters preceded by "L" are
cited in parentheses in the text according to Johnson's numbering.

American Literature, Volume 59, Number 3, October 1987. Copyright © 1987 by the
Duke University Press. CCC 0002-9831/87/$1.50.

acceptance of such données as the Trinity, the Incarnation, and the Redemption. They regard the life of Christ as not merely a picturesque fable providing vivid metaphors but rather as their model. In the language of Christian typology, they see both a fulfillment of Old Testament figures and a prefiguration or fore-shadowing of the lives of His followers.[3] Dickinson's Christology in her poems on the life of Christ is that of the devotional tradi-tion and so are many of her most arresting tropes in portraying Him, her own versions of recurring Christian figures.

Paradigmatic of her way of imaginatively recreating while maintaining the essence of traditional material is the follow-ing meditation's epithet for Jesus, "Tender Pioneer," summing up her loving portrait of Him in this poem and throughout the canon. According to the "Lexicon," whose importance to her poetic thought she herself acknowledged (L-261), "tender" means loving, compassionate, kind, and "anxious for another's good"; a "pioneer" is "one that goes before another to remove obstruction or to prepare the way for another."[4] Dickinson thus describes Jesus in her own words, but her underlying meaning is that of the New Testament and of other devotional poets: Jesus Christ is the loving and courageous Redeemer.

> Life – is what we make it –
> Death – We do not know –
> Christ's acquaintance with Him
> Justify Him – though –
>
> He – would trust no stranger –
> Other – could betray –

[3] I am indebted here and throughout for my definition of the poetic tradition of devotion to Miriam K. Starkman, director of my 1980 doctoral dissertation. See her "Noble Numbers and the Poetry of Devotion" in *Reason and the Imagination: Studies in the History of Ideas 1600–1800*, ed. J. A. Mazzeo (New York: Columbia Univ. Press, 1962), pp. 1–27, and "The 'Grace of the Absurd': Form and Concept in W. H. Auden's *For the Time Being*," *Harvard Theological Review*, 67 (1974), 275–88. Donald Davie, ed. *The New Oxford Book of Christian Verse* (New York: Oxford Univ. Press, 1981), p. xxi, stresses the centrality of attention to the life of Christ and acceptance of Christian doctrines to a definition of Christian poetry. For a discussion of Christian typology, see A. C. Charity, *Events and Their After-life: The Dialectics of Christian Typology in the Bible and Dante* (Cambridge: Cambridge Univ. Press, 1966).

[4] Noah Webster, *An American Dictionary of the English Language* (1848 ed.; rpt. Ann Arbor: University Microfilms International, 1979). Hereafter, definitions are Webster's.

Just His own endorsement –
That – sufficeth Me –

All the other Distance
He hath traversed first –
No New Mile remaineth –
Far as Paradise –

His sure foot preceding –
Tender Pioneer –
Base must be the Coward
Dare not venture – now – (698)

This meditation's meaning centers on its astonishingly varied verb forms. The first two sentences, in the general present, introduce the themes of life, created by our own choices, and death, as yet unknown. But "Christ's acquaintance" with death "Justify Him." "Him" punningly refers not only to death, personified as "Him" in line 3, but to Christ, "He" in line 5. Christ's Atonement both vindicated God by proving His love and vindicated death by transforming its meaning, a recurring Christian donnée expressed less succinctly and more prosaically in the title of Isaac Watts's hymn, "A Prospect of Heaven makes Death easy."[5] Dickinson's uninflected verb, "Justify," expresses grammatically the eternal meaning of Christ's redemptive death: it did, does, and always will prove His love and transform the meaning of death.

Returning to the theme of choice in the first two lines of the second stanza, the single sentence's verbs are conditional: Christ "would" trust no other because another "could" betray. Though He "could" have done otherwise, He willingly chose human life and death, another donnée of the poetic tradition of devotion. As George Herbert's Jesus "sweetly took / Our flesh" and the "Dream of the Rood" poet's Jesus was "eager to mount the gallows,"[6] Dickinson's "Savior" voluntarily chose to come to earth for the sake of His "little Fellowmen" and even

[5] In Davie, *Oxford Book of Christian Verse*, p. 149.

[6] "Faith," *The Works of George Herbert*, ed. F. E. Hutchinson (Oxford: Clarendon Press, 1941), p. 49. "The Dream of the Rood" in Davie, *Oxford Book of Christian Verse*, p. 1.

"coveted" the Crown of Thorns (1487, 1735, to be discussed later). The third and fourth lines of stanza 2 return from the conditional to the present tense but in the specific rather than general sense: Christ's endorsement "sufficeth" for the speaker who here therefore accepts death.

Beginning with the third stanza, Jesus is conqueror of life as well as death. When the reader regularizes its syntax and supplies its elliptical words, stanza 3 reads, "[Because] He hath traversed first / All the other Distance [of human life,] / No New Mile remaineth [from birth, through life and death, and ultimately as] Far as Paradise." The initial spondee, "No New Mile" underscores the importance of Christ's having "traversed first": by typologically foreshadowing His followers' pilgrimage, He has provided a model for their imitation and extended the way as far as Paradise. The meaning of the Incarnation is re-stated but intensified in stanza 4: "[Because] His sure foot is preceding [,] / Tender Pioneer [,] / Base must be the Coward [who does not] / Dare [to] venture – now – ." "His sure foot," another spondee, is one of many Dickinson synecdoches draw-ing attention to the actual physical body of Christ and His real humanity; in other poems, He has a "second [human] face" (225), the "highest head" (1735), and even stands on "divinest tiptoe" (317). The past biblical form "hath traversed" becomes in stanza 4 "[is] preceding," placing Christ's life in the ongoing present. Here Dickinson adapts the recurring devotional figure of anachronism to stress the ever-present significance of Christ's life; as Herbert's speaker is present at both the Nativity and the Crucifixion and Auden's Nativity takes place in twentieth-century New York City, Dickinson's Christ is preceding now and as "Pioneer," with its connotations of the American frontier, on this very continent.[7]

"Tender Pioneer," foregrounded as a single line, is one of Dickinson's many original, often witty kennings for Christ. As Robert Alter points out, the kenning, a recurring biblical fig-ure, is in reality a riddle that has been transformed from the interrogative into the declarative. This is obvious, as Alter ex-

---

[7] Herbert, "Christmas" and "Redemption," *Works*, pp. 80, 40. Auden, "For the Time Being," *Collected Poetry* (New York: Random House, 1945), pp. 407–66.

plains, when one turns the declarative back into the interrogative: "What is a whale-road? The sea. What is fruit of the loins? A child."[8] Dickinson's kennings for Jesus are similarly illuminated when returned to the interrogative: Who is the "Tender Pioneer," the "docile Gentleman," the "Largest Lover"? The reader must then in the context of the poem answer, Jesus Christ, of course (1487, 573, to be discussed later).

Concluding as it began with the theme of choice and in the general present, the meditation's final two lines retrospectively draw together the poem's widely disparate verb forms: because Christ did, does, and will "Justify" death as well as His love; because He who could have done otherwise willingly chose human life and death; because He "hath traversed" first, defeating both life and death; because "His sure foot [is] preceding"; in short, because He is the "Tender Pioneer," "Base must be the Coward" who does not choose to imitate Jesus' courage and "dare venture" both life and death—"now."

As "Tender Pioneer," Jesus thus tested the "Bridge" of faith for the sake of the "Crowd" who follow:

> How brittle are the Piers
> On which our Faith doth tread –
> No Bridge below doth totter so –
> Yet none hath such a Crowd.

> It is as old as God –
> Indeed – 'twas built by him –
> He sent his Son to test the Plank,
> And he pronounced it firm. (1433)

An emblem poem, a form favored by the religious poets of the seventeenth century as well as by Dickinson, its visual image for meditation is the bridge of faith. One of her many inner dialogues, its two quatrains are united by this visual image, by their identical metrical and rhyme patterns, and by the regularity of the poem's iambic trimeters and tetrameters expressing the steady, ongoing "tread" of the faithful. Yet each stanza concludes with a period, and the two voices assume opposing attitudes toward the bridge. The bridge is "brittle," vacillating, and crowded, reflects the first voice; the second responds, reminding the first voice (as well as the reader), the bridge was built by God and tested and endorsed by Jesus. That God the Father is the craftsman who built the bridge and Jesus the "Son" sent to test it manifests Dickinson's acceptance of the Christian Trinity, implicit in all her Christocentric poems but more specifically stated here and elsewhere. In a seldom-considered meditation on prayer, Deity is both the singular "God" and the plural "Jehovahs," including Father, "Son," and "Spirit" (626); in another, the speaker declares herself "Bride" of the Trinity, naming in turn "Father," "Son," and "Holy Ghost" (817).

In a Nativity poem, Dickinson's kenning for the "Son" is "docile Gentleman." Far less solemn than the "Tender Pioneer" and bridge of faith meditations, its reverential-playful tone brings to mind the "saintly impertinence" often attributed to George Herbert.[9] After wittily titling the meditation "Christ's Birthday," she is believed to have sent it next door to her best friend and sister-in-law, Susan Dickinson, at Christmas 1876 with an iced cake, presumably intended as the Savior's birthday cake:[10]

> The Savior must have been
> A docile Gentleman –
> To come so far so cold a Day
> For little Fellowmen –
>
> The Road to Bethlehem
> Since He and I were Boys
> Was leveled, but for that twould be
> A rugged billion Miles – (1487)

The first stanza focuses on the Nativity, the second more generally on the meaning of the Incarnation. The witty near-rhyme, "docile Gentleman" / "little Fellowmen" stresses that Jesus' pilgrimage was human but precedes those of His followers in importance as well as in time. In other poems, she similarly con-

---

9 William Empson, *Seven Types of Ambiguity*, 3rd ed. (New York: New Directions, 1955), p. 238.

10 See my "In Defense of Sue," *Dickinson Studies*, No. 48 (Bonus 1983), pp. 1–25, for a refutation of the widely held belief that Emily and Susan Dickinson's girlhood friendship ended in indifference or even hostility.

trasts Him with His followers in terms of size: our crucifixions are "smaller" versions of His (225); His is the "highest head" (1735); the speaker's attempts to imitate Him are of necessity "smaller" because she has "less Infinity" (573). Here Dickinson's "Savior" willingly came to earth for the sake of His "little Fellowmen" on a cold New England day, another instance of her use of anachronism, a figure further developed in the second stanza where the speaker and the "Savior" were "Boys" together.

The second stanza's "Bethlehem," puzzling at first because it seems to refer to the scene of Jesus' birth, is a metonymy for the entire human life and death of Christ and typologically for those of His followers. By conflating Jesus' birth, life, and Crucifixion, Dickinson stresses that in choosing birth He chose human life, suffering, and death, another recurring devotional theme, as in Eliot's "Journey of the Magi" where the kings journey to Bethlehem to find upon their arrival a foreshadowing of the Crucifixion, "three trees on the low sky" and men "dicing for pieces of silver." [11] Dickinson similarly conflates Christ's entire life in a dialogue between Jesus and Daisy, often the speaker of her Christocentric poems. The poem begins with Jesus' saying, " 'They have not chosen me . . . But I have chosen them!' ", according to Daisy, the "Broken hearted statement [He] Uttered in Bethleem!" (sic, 85). Jesus spoke these words, of course, not as an infant, but in Jerusalem shortly before His Crucifixion.[12] Elsewhere, "Bethlehem" refers typologically to the lives of Christ's followers whose birth, like His, necessitates suffering and death. In a meditation on I Corinthians 15.35, "Paul knew the Man that knew the News," another kenning for Jesus, because "He passed through Bethlehem," not meaning that he was present at Jesus' birth but that he followed the way of the Cross (1492). "The Road to Bethlehem," then, refers both to Jesus' human life and death and to those of every human pilgrim whose "Road" would be a "rugged billion Miles" had Jesus not "leveled" the way.

The speaker of the following meditation reflects upon the

[11] T. S. Eliot, *The Complete Poems and Plays, 1909–1950* (New York: Harcourt, Brace, and World, 1952), p. 68.

[12] John 15.16, King James version. Hereafter biblical references are noted in parentheses in the text.

Cross that proved God's love, asserts that she attempts to imitate
His love, confesses her imitation is imperfect, and finally asks
for salvation not because she has earned it but because Christ
promised and won it:

> The Test of Love – is Death –
> Our Lord – "so loved" – it saith –
> What Largest Lover – hath –
> Another – doth –
>
> If smaller Patience – be –
> Through less Infinity –
> If Bravo, sometimes swerve –
> Through fainter Nerve –
>
> Accept it's Most –
> And overlook – the Dust –
> Last – Least –
> The Cross' – Request – (573)

The first stanza is meditatively spoken by the speaker to herself,
the second and third are prayerfully addressed to the "Largest
Lover." The first line echoes Jesus' words, "Greater love hath no
man than this, that a man lay down his life for his friends" (John
15.13). The second blurs the distinction Dickinson usually makes
between Father and Son. By "Lord," she almost always means
Jesus, as in number 538 where "Christ" is the variant word for
"Lord" and 571 where "Our lord – thought no / Extravagance /
To pay – a Cross –"; yet the apparent biblical analogue for "so
loved" is John 3.16, "For God so loved the world, that he gave
his only begotten Son." The "Largest Lover" whom the speaker
subsequently addresses is thus the Son, but it also alludes to
that New Dispensation's loving Father described by Jesus. She
"doth" / He "hath" is a near-rhyme drawing attention to her
imperfect imitation. In turn, "doth" / "hath" nearly rhyme with
the first two lines' "Death" and "saith," drawing attention to
what it is she attempts to imitate, the love Christ proved by His
death and attributes to God the Father.

   She then apologizes to the "Largest Lover" for her imperfect
imitation and asks His forebearance: "If smaller Patience – be
– / Through [my having] less Infinity [than you, and] / If Bravo,
sometimes swerve – / Through [my having] fainter Nerve – /

[Please] Accept it's Most [my imperfect attempt] / And over-look – the Dust." The uninflected "be" and "swerve" express the ongoing nature of the human condition. As representative of humanity, the speaker was, is, and always will be imperfect because she is after all only "Dust," a recurring trope for imper-fect mortality in Dickinson, the Bible, and the poetic tradition of devotion.

In the poem's penultimate line, like the first a highly con-densed biblical allusion, the speaker boldly quotes Scripture to the "Largest Lover" to support her plea, reminding Him that He Himself promised "the last shall be first" and the "least among you . . . great" (Matthew 19.30, Luke 9.48). Foregrounded as a spondee and the poem's only monometer, "Last – Least" allitera-tively recalls "Largest Lover," contrasting her "Dust" with His "Infinity," a juxtaposition underscored by the poem's intricate rhyme pattern. "Last – Least," an internal near-rhyme, nearly rhymes with "Most" and "Dust," referring to human imperfec-tion. All are near-rhymes with the poem's first accented word, "Test," and its final word, "Request," true rhymes referring to Christ's redemptive Crucifixion. Though the speaker attempts to imitate the "Largest Lover," she does not rely upon her own merit for salvation but rather upon the "Cross' Request," the unexplainable but all-consuming love for His creatures Jesus proved by His Atonement.[13]

As in the "Tender Pioneer" meditation, Christ's Atonement proves His love and promises redemption, but His Passion is also for Dickinson as for other devotional poets an awesome event of unparalleled significance to be contemplated sorrow-fully. The hieroglyph and meditational focus of the following emblem poem is the Crown of Thorns Jesus wore when pre-sented to Pontius Pilate, who then turned Him over to the mob to be crucified (John 19.2):

> One crown that no one seeks
> And yet the highest head

---

[13] Compare Richard Strier's discussion of Herbert's "Artillerie," *Love Known: The-ology and Experience in George Herbert's Poetry* (Chicago: Univ. of Chicago Press, 1983), pp. 97–104.

Its isolation coveted
Its stigma deified

While Pontius Pilate lives
In whatsoever hell
That coronation pierces him
He recollects it well. (1735)

As the initial spondee, "One crown," juxtaposed alliteratively
with the spondee, "no one," contrasts human reluctance to suffer
with Christ's uniquely coveting its "isolation," so "coveted" and
"stigma deified" contrast Old Testament with New Testament
connotations. According to Christian typology, Old Testament
figures foreshadow those of the New, but often there is considerable tension between old and new meanings. In the Tenth Com-
mandment, "covet" means "to desire inordinately" in a negative
sense, but in the New Testament the word is used in a positive sense, as in I Corinthians 12.31 where Paul advises, "covet
earnestly the best gifts." Similarly, the oxymoron "stigma deified" contrasts the usual negative biblical connotation of "thorns"
with their meaning when worn by Christ. "Thorns" in the Old
Testament signify God's anger; after the Fall, He tells Adam,
"Cursed is the ground for thy sake. . . . Thorns also and thistles
shall it bring forth to thee" (Genesis 3.17–18). The word retains
some of its negative meaning in the New Testament; even Jesus
asks, "Do men gather grapes of thorns?" (Matthew 7.16). But by
wearing the Crown, Christ transformed "thorns" into a symbol
of His glory—though they retain their old meaning for Pontius
Pilate who in hell is still "pierced" by them.[14]

Neither the meditation on the Crown of Thorns, the "Tender Pioneer," the bridge of faith, the "docile Gentleman," nor
the "Largest Lover" has received more than passing critical attention, yet these poems where Dickinson's discourse is most
clearly that of Christian devotion are crucial to understanding
her other poems on the life of Christ. One better known poem
whose secular interpretations are called into question when read

[14] See Chana Block, *Spelling the Word: George Herbert and the Bible* (Berkeley: Univ.
of California Press, 1985), pp. 50–51, for a discussion of Old and New Testament
meanings for "thorn."

in light of these five includes a dramatization of Peter's denial of Christ:

> He forgot – and I – remembered –
> 'Twas an everyday affair –
> Long ago as Christ and Peter –
> "Warmed them" at the "Temple fire".
>
> "Thou wert with him" – quoth "the Damsel"?
> "*No*" – said Peter, 'twas'nt me –
> Jesus merely "looked" at Peter –
> Could I do aught else – to Thee? (203)

This poem has elicited much speculation as to who it was that forgot Dickinson, John Cody supposing it a lover and Rebecca Patterson a woman friend.[15] But Dickinson does not disclose what if any personal event inspired the poem; nor does it concern the speaker's experience, mentioned only in the first and final lines, but rather her mental process in a disappointing situation.

She begins, "He forgot," reflects such experiences are common, then in line 3 turns to the typic denial of Peter. Again, "No New Mile remaineth" because Jesus has experienced denial first. Vividly recreating Peter's denial in lines 3 through 7, she draws attention to its contemporary relevance by fusing American colloquial language with the biblical language of all four Evangelists: The "damsel" appears in Matthew and John, Peter "warmed himself" in Mark and John, "the Lord . . . looked upon Peter" in Luke (Matthew 26.69–75, Mark 14.66–72, Luke 22.55–62, and John 18.16–27), yet Peter responds to the damsel's charge in unmistakably nineteenth-century American colloquial terms: " 'No'—said Peter, ' 'twas'nt me.' " Remembering Jesus' response to Peter solves the problem of how to respond to her delinquent friend whom she directly addresses in the final line: she will imitate Jesus and "merely" look at him.

Secular interpretations of another better known poem, a meditation on the Crucifixion, are similarly called into question when

---

[15] John Cody, *After Great Pain: The Inner Life of Emily Dickinson* (Cambridge: Harvard Univ. Press, 1971), p. 374; Rebecca Patterson, *The Riddle of Emily Dickinson* (Boston: Houghton Mifflin, 1951), p. 203.

read in light of the Bible, the poetic tradition of devotion, and the five clearly devotional meditations:

> One Crucifixion is recorded – only –
> How many be
> Is not affirmed of Mathematics –
> Or History –
>
> One Calvary – exhibited to Stranger –
> As many be
> As Persons – or Peninsulas –
> Gethsemane –
>
> Is but a Province – in the Being's Centre –
> Judea –
> For Journey – or Crusade's Achieving –
> Too near –
>
> Our Lord – indeed – made Compound Witness –
> And yet –
> There's newer – nearer Crucifixion
> Than That – (553)

Brooks, Lewis, and Warren see this meditation biographically as "a fine instance of Emily Dickinson's capacity to bend the Biblical vocabulary to an account of her own psychic condition." Robert Weisbuch, too, diminishes Christ's importance to the poem, arguing that Dickinson finds His Crucifixion "unique only in that it was made historically public" and "'newer-nearer Crucifixion' . . . most worthy of attention."[16] But, though crucifixion is here the common lot for all humanity as well as for the human-divine Jesus and though in the final stanza the speaker alludes obliquely to her own, Dickinson keeps the Crucifixion of Christ before the reader's attention throughout the poem.

As number 1735 begins "One crown," this meditation begins "One Crucifixion." "One Calvary" and "Our Lord" are similarly stressed as initial spondees. "Calvary," "Gethsemane," "Province," and "Judea" metonymically allude to the geographical place where Christ's life and death took place. Even the poem's shape is that of the typic Cross, its long pentameters and

16 Cleanth Brooks, R. W. B. Lewis, and Robert Penn Warren, eds. *American Literature: The Makers and the Making* (New York: St. Martin's, 1973), pp. 1245–46. Weisbuch, *Emily Dickinson's Poetry* (Chicago: Univ. of Chicago, 1975), pp. 80–81.

tetrameters the upright post, its short alternating dimeters and monometers the transverse piece. The uniqueness of Christ's sacrifice is expressed by the uniqueness of the ringing first line of the last stanza, "Our Lord – indeed – made Compound Witness." The other stanzas begin with a pentameter, but this is a tetrameter; the other verbs are either in the passive voice or forms of "to be," but this line is in the active voice and contains the poem's only strong verb, "made," accented by "indeed." The line's apparent biblical analogues are 1 John 5.6–9 where Christ is He that "beareth witness" (Dickinson's variant for "made" is "bore") and Revelation 1.5 where He is the "faithful witness and the first begotten of the dead." To the biblical "Witness," Dickinson adds "Compound," creating another kenning. Christ's "Witness" is "Compound" because, as in the "Tender Pioneer" and "Largest Lover" meditations, He gave His life both as evidence of God's love and of His transformation of death.

Stanza 1, the first three lines of stanza 2, and stanza 4 are parallel, each beginning with a clause concerning Christ's Crucifixion, then the adversative "And yet" (specifically stated in stanza 4 and understood in 1 and 2), and finally a clause concerning those unrecorded. The uninflected "be" of stanzas 1 and 2 and "is" of stanza 3 assert the universal nature of personal suffering both before and after Christ, typologically placing His at the center of time.[17] Thus, "One Crucifixion is recorded," and yet how many there have been, are, and will be remains unknown; "One Calvary" is exhibited, and yet there are as many as have been, are, and will be persons. "Our Lord – indeed – made Compound Witness," and yet there is antitypical crucifixion taking place right now, presumably including that of the speaker.[18]

These parallel stanzas provide an envelope structure for the poem's central insight: "Gethsemane – / Is but a Province – in the Being's Centre." As Christ in "One crown" suffered in "isolation," so all human suffering takes place alone and within. Seven lines precede and seven follow this sentence, Dickinson's pun, "Centre," drawing attention to its centrality in form as well

---

[17] Weisbuch, pp. 80–81, argues that for Dickinson, Christ is no longer the center of time.

[18] Note that "antitype" does not mean opposite type, but fulfilled type.

as meaning. "Province," another pun, uniting all crucifixion with
that of the human-divine Jesus, is a verbal play she explains in
the following lines: one does not have to journey to the province
of Judea because the province of suffering is within. The poem's
metrical pattern underscores this epiphany: up to and including "Gethsemane," the short alternating lines are dimeters, but
thereafter monometers, expressing union with Christ, a union
all humanity attains through the sameness of their crucifixions.

Dickinson thus internalizes the meaning of the Crucifixion,
but not in the sense of "bend[ing] the Biblical vocabulary to
an account of her own psychic condition." Nor, as Weisbuch
argues, does her "internalization" of biblical texts and Christian
typology distinguish her from other religious poets.[19] Robert
Alter cites George Herbert, "arguably the greatest Protestant
poet in English," as adapting not only biblical ideas and phrases
but the "dynamics of biblical poetry and its relation to the life of
the spirit." Noting that even the Psalms include many poignantly
personal allusions, Alter explains that there is a tendency in
biblical poetry to move "from outer to inner," "from heaven
to earth . . . to [the human] heart" standing at the "center
of the great picture" recorded in biblical poetry.[20] Dickinson's
internalization of biblical texts is thus not that of an eccentric
nineteenth-century American spinster searching for metaphors
to express her personal angst but that of the great poets of
the Bible and that of the epitome of Christian poets, George
Herbert.

As type, awesome event demanding sorrowful contemplation,
and "Compound Witness" to Christ's love and transformation of
death, the Crucifixion is Dickinson's most frequent subject and
allusion in her poems on the life of Christ. His Resurrection,
understood in the preceding poems by His transformation of
death, is the subject of the previously undiscussed retrospective
narrative concluding this study. Drawing on all four Evangelists'
accounts, Dickinson recreates the first Easter. After announcing
the enormous import for all time of Christ's gift of Himself, the
narrator recounts the aftermath of the Crucifixion, the disciples'

19 Weisbuch, pp. 80–81.
20 *Art of Biblical Poetry*, pp. 209–11.

discovery of the empty tomb, their despair when believing their Master dead, and their ultimate joy when He suddenly appears among them:

> He gave away his Life –
> To Us – Gigantic Sum –
> A trifle – in his own esteem –
> But magnified – by Fame –
>
> Until it burst the Hearts
> That fancied they could hold –
> When swift it slipped it's limit –
> And on the Heavens – unrolled –
>
> 'Tis Ours – to wince – and weep –
> And wonder – and decay
> By Blossoms gradual process –
> He chose – Maturity –
>
> And quickening – as we sowed –
> Just obviated Bud –
> And when We turned to note the Growth –
> Broke – perfect – from the Pod – (567)

Though not named, Christ is obviously He who "gave away his Life" and "Broke – perfect from the Pod," but the identity of the similarly unnamed narrator, a far more fully drawn dramatic figure than the preceding poems' speakers, is less clear. As her first person plural pronoun indicates, she participated in the events she describes. Though Dickinson may have had in mind Mary Magdalene, a favorite protagonist of Christian poets in poems about the Resurrection, more likely, as line nine's colloquial "'Tis" suggests, she anachronistically painted into the biblical scene a nineteenth-century American disciple, perhaps "little 'John'" or Daisy (497, 85).[21] Whether a nineteenth-century disciple, Mary Magdalene, or a fusion of both, the narrator has a complex point of view. From the beginning, she knows the narrative's happy outcome, but she shifts between this omniscient perspective and the first person view of a participant. This double perspective heightens the ironic disparity between what the disciples perceive and what in reality is taking place.

[21] Bloch, *Spelling the Word*, p. 30, describes Herbert as "painting himself into the biblical scene."

From a universal viewpoint, she begins with the "Gigantic Sum" or summary of the meaning of Christ's Atonement, "He gave away his Life – / To Us," a variation of Jesus' saying He "came . . . to give his life a ransom for many" (Matthew 20.28, Mark 10.45). But He spoke these words as a prediction of His approaching death and Resurrection, and the narrator speaks after His prediction has been fulfilled. As the poem later makes clear, however, she no more than the others remembered while the events were taking place that He not only predicted His death but that on the third day He would rise again (Matthew 20.19, Mark 10.34). "Gigantic Sum," foregrounded as a kenning, is a pun meaning both summary and the enormous price or value of Christ's life given as ransom, its second meaning the subject of the following sentence and the referent of its three third-person-singular pronouns.

This sentence works as a kind of zoom lens, quickly relating what happened after the Crucifixion until the disciples found the empty sepulchre. Decompressed, it reads, "[The 'Gigantic Sum' of Christ's life given as ransom was] A trifle – in his own esteem – / But [it was] magnified – by Fame – / Until it burst the Hearts / That fancied they could hold – / When swift it slipped it's limit – / And on the Heavens – unrolled." The first line counters the narrator's estimate of the enormous value of Christ's gift of Himself with His own: He "thought [it] no / Extravagance / To pay – a Cross" (571). "But," she continues, His death on the Cross was "magnified – by Fame," a dark fame so great that when Christ appeared unrecognized and asked the disciples why they were sad, ironically pretending not to know what had taken place, Cleopas replied He must be a stranger in Jerusalem not to have heard of the Crucifixion (Luke 24.17–18). The disciples were overwhelmed with grief at Christ's awful death, their courage further eroded by its notoriety "Until" their hearts finally "burst" "When" they discovered the empty sepulchre, though as Dickinson interjects they had incorrectly believed they could "hold" the faith in face of any adversity. From the enlightened viewpoint of one who knows why the tomb is empty, the narrator explains its meaning: Christ "slipped it's limit." Though the disciples saw the stone "unrolled" ("rolled away" in Matthew 28.2, Mark 16.4, Luke 24.2) and assumed

His body stolen, in reality Christ "unrolled" on the heavens as the bird of another Dickinson poem "unrolled" his feathers in flight (328).

The first three lines of stanza 3, the poem's only lines in the present tense, are spoken in both the immediate and general present. On one level, the narrator intensifies her story, reliving it in the telling; on another, she succinctly and powerfully describes the despair of all who live without the hope of salvation. Dickinson accentuates the lines' dual biblical-contemporary significance by interweaving Gospel words with her own. The colloquial " 'Tis" sounds more contemporary than biblical, and two of the sentence's four verbs are Dickinson's. By alliterating biblical words with her own, she further fuses the lines' biblical and contemporary meanings: "weep" echoes Mary Magdalene's "weeping" outside the sepulchre (John 20.11) and "wonder" Peter's "wondering in himself" after discovering the empty tomb (Luke 24.12). However, "wince" is Dickinson's, though as a tactile verb it recalls how the women "trembled" when they fled from the sepulchre (Mark 16.8). Her own verb "decay" introduces the poem's concluding botanical imagery. The disciples (including the narrator) expect their bodies to decay with their hopes, like "Blossoms." But in the stanza's final line, the narrator, resuming the omniscient perspective, tells how Christ countered this expectation: "He chose Maturity," a pun drawing together the poem's initial commercial language inspired by Christ's "ransom" and its concluding botanical language. By choosing "Maturity," defined both as "the time when [a note or bill of exchange] becomes due" and as a state of "ripeness . . . as of corn or grass," Christ fulfilled His promise alluded to in lines 1 and 2 of rising on the third day and assured His disciples—then and now—they would not die like "Blossoms."

The final stanza contrasts the disciples' perceptions with what, unknown to them, was taking place: even "As [we buried Christ] we sowed [because He was even then] quickening." "Sow" and "quicken" are not words used in the Evangelists' accounts, but they are biblical words. Celebrating the Israelites' release from captivity, the Psalmist exults, "They that sow in tears shall reap in joy" (126), a line summing up the meaning of Easter: the disciples sowed tearfully and reaped joyfully when Christ "slipped" the "limit" of the grave. Paul, too, uses "sow" as well as "quicken" in a sermon on Christ's resurrection as testimony to the resurrection of all: beginning with Christ who "was made a quickening spirit," the dead are "sown in dishonour [but] raised in glory" (I Corinthians 15.42–45). By introducing references to the Psalms and to Paul's sermon on Christ's defeat of death, Dickinson once more places Christ at the center of time as fulfillment of Old Testament figures and prefiguration of the lives of His followers.

Her concluding lines echo three of the Evangelists' sentences describing Christ's sudden appearance among the dejected disciples. According to Matthew, "And as [the women] went to tell his disciples, behold, Jesus met them" (28.9). According to Luke, "And as [the disciples] spake, Jesus himself stood in the midst of them" (24.36). According to John, "And when [Mary Magdalene] had thus said, she turned herself back and saw Jesus standing" (20.14). According to Dickinson, "And when We turned to note the Growth [,] [Jesus] Broke – perfect – from the Pod."

Dickinson's agon in her poems on the life of Christ is with the Bible and the poetic tradition of Christian devotion. Her kennings for Jesus illustrate most dramatically her way of waging this agon, of considering biblical and devotional texts, then responding with her own condensed, original versions. Christian tradition portrays Jesus Christ as the loving courageous Savior, typological prefiguration of the lives of His followers, perfect model for imitation, and herald of the New Dispensation. Dickinson responds that Jesus Christ is the "Tender Pioneer," the "docile Gentleman," the "Largest Lover," and the "Man that knew the News" who gave the "Gigantic Sum" of His life as "Compound Witness" to God's love for His creatures and to the good news that the grave is now only a seed "Pod." By recreating the Gospels, Dickinson makes them freshly available to modern readers and forcefully affirms their ongoing relevance.

The Development of Dickinson's Style

Timothy Morris

Iᴛ has become a given of Dickinson criticism that the poet's style never changed. A recent study begins: "As more than one critic has observed, Emily Dickinson's poetry reaches its maturity almost immediately. Beginning with the verse valentine of 1850 (P-1), she is in full possession of the technical and thematic powers that distinguish her finest lyrics."[1] Most critics in the last twenty years have accepted this view; several of the most distinguished writers on Dickinson agree that her style was unchanging, including Barbara Antonina Clarke Mossberg, David Porter, and Robert Weisbuch.[2] The thesis that Dickinson's style never developed owes a great deal to Charles R. Anderson. In 1960 Anderson wrote: "The chronological arrangement of the new edition [Thomas H. Johnson's 1955 variorum] has been useful in minor ways, but not for selecting or ordering the poems. There are no marked periods in her career, no significant curve of development in her artistic powers, such as might furnish the central plan for a book on Milton or Yeats."[3] Hence, Anderson arranged his readings by theme, an approach that has been followed by many of Dickinson's interpreters.

The thematic reading of Dickinson's poetry has produced a great deal of valuable and provocative criticism; it is not my purpose to argue with the fine readings of Mossberg and Weisbuch, or to undermine the method that led to those readings. But the development of Dickinson's style deserves more critical attention.

---

[1] Douglas Anderson, "Presence and Place in Emily Dickinson's Poetry," *New England Quarterly*, 57 (1984), 205.

[2] See Mossberg, *Emily Dickinson: When a Writer Is a Daughter* (Bloomington: Indiana Univ. Press, 1982); Porter, *Dickinson: The Modern Idiom* (Cambridge: Harvard Univ. Press, 1981); Weisbuch, *Emily Dickinson's Poetry* (Chicago: Univ. of Chicago Press, 1975).

[3] *Emily Dickinson's Poetry: Stairway of Surprise* (New York: Holt, Rinehart, and Winston, 1960), p. xii.

American Literature, Volume 60, Number 1, March 1988. Copyright © 1988 by the Duke University Press. CCC 0002-9831/88/$1.50.

By measuring Dickinson's patterns of rhyme and enjambment, we can see that these formal contours of her verse changed over time, especially from 1858 to 1865. As Dickinson refined her verse technique, her approach to the subjects of her poems changed as well. But her poetry did not develop in the ways we are accustomed to see with poets whose work is published during their lifetimes and subjected to criticism and editorial advice.

Dickinson's poetic development consists mainly of two achievements that mark her work as unique and have established her as a great and difficult poet. First, she revised the hymn quatrain and made of it a more purely literary genre than it had ever been before. By "literary genre" I mean one where the work is intended to exist on the page alone and to be read silently. Dickinson's quatrain poems go even farther beyond the musical hymn of Isaac Watts than the literary ballad of Cowper, Coleridge and others goes beyond the sung ballad. Far from being constrained by her form or immured within the tradition of the hymn, she escaped that tradition completely, to the point where most of her poems no longer bear even a parodic or contrasting relationship to hymns.

Dickinson's second achievement is even more radical. In moving to her late manner she commented on her own texts, producing poems that were adaptations of earlier texts in her growing collection of manuscript fascicles. Having created a genre unique to her own work, she spent her career exploring and redefining that genre. Her reworkings of the subjects of her earlier poems show her concern with the interrelations between texts and with the effects of her own characteristic diction on her subjects. Her use of later poems to comment on earlier ones gives rise to those problems of interpretation that confront any reader of reworked material—except that here the poet is not adapting another's work but her own.

The most striking thing about Dickinson's work is that it is not directed outward. Although her letters teem with references to and talk about literature, there are hardly any uses in her poetry of the language of other poets. Even her few allusions to Shakespeare are mostly character names, except for "Mail from Tunis" in 1463, used for an impossibly long haul, as in *The Tem-*

pest.[4] One of her poems, 960—"Lay this Laurel on the One"—is an adaptation of T. W. Higginson's "Decoration." There is one possible use of Emerson (214), one of Percy Shelley (1620). Her only use of the language of Elizabeth Barrett Browning is in 449, "I died for Beauty—"; and it is a commonplace equation of Beauty and Truth which obviously owes at least as much to Keats, or to dozens of other poets.[5] Criticism has traced powerful undercurrents of the influence of Dickinson's wide reading on her poetry, and of the implicit relation of her style to that of her precursors.[6] But in the language of her poems, Dickinson never appropriated the language of another poet and never used the characteristic diction of a school or movement.

The state of Dickinson's surviving manuscripts confirms this picture of her as an inward-directed artist. There are no prose jottings on the construction of poems, no notebooks on art. We have no idea what her philosophy of composition was. We know that she revised carefully, sometimes taking great pains to find the right word.[7] But she left no explicit clue to her creative process. Her fair copies, bound into fascicles, are a vast and enigmatic book that has evoked many competing interpretations. But that book is not externally a record of artistic experiment. Aside from changes in handwriting over the years, the fascicles are uniform in presentation. They are featureless aside from the texts of the poems and variant readings recorded, without comment, by the poet herself.

But of course this very featurelessness of the fascicles is silent testimony to Dickinson's concern with the status of her texts. Many of the fair copies contain text alone. But the fair copies that contain variant readings are problematic. Johnson considers

[4] All quotations from Dickinson's poetry are from *The Poems of Emily Dickinson*, ed. Thomas H. Johnson (Cambridge: Harvard Univ. Press, 1955). They are referred to by the numbers given them in that edition.

[5] See Jack L. Capps, *Emily Dickinson's Reading: 1836–1886* (Cambridge: Harvard Univ. Press, 1966), pp. 147–88.

[6] See Joanne Feit Diehl, *Dickinson and the Romantic Imagination* (Princeton: Princeton Univ. Press, 1981), which treats Dickinson's responses to her major Romantic precursors; Susan Howe, *My Emily Dickinson* (Berkeley, Cal.: North Atlantic Press, 1985), which examines far-reaching networks of associations between Dickinson's reading and her poetry; A. R. C. Finch, "Dickinson and Patriarchal Meter: A Theory of Metrical Codes," *PMLA*, 102 (1987), 166–76, looks at Dickinson's choice of the quatrain in relation to the tradition of pentameter in English verse.

[7] See *Poems*, I, xxxiii-xxxviii.

these manuscripts to be poems in "the semifinal stage"; the variants, carefully written at the end of each poem and keyed to
crosses over the words in the poem's text, seemed to him to be
suggested changes.[8] This may be true; but it may just as well
be true that Dickinson was preserving not future possibilities
but stages in the composition of the poem, recording alternatives she had considered but rejected. Most semifinal drafts of a
poet's work contain crossings-out and lists of alternatives; many
of Dickinson's manuscripts are in this state. But the variants in
the meticulously transcribed fair copies do not seem like inter-
mediate draft alternatives but like part of the poet's attempt to
preserve her own handwritten variorum edition. It is possible
that the careful preservation of variants indicates great attention
by Dickinson to versions of her poems and to the consequent
refinements in diction that different versions entail.

The manuscript books offer a blank face in terms of the
poet's own discussion of her poetics; but they do allow for
the establishment of a chronology of Dickinson's poems from
1858 to 1865 (nearly all the fascicles are from these years). The
chronology, in turn, can be used to show how Dickinson's use
of rhyme and enjambment developed over time. The efforts of
Johnson, Theodora Ward, and R. W. Franklin have established
a sound, approximate dating of the fascicle poems.[9]

Table 1 presents this chronology. Only the years 1850–1865,
the crucial ones for Dickinson's poetic development, are included.

Table 1

Chronology of Dickinson's Poems

1850–54	1–5
1858	6–57, 323, 1729–1730
1859	58–151, 216
1860	152–215, 318, 324
1861	217–298, 317, 319, 322, 325, 330, 687, 1737
1862	299–316, 320–321, 326–329, 332–432, 434–608, 610–664, 678, 683, 688, 712–717, 759–770, 1053, 1072, 1076, 1181, 1710, 1712, 1725, 1727, 1739

[8] *Poems*, I, xxxiii.

[9] The chronology of Dickinson's poems is from *Poems* with corrections from *The Manuscript Books of Emily Dickinson*, ed. R. W. Franklin (Cambridge: Harvard Univ. Press, 1981).

1863	665–677, 679–682, 684–686, 689–711, 718–758, 771–807
1864	808–981, 1114
1865	433, 982–991, 993–1052, 1054–1066, 1070, 1073, 1177, 1540

The analysis of Dickinson's rhymes is made straightforward by the conventionality of her poems in terms of meter and rhyme-scheme. She did write a small number of poems in a "free-rhyming" verse that rhymes erratically, with no regular meter or rhyme-scheme, and I have excluded those poems from this analysis.[10] And of course some of her poems are fragmentary or in very rough drafts; these have also been excluded. But apart from these exceptions, all of her poems are in hymn stanzas and rhyme in one of the basic hymn rhyme-schemes: *aab ccb* or *xaxa*. Nearly all the places where rhyme would be expected in these poems have some type of rhyme; Dickinson wrote very little unrhymed or free verse (she approaches free verse only in 690 and in parts of 252, 253, 352, and 1720).

Eighty-eight percent of Dickinson's rhymes are of three phonetic types: exact, consonantal, and vowel rhymes.[11] Exact rhyme is the most common type, as in 67:

> Success is counted sweetest
> By those who ne'er *succeed*.
> To comprehend a nectar
> Requires sorest *need*. (Italics mine here
> and in the next two examples.)

Nearly as common is consonantal rhyme, where the final consonants, but not the preceding vowels, are identical:

[10] See Timothy Morris, "The Free-Rhyming Poetry of Emerson and Dickinson," *Essays in Literature*, 12 (1985), 225–40.

[11] Of 4,840 rhymes in Dickinson's poems, 2,006 (41.4%) are exact (of the type see/me, 1732); 167 (3.5%) pair a vowel with a reduced version of itself (me/immortality, 712); 80 (1.6%) are assonantal (breath/quench, 422); 731 (15.1%) are vowel (blew/sky, 354); 1,535 (31.7%) are consonantal (mean/sun, 411); 164 (3.4%) pair a consonant with a cluster containing that consonant (night/erect, 419); 23 pair a cluster with another cluster that shares one consonant with it (disclosed/blind, 761); 2 rhyme a cluster with the same cluster reversed (used/birds, 430); 84 (1.7%) rhyme one nasal consonant with another (thing/begun, 565); 20 rhyme one fricative with another (breeze/divorce, 896); 2 rhyme one voiced stop with another (sob/wood, 45); 5 rhyme one unvoiced stop with another (frock/night, 584); 21 rhyme-positions show less close approximations to exact rhyme, and cannot be considered rhyme at all (for instance, blaze/forge in 365).

One dignity delays for all—
One mitred After*noon*—
None can avoid this purple—
None evade this *Crown*! (98)

Dickinson also frequently uses vowel rhyme, where any vowel rhymes with any other:

I stepped from Plank to Plank
A slow and cautious *way*
The Stars about my Head I felt
About my Feet the *Sea*. (875)

Table 2

Dickinson's Rhymes by Year and Rhyme-Type

	Exact	Consonantal	Vowel
1850–54	80.4	10.7	—
1858	68.1	14.4	7.5
1859	57.7	19.1	10.0
1860	45.5	25.8	13.4
1861	40.0	34.6	13.1
1862	34.5	33.8	17.2
1863	30.5	36.1	18.8
1864	28.3	35.5	17.5
1865	29.9	36.5	16.8

(The percentages given are of *all* rhymes in a given sample, and exclude less common types of rhyme, so totals are less than 100%.)[12]

Table 2 shows the development of Dickinson's technique in terms of rhyme. For each year, the percentage of all rhymes is given for each of the three most common phonetic types. In her earliest surviving poems (1–5, from 1850–54) Dickinson uses mainly exact rhymes; the poems are Valentines, or bits of verse incorporated into letters, and are highly conventional in diction. By the time when she was first binding poems into fascicles, in

[12] I have not found it worthwhile to give a fascicle-by-fascicle analysis of Dickinson's rhymes. The broad trends of the change in her style do show, of course, in such an analysis: for example, she uses 78.1% exact rhyme in Fascicle 1 and only 24.3% exact rhyme in Fascicle 24. But the trend would only be obscured by noting the very small variations from fascicle to fascicle. The dating of the fascicles can never be precise enough to permit statements about development over very brief intervals of time anyway; the year-by-year dating shows Dickinson's stylistic development in general terms, which is my aim here.

1858–59, she had developed a much less conventional rhyming technique. Unfortunately, we have no evidence about how she created these early fascicle poems; none of her manuscripts from the years 1855–57 survive. We see her now in the manuscripts, after four years of silence, as a poet who had broken with the cónventional rhyming of her earliest verse.

After 1865, Dickinson wrote so little poetry that analysis of trends is not reliable. There are few fascicles from 1866 and after; most of the later poems survive in isolated copies and transcripts. Dickinson stopped her great outpouring of poetry in 1866, and the technique she had developed through so many hundreds of poems shows no strong growth in any direction thereafter.

Even more than her rhyme, Dickinson's characteristic enjambment is probably the one formal element that makes her quatrains sound so distinctive. Hymn quatrains are always end-stopped. The hymns of Watts, though they employ inexact rhyme, are entirely unenjambed. In performance, it would be intolerable for a syntactic phrase to be broken at the end of one stanza and picked up at the beginning of the next after an instrumental passage or chorus. But the quatrains of purely literary poems that are meant to be read silently or recited in a speaking voice need not be end-stopped. And in Dickinson's hands, the quatrain became a form meant to be read silently, similar in diction to that of the unenjambed couplets of Keats (as in "Sleep and Poetry") or Browning (*Sordello* or "My Last Duchess"). With their frequent inexact rhyme and their true syntactic verse-paragraphs, Dickinson's quatrains are a new genre, one unique to her own poetry.

Table 3 shows how Dickinson's use of enjambment developed from her earliest verse until 1865. (The final quatrains of poems are not included, as it makes no sense to speak of them as being enjambed or not.)

Table 3

Dickinson's Enjambment

	percentage of enjambed quatrains
1850–54	5.6
1858	16.7
1859	14.6

1860	15.4
1861	20.4
1862	29.8
1863	27.1
1864	34.1
1865	36.7

Dickinson began by using conventional hymn-like end-stopping. Her earliest poems are heavily end-stopped, and the first fascicle poems, in 1858–59, show only infrequent enjambment. But from 1860 to 1865, the amount of enjambment in her poetry grows steadily. By 1864, more than one-third of her quatrains are enjambed.

Dickinson used her later style, enjambed and using frequent inexact rhyme, to write adaptations of her earlier poems. The themes and subjects of these earlier poems reappear in the late style, but Dickinson adapts them by compressing or expanding the diction, changing the amount and nature of subordinate detail, and shifting—or often suppressing—key symbolic references.

Several readers have noticed compression in Dickinson's later poetry. George Frisbie Whicher discusses the condensation of the hummingbird poem "Within my Garden, rides a Bird" (500, dated 1862) into the famous "A Route of Evanescence" (1463, dated 1879).[13] Richard B. Sewall notes the impact of the boiling-down of the nine-stanza "I watched the Moon around the House" (629, dated 1862) into the two-stanza "The Moon upon her fluent Route" (1528, dated 1881).[14] The ultimate of this compressing process is what Gérard Genette calls haïkaïsation.[15] No matter how far haïkaïsation goes, the central referent of the original text (hummingbird, moon) remains present in the rewritten text. And so, the essential element of what Genette calls the "hypotext," the original version, is still present in the "hypertext," the revised version.

But Dickinson did not always condense; she often chose more complex ways of adapting her earlier work. Particularly problematic is the kind of hypertext produced by what Genette calls

---

[13] *This Was a Poet* (New York: Scribners, 1939), p. 262.
[14] *The Life of Emily Dickinson* (New York: Farrar, Straus, and Giroux, 1974), I, 240–43.
[15] *Palimpsestes* (Paris: Seuil, 1982), chap. 9.

demotivation.[16] In this type of adaptation, the presence of the hypotext is absolutely necessary for the reading of the hypertext. There is no sense in which otiose material has been removed from the hypotext; or rather, the otiose and the essential are both removed, or essential material is replaced by new otiose material. In Flaubert's tale "Hérodias," Genette explains, the author retells the Biblical story. But he omits a vital part of the story, the crucial act of Hérodias that dooms John the Baptist. When adapting a Biblical story, Flaubert takes advantage of the fact that every reader knows the hypotext. But it is entirely possible for an author to practice demotivation of a text that is not well known, or that is unknown to every reader but herself; and this is what Dickinson does in reworking 72, "Glowing is her Bonnet" (about 1859), into 978, "It bloomed and dropt, a Single Noon—" (about 1864). Here is the earlier poem:

> Glowing is her Bonnet,
> Glowing is her Cheek,
> Glowing is her Kirtle,
> Yet she cannot speak.
>
> Better as the Daisy
> From the Summer hill
> Vanish unrecorded
> Save by tearful rill—
>
> Save by loving sunrise
> Looking for her face.
> Save by feet unnumbered
> Pausing at the place.

These quatrains are typical in form for an early Dickinson poem. They rhyme exactly, and the only enjambment comes between the second and third stanzas, at a break between paratactic phrases.

The first stanza establishes that someone is dead. It does so indirectly; but the central referent is clear. The following two stanzas express a preference for the way flowers die. The diction of the poem is characteristically Dickinson's, especially in its terse obliqueness; many of her early poems are terse and telegraphic in a similar way.

---

[16] "Demotivation in *Hérodias*," in *Flaubert and Postmodernism*, ed. Naomi Sekori and Henry F. Majewski (Lincoln: Univ. of Nebraska Press, 1984), pp. 192–201. Trans. Marlena Corcoran.

This early poem is marked strongly by the absence of tension. The poem, with its stock metrical phrases—"tearful rill," "loving sunrise"—and its conventional meter, rhyme, and end-stopping, is a metaphoric cliché. This is true despite Dickinson's metonymic evasiveness, her reluctance to name the central referents. And it is also clear that no amount of compression could complicate the poem much. In fact, not much compression is possible, given the poem's already small bounds.

In reworking the material of this poem, then, Dickinson elaborated rather than compressed it. But as she elaborated the detail and the rhetorical structure of the poem (by adding "I," in this case), and as she loosened the prosody by means of inexact rhyme and enjambment, she also removed the initial reference to a human death that motivates the consideration of the flower. The result is the demotivated text of 978.

> It bloomed and dropt, a Single Noon—
> The Flower—distinct and Red—
> I, passing, thought another Noon
> Another in its stead
>
> Will equal glow, and thought no More
> But came another Day
> To find the Species disappeared—
> The Same Locality—
>
> The Sun in place—no other fraud
> On Nature's perfect Sum—
> Had I but lingered Yesterday—
> Was my retrieveless blame—
>
> Much Flowers of this and further Zones
> Have perished in my Hands
> For seeking its Resemblance—
> But unapproached it stands—
>
> The single Flower of the Earth
> That I, in passing by
> Unconscious was—Great Nature's Face
> Passed infinite by Me—

In contrast to 72, 978 contains all the features of Dickinson's later style. In the variation of rhyme and enjambment and in its verse-paragraphing, the poem avoids the stock phrases that fill out 72.

Poem 72 compares a human death and the death of a flower;

978 expands on the death of the flower and removes the human death altogether. Dickinson expands the terseness of the narrative detail in the earlier poem; "Vanish unrecorded" becomes "came another Day / To find the Species disappeared— / The Same Locality— / The Sun in place—no other fraud / On Nature's perfect Sum—." But no similar refinement is applied to the first stanza of 72. It is simply dropped. The result of this demotivation is to throw great emphasis on the disappearance of the flower, and to demand a symbolic referent for it. But the poem refuses to associate the flower with anything else. The extremity of the speaker's emotions becomes extremely puzzling: "retrieveless blame" and "Great Nature's Face / Passed infinite by me" suggest a psychological depth that the literal situation doesn't call for. The reader is left wondering what so extreme an emotion could be evoked by, and what the hidden connection between the flower and the unknown symbolic referent could be. One is led, when reading such a poem, to a state of *presque vu* about the poet's intentions and private associations. The powerful suggestiveness of the poem results from its being a demotivation of a hypotext that was more explicit about these associations.

Over the course of Dickinson's career, she returned again and again to the basic themes that figure in her early poems— hence the observation by many critics that her subject matter remained static. But while the early poems tend to be simply descriptive or to present stock conclusions (even when they are paradoxical or ironic stock conclusions), the later poems employ compression, or demotivation, or a shift in symbolic direction, to cause problems of interpretation. Dickinson's later style demands that the intricacy of her early hymn-like poems be doubled back on itself to produce a problem of interpretation every time the poem is read. The style in itself becomes the argument. This pattern can be observed in the large clusters of poems on death, marriage, loneliness, and other subjects; one small cluster of poems that shows it well is on Indian Summer, the period of warm weather after the first frost. Dickinson's first Indian Summer poem is 130:

> These are the days when Birds come back—
> A very few—a Bird or two—
> To take a backward look.

These are the days when skies resume
The old—old sophistries of June—
A blue and gold mistake.

Oh fraud that cannot cheat the Bee—
Almost thy plausibility
Induces my belief.

Till ranks of seeds their witness bear—
And softly thro' the altered air
Hurries a timid leaf.

Oh Sacrament of summer days,
Oh Last Communion in the Haze—
Permit a child to join.

The sacred emblems to partake—
Thy consecrated bread to take
And thine immortal wine!

The poem is far from being a simple appreciation of the season. Even though the final stanza seems like an ecstatic acceptance of Indian Summer, the poem is, centrally, ambiguous. Indian Summer is a "Sacrament," but it is also a "fraud" and a "mistake": it is a repetition of the "sophistries of June." And if June itself, the real summer, is full of sophistries, a false June must be even falser. The speaker seems weary of the summer itself, because it is necessarily transient, and even wearier of the final deceit of the Indian Summer.

And yet, paradoxically, the speaker regains her faith at the very moment when she is made certain that the false summer is false: when "ranks of seeds their witness bear." Now that the season has stopped pretending to be anything other than summer's last gasp, she is ready to participate, and the poem slips into the devotional language of the last two stanzas. Or maybe it doesn't; maybe the last two stanzas are a satire on a type of attitude toward faith that embraces faith despite a deep-rooted skepticism. This satiric logic is papered over by the end-stopped hymn stanzas and the light tone. The satirical level is there, but it remains smirking, not serious; mock-devotional, not anti-devotional. Above all, the poem does not confront the problem of faith. It poses outside the problem, and we can either appreciate or reject that pose, but not engage it in an argument.

Poem 130 was written about 1859. Five years later, Dickin-

son returned to the theme of Indian Summer to write a more
problematic poem, 930:

> There is a June when Corn is cut
> And Roses in the Seed—
> A Summer briefer than the first
> But tenderer indeed
>
> As should a Face supposed the Grave's
> Emerge a single Noon
> In the Vermillion that it wore
> Affect us, and return—
>
> Two Seasons, it is said, exist—
> The Summer of the Just,
> And this of Ours, diversified
> With Prospect, and with Frost—
>
> May not our Second with its First
> So infinite compare
> That We but recollect the one
> The other to prefer?

The problems of interpretation in this poem come from its
piling up of comparisons, comparisons that at each level embody
paradoxes. The enjambment from the first stanza to the second
makes the first comparison, between Indian Summer and the
brief reappearance of someone buried. Indian Summer itself is
presented paradoxically, as a "June when Corn is cut," instead of
simply as "the days when Birds come back." And the season is
not merely accused of sophistry, as in 130; it is directly compared
to an experience that is impossible: someone coming back from
the dead not as a ghost but "in the Vermillion," in the flesh. Most
similes present the unfamiliar in terms of the familiar, but this
one presents the familiar in terms of the impossible. In the third
stanza, Indian Summer, in its impossible beauty, is compared to
the bliss of heaven, the "Summer of the Just." Which is better?
The fourth stanza should tell us, but it doesn't quite manage
to; its syntax is as baffling as anything Dickinson ever wrote.
"Our Second" is Indian Summer, and "its First" is heaven, but
which of these is "the other" that we have recollected "the one"
to prefer?

The answer, I think, lies not in any internal evidence, but
in an echo of 130 that the whole situation of 930 brings to

mind. Remember that both June and Indian Summer in the earlier poem are accused of "sophistries," in an offhand way that the speaker does not elaborate. The speaker instead drifts into a formulaic appreciation of the season she has accused. Here in 930, though, the sophistry is examined and explained. The reappearance of someone buried in the second stanza is, of course, only humanly impossible; there is a notable example of it, beyond human power, in the Resurrection. And we are certainly reminded of the Resurrection in the second stanza, because the very impossibility of the simile demands it. After the end-stopping at the end of the second stanza, the poem picks up the same comparison that it made in that second stanza, because the Resurrection and the "Summer of the Just" are, after all, identical. The Resurrection defeated death and made this summer that is not "diversified" possible.

So when we "recollect the one," we are recollecting that Resurrection and its promise of eternal summer. But we are preferring "the other," the Indian Summer that so paradoxically can only be appreciated because it is false—palpably, not metaphysically, false. Poem 930, welded together out of a tremendous tension of style and symbol, is a rejection of the whole mystery of immortality in favor of a confidence trick by Nature that seems honest in comparison. But the poet is not merely expounding a position here; she is arriving at it by the process of adapting an earlier text. In another poem or set of poems she may very well—she certainly did—arrive at other conclusions about Christ and about immortality. But here, she takes what is only hinted at in the contradictions of 130, and by pressing those contradictions to their limit, she arrives at the agonizing puzzle of 930.

Dickinson continued to rework the theme of Indian Summer, and her 1364, written about 1876, is a late haïkaïsation of the subject. As in many of these extremely compressed poems, the central term has become enigmatic:

> How know it from a Summer's Day?
> Its Fervors are as firm—
> And nothing in its Countenance
> But scintillates the same—
> Yet Birds examine it and flee—
> And Vans without a name

Inspect the Admonition
And sunder as they came—

The first five lines of the poem are a simple compression of
Dickinson's earlier descriptions of Indian Summer. The speaker
knows that it is not summer; the only difficulty is in proving it,
and this is accomplished by noting that the birds aren't fooled.
(In 130, the proof was the "ranks of seeds." Also in that poem,
it was the bees, not the birds, that couldn't be fooled; but bees
actually are very active on warm autumn days, perhaps leading
Dickinson to drop that element of the treatment.) The problem
of the poem lies in lines 6-8. "Vans without a name" is an
impossibly obscure phrase, and deliberately so. These Vans are
only named by their lack of a name, and their only action in
the poem is to refuse to appear in it. They might be insects; the
vaguely visual evocation of them makes them "look" like insects;
but why would insects lack a name when birds are given one?
As they appear, nameless, almost in the poem, they are spiritual
presences of some sort, hovering on the edge of the poem's
consciousness. Their sundering, in the last line, is a melting into
silence of all the sarcasm and anguish that surrounded Indian
Summer in 130 and 930, and 1364 is eerier and more cryptic
than either of its predecessors.

The Indian Summer poems chart, in miniature, the development of Dickinson's style, from something resembling a hymn,
at least in formal outline, to a far more individual treatment of
the same subjects, made possible by inexact rhyme, enjambment,
verse-paragraphing, haïkaïsation, demotivation—in general, by a
ceaseless reworking of the one book that meant more to Dickinson than any other, even the Bible: the book of her own poetry.
R. P. Blackmur accused Dickinson of "revolving in a vacuum"
when she wrote her unconventional verse, and the accusation
is true.[17] She never adopted conventional technique, but started
very early with something idiosyncratic and then revised her
own idiosyncrasies. Probably it is fortunate that she did, as she
was led to complicate rather than to polish her early work. An
editor would have noted very early on that she had gotten the
bees and birds mixed up in 130, and while she was smoothing
that out, she might never have composed 930.

[17] "Emily Dickinson: Notes on Prejudice and Fact," *Southern Review*, 3 (1937), 323-47.

Picasso is supposed to have said that he didn't care who influenced him, so long as he didn't influence himself. Dickinson proceeded oppositely; she was vigorously anti-eclectic. This leads to the difficulty of considering her work as a single integrated corpus. In the Indian Summer poems, Dickinson certainly has her earlier poems—carefully preserved in the fascicles—in mind as a context for the later ones. But for other sequences of poems, such as the many that affirm faith and immortality, her manuscript books provide different contexts. It is customary to think of lyric poems as being strictly independent utterances, or as being elements in a narrative or meditative sequence. But Dickinson's fascicles are neither. The logic of clusters on different themes— or even, sometimes, of different poems within a cluster on the same theme—develops in different directions. When interpreters attempt to capture her thought on a given subject by referring to poems written over a twenty-five-year period, they are not proceeding incorrectly—very often there is no other way to proceed if we want to make sense of Dickinson—but they are compiling provisional indexes to what was still, in its final "edition," very much a work in progress.

So was *Leaves of Grass*, of course, but the difference is that Dickinson was not making a book for anyone but herself. Her work is inward-directed to a unique extent, and not just in its lack of appropriation of the language of others and in her lack of interest in publication. The most distinctive thing about her poetry is, finally, the intensely problematic nature of her painstaking and often enigmatic adaptation of her private texts.

Emily Dickinson and the Economics of Desire

Joan Burbick

THE writings of Emily Dickinson are often interpreted as a
pristine expression of individual consciousness or a narrative
of the autonomous self bent on an ever-deepening quest for power
and freedom. As such, her voice stands beyond culture in the lyric
landscape of mythic yearning. Instead, this study presumes to read
Dickinson's words as a cultural text that attempts to explore and
resolve on an aesthetic level pressing ideological conflicts of her
social class.[1] Dickinson's Amherst, no matter how disembodied we
would like to perceive her participation, was marked by the fervor
of evangelical Christianity, the ethos of the Christian Gentleman
and Lady, and the determined desire for social order and class
stability, emerging from the Protestant vision of industrial capitalism.[2]

At the heart of the developing managerial and professional class
was a strongly articulated need for the rational control of human
actions and emotions whose language was frequently encased in an
economic metaphor of use.[3] As Henry May has reminded us, the
language of rational control is not unique to nineteenth-century

[1] As Fredric Jameson, *The Political Unconscious: Narrative as a Socially Symbolic Act*
(Ithaca: Cornell Univ. Press, 1981), writes, the literary act is "a way of doing something to
the world, to that degree what we are calling 'world' must inhere within it, as the content it
has to take up into itself in order to submit it to the transformation of form," p. 81.

[2] Besides the biography of Richard B. Sewall, *The Life of Emily Dickinson*, 2 vols. (New
York: Farrar, Straus and Giroux, 1974), of relevance to an understanding of Dickinson's
social context is Polly Longsworth's book, *Austin and Mabel: The Amherst Affair and Love
Letters of Austin Dickinson and Mabel Loomis Todd* (New York: Farrar, Straus, and Giroux,
1984) in which the language of desire is justified in a highly antinomian manner by means of
the rhetoric of evangelical Christianity.

[3] Of general interest see in particular, Gilles Deleuze and Felix Guattari *Anti-Oedipus:
Capitalism and Schizophrenia* (New York: Viking, 1972); Albert O. Hirschman, *The Passions
and the Interests: Political Arguments for Capitalism before Its Triumph* (Princeton: Princeton
Univ. Press, 1977), and Max Weber, *The Protestant Ethic and the Spirit of Capitalism* (New
York: Scribner's, 1958). More specifically, Dickinson's father, Edward Dickinson, is fairly
representative when he writes to Emily Norcross two months before their marriage: "Let us

American Literature, Volume 58, Number 3, October 1986. Copyright © 1986 by the Duke
University Press. CCC 0002-9831/86/$1.50.

America, having a long history in enlightenment thought.[4] What is distinctive, however, is its increasing emphasis on cultural prescriptions concerning sexual behavior. Charles Rosenberg points out that during the years between 1830 and 1870, after the Second Great Awakening, a new interest was placed upon the social need to manage sexuality, both within and without marriage. He identifies the medical and biological literature of this period as at first expressing a "tone of repressiveness" which by the 1870s has "moved from the level of individual exhortation to that of organized efforts to enforce chastity upon the unwilling."[5] By analyzing the mode of authority used by these social commentators, Rosenberg notes how "apparent is the emotional centrality of a fundamental expository metaphor, one which might best be called 'mercantilist.' " This economic language led to, what Rosenberg calls, a "logic of sexual frugality."[6]

In the economic language of sexual frugality, the unmarried woman represented a puzzling, if not disturbing, cultural fact. As a woman, she was equated with sexuality, having access to its use,

---

prepare for a life of rational happiness. I do not expect, neither do I desire a life of *pleasure*, as some call it—I anticipate pleasure from engaging with my whole soul in business," Sewall, *The Life of Emily Dickinson*, I, 47.

[4] *The Enlightenment in America* (New York: Oxford Univ. Press, 1976).

[5] *No Other Gods: On Science and American Social Thought* (Baltimore: Johns Hopkins Univ. Press, 1976), p. 73.

[6] *No Other Gods*, p. 87. In addition, John S. Haller and Robin M. Haller, *The Physician and Sexuality in Victorian America* (Urbana: Univ. of Illinois Press, 1974), pp. 91–137, claim that seventeenth- and eighteenth-century manuals of love and marriage stress "pleasure" as a legitimate need and emotion between marriage partners, but that mid-nineteenth century manuals stress the utilitarian aspects of sex. Women are accordingly seen as "indifferent" to both desire and sexual activity. Carl N. Degler, *At Odds: Women and the Family in America from the Revolution to the Present* (New York: Oxford Univ. Press, 1980), however, considers the portraits in health manuals as idealized renderings of how woman should behave. Instead, Degler claims that women increasingly controlled the means of reproduction through policies of sexual purity and male self-restraint. Gerda Lerner, ed. *The Female Experience: An American Documentary* (Indianapolis: Bobbs-Merrill, 1977), also points out that nineteenth-century feminists often attacked sexuality because "for most women, the perils, travails, and hardships of frequent pregnancies far outweighed the benefits and pleasures of sexual intercourse," p. 47. Sexual abstinence was turned to as the most reliable form of birth control. But Lerner does not see the drop in birth rate at the end of the nineteenth century as a signal of women's power in domestic matters. Rather she cites economic reasons for restricting the size of families. Desire in this historical debate, however, quickly becomes subservient to the issues of birth control and the functions of adult marital sexuality. See also Nancy Cott, "Passionlessness: An Interpretation of Victorian Sexual Ideology, 1790–1850," *Signs: Journal of Women in Culture and Society*, 4 (1978), 223; and Anita Clair Fellman and Michael Fellman, *Making Sense of Self: Medical Advice Literature in Late Nineteenth-Century America* (Philadelphia: Univ. of Pennsylvania Press, 1981), p. 105.

but as a single woman without the sanction of marriage, she had no proper guidelines for how to "manage" its use.[7] As a result, the unmarried woman was in need of severe regulation: all sexual feelings, thoughts, and actions had to be contained. In particular, desire, if it existed for the unmarried woman, was "dangerous" and, as Dickinson would write, needed to be "handled with a Chain." Without the legitimation of marriage, the single woman was forced into a controlled abstinence of both her emotional and social self. Desire must not be felt or thought, let alone acted upon.

Recent critics have shown how Dickinson transforms religion, art and death into Eros and how she rivals Walt Whitman's litanies to the senses.[8] Yet few have bothered to examine how Dickinson often analyzes desire through economic tropes that ultimately determine the "cost" of longing.[9] Through what might be called her "economics of desire," Dickinson describes longing in terms of poverty and wealth, loss and gain, producing poems that both mimic and deprecate the mercantilist vision of her social class.[10]

In general, Dickinson's writings can be seen as expressing four logical, not chronological, visions of desire that imply a specific

---

[7] A revealing set of letters between Lucy Stone, the nineteenth-century women's rights leader who early in her life embraced spinsterhood, and her family shows how strongly women were considered "unnatural" if they did not marry. Luther Stone wrote to Lucy these words of wisdom, telling her that it was "As Great A Sin To Not Suffer These Organs To Be Used At All As To Use Them To Much." Gerda Lerner, ed., *The Female Experience: An American Documentary* (Indianapolis: Bobbs-Merrill, 1977), p. 85.

[8] Rebecca Patterson, *Emily Dickinson's Imagery* (Amherst: Univ. of Massachusetts Press, 1979), claims that there is "no more erotic poetry in the English language" than Dickinson's, p. 30. While Karl Keller, *The Only Kangaroo Among the Beauty: Emily Dickinson and America* (Baltimore: Johns Hopkins Univ. Press, 1979), compares Dickinson directly to Whitman and finds her vision of sex "as many things: overwhelming monster, plaything, object of perplexity, escapist high, symbol of disillusionment, spiritual tease, productive pain—any and all of these," p. 267.

[9] Some critics have written on Dickinson's economic language as it pertained to family, friends, and New England society. Robert Meredith, "Emily Dickinson and the Acquisitive Society," *New England Quarterly*, 37 (1964), 436, suggests that her language attacks "the counterfeit values of her time." Vivian R. Pollak, " 'That Fine Prosperity': Economic Metaphors in Emily Dickinson's Poetry," *Modern Language Quarterly*, 34 (1973), 171, also finds that Dickinson's economic language functions as "oblique social criticism." It establishes "the resistance of the private self to public values, the resistance of the self to any form of authority, human or divine." But Cynthia Chaliff, "The Psychology of Economics in Emily Dickinson," *Literature and Psychology*, 18 (1968), 93, finds instead that the "capitalistic system" became a part of Dickinson's "psychological dynamics." Though these studies connect Dickinson's language with the terms of mercantile New England culture, they overlook the specific tension between economic language and expressions of desire.

[10] As an unmarried woman, Dickinson was in a particularly acute social role. Degler, *At Odds*, points out that the "highest proportion of women who never married for any period

theory of use or economy. The first dreams about an extravagant wealth and joyful consumption of pleasure without regulation: delight becomes an end in itself, producing nothing other than its own "greedy" enjoyment. The second ponders the tension of not-having: loss and restraint promise greater "gain" by deferring possession and, at times, by embracing asceticism. The third analyzes and renders ironic patterns of not-having until they assume nightmare proportions of need: the "true cost" of restraint is revealed to be the mutilation of the body. The fourth pushes even further into irony: desire is denied until only the "dead" body remains as the "price" of wanting.

As presented in this study, each successive voice widens further the gap between desire and delight until the power to have is eliminated. At its worst, delight rests finally within death. Nonetheless, what is remarkable about her poetry is the extent to which Dickinson depicts the bliss of consummatory pleasure and constructs an economy that equates it with absolute "riches." As "Debauchees of Dew," her speakers exist in a state of animated sensuality. She knew that the "Heart" asks "Pleasure" first but also described how afterward comes the menacing "will of its Inquisitor." Her work is never far from describing the tension of delayed desire as well as the horror of deprivation. In her quest for adequate expressions of delight, spectres of regulation stalk the poetry. They can appear at any moment as the frowning mask of the "Keeper" or the "Sexton" who guards the keys to life. But most provokingly, they figure as economic metaphors that imply a system of controlled "values." Desire is often encased in a "costly" standard of measure that robs the body of delight.

I

Hardly a strategy of restraint, this lyric voice, tinged with "greed," unabashedly proclaims the desire to "hoard" the love of

between 1835 and the present were those born between 1860 and 1880," p. 152. There was a rising incidence of single women during the second half of the nineteenth century, but despite this increase, these women were still generally characterized as living in an "unnatural" state, conducive to "unpleasant eccentricities" and "queer fancies." In this regard, Thomas Wentworth Higginson is famous but hardly unique for his "dread" of printing "Wild Nights." His inability to reconcile the psyche of an unmarried woman with expressions of desire is merely symptomatic of the times. See Millicent Todd Bingham, *Ancestor's Brocades: The Literary Debut of Emily Dickinson* (New York: Harper, 1945), p. 127.

family and friends. This opulent language that describes those desired as gold and priceless jewels, challenges the world of carefully measured mercantilist wealth. Not uncommonly, women writers at mid-nineteenth century often described their domestic spheres as the locus of value in the culture, equating wealth with home and friends bound together by love. The wealth of men in the marketplace was, hence, inferior to the wealth of women in extended households.[11] Dickinson too, from an early age, links her family and friends with gold, the ultimate social sign of value, and declares the domestic sphere the citadel of wealth. She writes to Jane Humphrey in 1842: "I miss my beloved Jane—I wish you would write to me—I should think more of it than of a mine of gold—."[12] Elsewhere her friends, as part of a domestic circle of love, are jewels and precious gems often bound together with golden chains which she covets as avidly as the greediest miser.[13]

These letters to her family and friends during the 1840s and 50s also express an economic language particularly imbued with biblical imagery. Equating extreme wealth with her friends, Dickinson frequently envisions them as precious treasures, echoing the language of Matthew: "For where your treasure is, there will your heart be also."[14] Dickinson, in turn, describes the heart as "such hard little creditors—such real little misers," without equal in the "whole, wide world" (L 85). In its greed, the heart yearns to possess its earthly treasure, and in this way, actually inverts the biblical language it echoes. In Matthew, the dictum is clear: "Lay not up for yourselves treasures upon earth, where moth and rust doth corrupt, and where thieves break through and steal: But lay up for yourselves treasures in heaven, where neither moth and rust doth corrupt, and where thieves do not break in and steal."[15]

[11] Nancy Cott, *The Bonds of Womanhood: Women's Sphere in New England, 1780–1835* (New Haven: Yale Univ. Press, 1977), p. 69, describes how women praised the value of the home, but she sees in their praise no direct challenge to "the modern organization of work and pursuit of wealth." Nina Baym, *Woman's Fiction: A Guide to Novels by and about Women in America, 1820–1870* (Ithaca: Cornell Univ. Press, 1978), pp. 48–49, however, assigns women a slightly more activist role. Their "special concept of home" with its perception of wealth as human bonds of affection attempts to reform the mercenary principles of larger American society.

[12] *The Letters of Emily Dickinson*, ed. Thomas H. Johnson and Theodora Ward, (Cambridge: Harvard Univ. Press, 1958) I, 7. Hereafter cited in the text with corresponding letter number.

[13] L 26; L 39; L 74; L 77; L 193.

[14] King James Version, Matthew 6:21.

[15] King James Version, Matthew 6:19–21.

Equating friends with gold is idolatrous, yet Dickinson continues
to evoke her desire for friendship and love with an earthly economy
of extravagant wealth. Writing to Samuel Bowles, she boldly
asserts: "My friends are my 'estate.' Forgive me then the avarice to
hoard them!" (L 193). This economy knows no restraint; friends
are "mints" and "precious stones" meant to be possessed entirely.

Dickinson clearly understands how she is inverting this biblical
language, and in a letter to Abiah Root, her conflict over where to
place "value" is apparent: "perhaps the treasure *here* would be *too
dear* a treasure—couldn't 'the moth corrupt, and the thief break
thro' and steal'—" (L 50). The "*subtle* moth" that has invaded her
"treasurehouse" performs an "errand," fulfilling its "mission"; "it
taught me dear Abiah to have no treasure here, or rather it tried to
tell me in it's little mothy way of another *enduring* treasure, the
robber cannot steal which, nor time waste away" (L 50). Ending on
a note that embraces the evangelical enthusiasm of her Abiah,
Dickinson nonetheless hints at another reason why the moth
exists. A fatal reminder of mortality, corruption warns against the
placing of value on earthly delights since, after all is experienced,
they may indeed be the most valuable treasure. Attempting to
restrain herself from desiring too strongly this earthly treasure,
Dickinson nonetheless cannot let go of its magical hold.

The earthly treasure is indeed so priceless, the theme of its
robbery and loss preoccupies Dickinson's poetic imagination. In "I
never lost as much but twice," the accused is the "Burglar!
Banker!—Father!" (P 49), who like other poetic marauders or
thieves continually pillages human life.[16] Friends are such precious
jewels that their loss leaves at best "an Amethyst remembrance" (P
245), at worst a searing emptiness: "Without this—there is
nought— / All other Riches be / As is the Twitter of a Bird— /
Heard opposite the Sea—" (P 655). Those desired are "Gigantic
Sums" whose value brings distress: "Heaven is so presuming that
we must hide our Gems" (L 535). In the economic and biblical
language of robbery, Dickinson seems particularly anxious: "No
Verse in the Bible has frightened me so much from a Child as 'from

---

[16] All quotes from the poetry are from *The Poems of Emily Dickinson*, ed. Thomas H.
Johnson (Cambridge: Harvard Univ. Press, 1955), cited in the text by the appropriate poem
number.

him that hath not, shall be taken even that he hath.' Was it because it's dark menace deepened our own Door?" (L 788).

Dickinson also carries economic metaphors of golden domestic treasure into the terrain of explicit sexual experience. Writing a "saucy page" to her future sister-in-law, Susan Gilbert, she dares to bring up the taboo topic: "How dull our lives must seem to the bride, and the plighted maiden, whose days are fed with gold, and who gathers pearls every evening. . . " (L 93).[17] This metaphor of extreme wealth as sexual knowledge informs her classic poem about desire: "Wild Nights—Wild Nights! / Were I with thee / Wild Nights should be / Our luxury!" (P 249).

Dickinson's speakers also supplicate and entreat the lover to experience a consummatory sexuality that implies total depletion. In P 211, the speaker entreats: "Come slowly—Eden!" and is eventually lost in the experience of sexual pleasure. Indeed, her speakers often dwell on the act of consummatory joy: "Oh Sumptuous moment / Slower go / That I may gloat on thee—" (P 1125). Some of her poetic voices eat and drink with abandon: they ask to be brought the "sunset in a cup" (P 128); their hands ache to practice "*Gem*-Tactics" in order to learn to possess jewels of love (P 320); they declare themselves "wives," claimants of sexual knowledge (P 461). And desire can ultimately become part of "nature," an aspect of being that like beauty "is." "Longing is like the Seed / That wrestles in the Ground" (P 1255); unavoidable, inexplicable, desire is one with life.

II

The language of hoarding, greed, and consumption stands in stark contrast to a strictly mercantilist language that "measures" desire in terms of "loss" and "gain," a closed system of monetary value in which gain is increased through not-consuming.[18] In an

[17] Rebecca Patterson, *Emily Dickinson's Imagery*, p. 86, thinks that "the most sexually charged of Emily Dickinson's jewels is the pearl—and from at least as early as the girlhood days when she first began to think of writing poetry."

[18] I am using Max Weber's concept of asceticism as a metaphor for consumption in the post-Reformation world, but it is a metaphor in the process of dissolving by Dickinson's time. As America is thrust into a world of necessary consumption, where consumer palaces dot the landscape of the late nineteenth century, great contradictions pervade the Victorian milieu. Rational restraint on sexuality stands in great contrast to the burgeoning affluence of the post-1870s.

economic language of asceticism, Dickinson's speakers often embrace a posture of self-denial for which they are rewarded. Only by not-having does that which is desired "gain" in value. A rationale for the management of wealth structures and regulates the emotions. The consumption of what is desired is continually deferred, and the activity of striving acquires value over the satisfaction of obtaining the goal. The second voice, unlike the first that consumes in excess, glorifies the language of economic restraint necessary for the accumulation of wealth.

These strategies of restraint, depicting "consummation" as the "hurry of fools,"[19] instead exalt the state of not-having. Writing to Susan Gilbert in 1871, Dickinson asserts: "To miss you, Sue, is power. The stimulus of Loss makes most Possession mean" (L 364). In "Go not too near a House of Rose—" (P 1434), the speaker concludes that "In insecurity to lie / Is Joy's insuring quality." On one level, such statements about desire fit into the larger schemas of opposition throughout her poetry. Critics have long analyzed the poems that base their tension on the enticement of polarities in which "Opposites—entice."[20] Her speakers thirst, hunger and fail and only through their state of deprivation truly value what they desire: "Water, is taught by thirst" (P 135) and "To comprehend a nectar / Requires sorest need" (P 67).

But what is of interest in this language of opposites is the way in which the desired goal "gains" through destitution. This economics of asceticism is often a way of allowing loss, danger, and uncertainty to increase both the cost and the value of what is desired. Dickinson's speakers can define desire as the mere realization of absence. Simply put, " 'Heaven'—is what I cannot reach!" (P 239). Striving for the unobtainable forms the very basis of incredible worth. Delight becomes "More fair—because impossible / That any gain—" (P 572). Elsewhere, Dickinson writes: "Danger—deepens Sum—" (P 807) and "That Possession fairest lies that is least possest" (L 359).

---

[19] Prose fragment noted in *The Letters of Emily Dickinson*, ed. Johnson, III, 922.

[20] See in particular the discussion of "compound vision" by Robert Weisbuch, *Emily Dickinson's Poetry* (Chicago: Univ. of Chicago Press, 1975), who writes that Dickinson's poetry "contrasts and sometimes, remarkably, combines a self which is powerful, autonomous, and godlike with a self which is all-vulnerable, limited, and victimized," p. xi.

This "spirit" of not-having that enhances the desired is also expressed as a series of obstacles, each provoking greater worth. In "I cross till I am weary," the speaker depicts the weariness of the mind confronted with "Mountains," "Seas," and a "Desert" while continuing to search and scan the horizon for the desired. Midway through the poem the following rationale is given for the deferment of satisfaction: "What merit had the Goal— / Except there intervene / Faint Doubt—and far Competitor— / To jeopardize the Gain?" (P 550). The logic of a carefully planned asceticism not only validates the struggle but claims that the goal will increase in "merit." Value increases in direct ratio to the threat of competition. Intervention, the necessary obstruction to the movement of desire, is found in "Faint Doubt" and "far Competitor." Whose doubt it is, however, is left in abeyance; Dickinson does not make clear whether it belongs to the desirer or the desired or if it is a shadow across the very act of the search. Hardly a conventional "rival," doubt nonetheless adds "value" to the goal.

The activity of not-having can, however, gain such importance that it begins to rival consumption. Each denial builds the prize to such proportions that actual possession pales in relation to the struggle to acquire. Consummation is denied, and instead asceticism emerges as a means to defer and increase the value of what becomes an impossible goal. In P 1430, the "Banquet of Abstemiousness" becomes so precious that it paradoxically "Defaces" the value of the inebriating wine. The "perfect Goal" is made transcendent and hence is never consumed; it exists in a perpetual state of denial. The speaker is finally left without the ability to have; only a fantasy about the ideal is possible.

III

Though it animates the search and adds value to the ideal, continually deferred goal, the economic language of restraint easily transforms into a third, deeply ironic vision in which self-denial becomes simply the expression of dire need. Temporary deferment, leading to a more valued or idealized gratification, becomes instead a permanent impoverishment, if not a psychic or physical wounding. The rationales for not-having become insidious and are exposed for their "true costs." In this economic description of desire, the system of deferred possession nullifies the purpose of the search and confines the pursuer within a maze of deprivation:

> From Blank to Blank—
> A Threadless Way
> I pushed Mechanic feet—
> To stop—or perish—or advance—
> Alike indifferent—
>
> If end I gained
> It ends beyond
> Indefinite disclosed
> I shut my eyes—and groped as well
> 'Twas lighter—to be Blind— (P 761)

By having the goal permanently out of reach, always one step beyond the speaker, the state of desiring and the object of desire create a terrifying impoverishment.

Restraint, a form of self-control or self-robbery, that regulates the desire to consume can as easily become a form of deprivation. In Dickinson's famous definition poem, "Renunciation—is a piercing Virtue—," the speaker who desires to drink and to see is required to thirst and blind herself for the sake of a goal beyond the reach of human hands. "Renunciation" becomes a "Not now— / The putting out of Eyes— / Just Sunrise—," a landscape of mutilation and envy. This form of renunciation is further expressed as necessary because "Sunrise" might have more value than "Day's Great Progenitor—." As a result, the activity of renunciation is presented less as a glorious triumph over earthly consumption than as a tormented process of self-denial: "Renunciation—is the Choosing / Against itself— / Itself to justify / Unto itself—" (P 745).

Vivian Pollak points out in her discussion on images of thirst and starvation in Dickinson's poetry that such moments of renunciation have too easily been labeled as "compensation." Renunciation implies for many critics the image of a suffering soul "who remains constant while waiting its ultimate reward." But Pollak finds that such labeling misses the "vulnerability and threatened deterioration of the self" that accompanies renunciation.[21] Such deteriora-

---

[21] "Thirst and Starvation in Emily Dickinson's Poetry," *American Literature*, 51 (1979), 48, finds that Dickinson's "starving self" wants the absence of food and drink but never

tion is not explained by labeling Dickinson's biographical sexuality "pathological"; rather she accurately describes the *effects* of a system of restraint endemic to female sexuality in the nineteenth century.[22] Dickinson sees clearly that the social demand of "renunciation," especially as it is interiorized by women, actually requires physical and mental wounding.

IV

Dickinson's most insidious voice involves the cost of desire as nothing less than death. Instead of displaying the scars of renunciation or remorse, Dickinson's speakers require death as the response to the mere thought of desire. Enthralling fantasies instantly kill (P 1291) and thrust the speaker into a deadly landscape of economic measure: "Utmost is relative— / Have not or Have / Adjacent Sums / Enough—the first Abode / On the familiar Road / Galloped in Dreams—." Desire for Dickinson's speakers, as for the heroines of Kate Chopin and Edith Wharton, ruins life and

---

"fully renounces the thirst and hungers of the social self." In general, she challenges the critical viewpoint of George Whicher, Albert Gelpi, William R. Sherwood and Richard Wilbur. Although I agree with much that Pollak writes, I believe that to free the social self from a system of restraint is to interiorize unnecessarily the problems of deprivation that Dickinson's speakers articulate. See also chap. 4 of Pollak's recent *Dickinson: The Anxiety of Gender* (Ithaca: Cornell Univ. Press, 1984). In addition, Robert Weisbuch has commented on how Dickinson's poetry bravely emphasizes "the hero's act of questing over against his successful completion of the quest." In his final interpretation, "Success is irrelevant." Poems that deprecate the quest are seen as "momentary" failures, laments of the "low comforts of the 'Daily mind,' " p. 166. Not only does this interpretation quickly overlook the pain and disillusionment of the failure while retaining an ideal of "heroism," but it also disregards the function of memory within quest activity. Dickinson's poems often depict the speaker's inability to control the memory of previous pleasure or desire. Restraint breaks down as the poem recreates the nightmare of a mind which cannot shut off memory. As one poem succinctly states, "No lid has Memory—," (P 939). The "Presence of Departed Acts" is a condition of consciousness equivalent to Hell. Hence, problems of consumption for Dickinson are not merely scenarios of struggles for unobtainable goals, enhancing the activity of the search and the value of the object; they rest also on the memory of past possession now lost. Restraints against consumption are torturously interiorized when they attempt to erase the memory of an earlier state of enjoyment.

[22] It is difficult today to look into the Victorian household without the eyeglasses of pathology, which we inherited from the medical sociology of the nineteenth century. In *The History of Sexuality* (New York: Random House, 1978), Michel Foucault notes that the nineteenth century found "sexuality" everywhere and produced a medical pathology to classify and hence regulate the "secret" of sex. He discusses this process as the "hysterization of women's bodies" where the feminine body was "analyzed—qualified and disqualified—as being thoroughly saturated with sexuality," p. 104. Not merely a repressive society, the nineteenth century was obsessed with the knowledge of sexual emotions and behavior and produced a *scientia sexualis* bent on differentiating and regulating all aspects of sexual experience. For the woman, and even the man, pathology and sexuality were

destroys the female body through suicide or fantasies of extinction.[23]

Dickinson also writes poems, however, in which the death of the desiring self becomes the necessary prerequisite to prove love. "The Test of Love—is Death—" (P 573) refers not only to the religious paradigm of Jesus's willingness to sacrifice his life for love, but also to the reality of "death" as the event which verifies desire. In another strangely tormented poem, the speaker urgently insists that her love can be proved in the face of impending doom. While the speaker watches the waters rise, threatening her extinction, the negation of her life is proof of love: "Oh Lover—Life could not convince— / Might Death—enable Thee—" (P 537).

Again, the cost of realizing desire is precisely self-annihilation. Desire is a fatal emotion for many Dickinson speakers; in a sense, it is much more dangerous than the Oedipal struggle. Whereas the son is threatened with castration, the daughter is threatened with the destruction of the entire body. The woman, of course, cannot be restrained through the cutting of a part. Her body in its entirety must be suppressed if she is to be made sexually ineffective. In working through the maze of wanting and the obstacles to desire, the woman must chart a system of punishment that does not seek to diminish power but to annihilate the body. The wounds on the body that "commemorate" its death are indeed the greatest threat to the attainment of desire. To want is to face intimately the "subtle suitor," Death. Put another way, what Dickinson seems to describe with unhalting repetition is the fact that restraint in its logical extreme demands as its price the total cancellation of the body.

---

wedded. Accordingly, many of Dickinson's critics and biographers find her living within a nexus of "pathological" female types: her mother, the "hysterical" married woman; her sister and herself, perverse "old maids"; her sister-in-law, the "frigid" wife; and her brother's mistress, the "libidinous" female. But as we have seen, these images of women reflect an economy of use, implying either the extremes of excess or inappropriate reserve. It is through her writings on desire that Dickinson explores the economic language underlying the tensions among desire, restraint, and use.

[23] Writing a number of years after Dickinson, Kate Chopin in *The Awakening* and Edith Wharton in "The Bunner Sisters" and *Ethan Frome* were also fascinated by the ruin of contentment. Their heroines are reasonably, though superficially, happy until the realization of desire sets off an inevitable wanting that leads to self-destruction. The fact alone of "more," the process of desiring, is in itself fatal. Desire destroys not only the basis of the heroines' social status and their expectations of duty, but also their desiring selves. A

Another variant to this economy that demands death for desire is the expression of desire in relation to the dead body. In some poems, the speaker imagines a space and time in which restraint from desire evaporates and the articulation of desire is allowed, if what one wants is dead. In a relatively early poem, Dickinson establishes how to "value" the lover without the presence of inhibiting restraint:

> As by the dead we love to sit,
> Become so wondrous dear—
> As for the lost we grapple
> Tho' all the rest are here—
>
> In broken mathematics
> We estimate our prize
> Vast—in it's fading ratio
> To our penurious eyes! (P 88)

In the language of exchange and measure, the other increases in price as it recedes into death. In a simple economy of desire, death ironically enhances the value of the desired; the corpse is most precious. In death all desire can be thought and spoken, freeing the speaker's voice to "value" the lover; but, of course, once spoken it cannot be acted upon in any other way than the drama of necrophilia. Basically, it frees only the voice: speakers are allowed to speak the words of desire to the dead precisely because they are dead and outside human action. In this way Dickinson describes how death ironically sanctions desire but forbids its consummation.

Some of Dickinson's speakers, however, often seek to outwit the threat of death. They envision a union of loved ones in the grave. Possession of the dead by the dead is a grim solution to an overwhelming social demand for the denial of pleasure:

---

tremendous fear of desire is interiorized in these stories; threats of punishment and agonizing guilt create situations in which desire sets off an inevitable process of destruction. In sharp contrast, according to Nina Baym, pp. 22–50, the women writers of the mid-century in America practically eliminated desire from their stories. The sexual purity of women in the home was assumed. Heroines were often portrayed as intelligent and moral, capable of surviving financial and personal hardship and of acquiring rational mates. Dickinson's poetry in this way prefigures Wharton's and Chopin's work. Dickinson was, of course, familiar with British and French women novelists whose works did not assume sexual purity. Ellen Moers, *Literary Women: The Great Writers* (Garden City, N. Y.: Anchor Books, 1977), pp. 84–95, stresses Dickinson's reading of Browning, Eliot and Sand as well as her preoccupation with the theme of love.

> If I may have it, when it's dead,
> I'll be contented—so—
> If just as soon as Breath is out
> It shall belong to me—
>
> Until they lock it in the Grave,
> 'Tis Bliss I cannot weigh—
> For 'tho they lock Thee in the Grave,
> Myself—can own the key— (P 577)

In the first two stanzas, the death scene not only lifts the sanctions against articulating desire but insures possession of it. Death frequently is seen as an interdiction to action, but here it becomes the place where desire is enacted. The dead body is capable of possession. "Back from the cordial Grave I drag thee / He shall not take thy Hand" (P 1625). Such aggressiveness is necessary because "Never the treasures in her nest / The cautious grave exposes" (P 141). If the speaker in the poem is also dead, her bliss is ensured by the death of the loved one. Conversing in their graves, these phantom lovers communicate by "signs" and freely admit their desire. The poem ends: "Forgive me, if the Grave come slow— / For Coveting to look at Thee— / Forgive me, if to stroke thy frost / Outvisions Paradise!" (P 577). For the fulfillment of desire, death is required. A middle space between earth and Paradise, the grave becomes a sanctioned meeting place for love. Celestial love in this bizarre poem is undone by the materiality of the body.

But necrophilism is not the only response to an internalized system of restraint. Death is also presented as a figure of intense power which stops desire, not merely robbing it of anticipated pleasure but transforming desire into dread. Like the "Sexton" or the "Keeper," death holds in check the experience of desire. In this way, horror can become the most menacing form of restraint. In P 512, desire is indeed haunted; it must "Sip, Goblin, from the very lips / The Lover—hovered—o'er— / Unworthy, that a thought so mean / Accost a Theme—so—fair." This frightening substitution, goblin for lover, immobilizes the speaker as she watches helplessly the advances of Death. The "Goblin" invades the intimate space shared by the lovers and accosts the lips, formerly warmed by love. The ability of the speaker's "Soul" to flip between images of lover and goblin is unnerving. To depict desire as always vulnerable to control by death equates desire with threat.

These elaborate, internalized systems of restraint, constraining desire and preventing its full enjoyment, are often reduced to a simple warning against consumption and joy: "For each extatic instant / We must an anguish pay / In keen and quivering ratio / To the extasy" (P 125). Desire is restrained merely through an inflated assignment of cost. The reason the cost of joy is so high is not disclosed; only the harsh ratio that rigidly extracts "years" of payment for "hours" of bliss is articulated. The punishment of joy by pain is measured in time and emotional strain. Ecstasy like life is fatal: " '*Tis* Costly—so are *purples*! / 'Tis just the price of *Breath*— / With but the 'Discount' of the *Grave* / Termed by the *Brokers*—'Death' " (P 234).

This reasoning, not dialectical but coldly mercantile, assigning clear-cut relationships of measure to human emotions, recurs throughout Dickinson's poems on immortality. Like joy, the cost of immortality is immense. Dickinson's speakers remind us of cultural heroes such as Christ who "thought no / Extravagance / To pay—a Cross—" (P 571). For the chance of immortality "All— is the price of All—" (P 772). Dickinson could parody the religio- business language of immortality (P 234) as well as take it with complete seriousness (P 522). She could also present a speaker aloof from the responsibility of the payment system of death: "Is Heaven an Exchequer? / They speak of what we owe— / But that negotiation / I'm not a Party to—" (P 1270). Someone outside the self has computed this economics of desire and life. In a number of the immortality poems, then, the original force behind restraint is not interiorized but belongs to a cosmic economy, planned by a "transcendent" actor. Although the speaker claims no responsibil- ity for assigning prices, she nonetheless must fall victim to the fatal demand that such eternal gains as immortality or ecstasy be paid in full.

The economics of immortality is, however, interwoven with that of desire, for implicit in the wish for life-after-death is the desire for reunion with earthly lovers. Immortality, then, is repayment not only for the loss of life, but for the loss of human bonds. Although

Dickinson sometimes resents and stands indifferent to the "new Equation" found in Heaven, she also presents speakers who demand specific repayments from the celestial Exchequer. Precisely, he must "refund us finally / Our confiscated Gods—" (P 1260). The God that extracts enormous sums for human joy and robs earth in jealous glee must at last return the stolen treasures.

Immortality becomes then, in one sense, deferred desire. The responsibility of union is placed on the will of the celestial banker who pillages life and is then appealed to for amends. Restoration of the desired is out of the hands of the poetic speakers. Possession of the desired is projected into a cosmic drama beyond life, and restraints against consumption are blamed on a competitor who makes human desire futile.

The origin of the ascetic economics of desire and its punishing system of restraint is identified in some of the poetry with the figure of a death-God—a "blond Assassin," a "Burglar," a "Thief"—who has set up a dictatorship of rules that produces an internal system of bondage. Obliquely pointing to the religious dictums of her class, Dickinson presents speakers of individual poems as victims within a value system that teaches the virtue of renunciation. As a result, this value system requires self-mutilation and finally death as payment for life.

Dickinson often leaves unnamed in the poems the power that defines these economic rules. Sometimes the controllers have social masks, like the "Keeper" and the "Sexton," at other times they appear as forces "within" the self that hold desire in check. At best, they attain focus as figures in a celestial economy. In one sense theology, society, and the personal psyche are indistinguishable players in the game of regulation. In this way, Dickinson's writings expose how mutilation and death stand as insidious checks within an economy of desire and are potent precisely because they cannot be projected easily beyond the self.

Late in her life, Dickinson writes to Judge Otis P. Lord: "I feel like wasting my Cheek on your Hand tonight—Will you accept (approve) the squander—Lay up Treasures immediately—that's the best Anodyne for moth and Rust and the thief whom the Bible knew enough of Banking to suspect would break in and steal" (L 843). To the end suspicious of celestial "gains," Dickinson parodies the religio-economic language of her social class. The dictum to "Lay up Treasures immediately" undoes both the evangelical fervor of heavenly reward and the mercantilist need for asceticism. Daring to dream a new economics of desire in which the cup is drunk and the joy consumed, Dickinson boldly asserts the right of the female body to speak and to have.

This economic system in which all life is finally reduced to a mortal payment is, at times, only redeemed by the voice of the poet. Through the magic of her art, Dickinson expresses "having" without the fear of deprivation or the necessity of restraint:

> Take all away from me, but leave me Ecstasy,
> And I am richer then than all my Fellow Men—
> Ill it becometh me to dwell so wealthily
> When at my very Door are those possessing more,
> In abject poverty— (P 1640)

Through the affirmation of "Ecstasy," often implying poetic reverie, the speaker poet stands beyond vulnerability, where even robbery cannot harm: "Himself—to Him—a Fortune— / Exterior-to Time—" (P 488).

We cannot, however, merely assume that Dickinson rests for long in this poetic triumph, compensating for life through a quest for aesthetic pleasure. More frequently, her poems and letters describe and expose an economic idiom of regulation that prevents "Ecstasy." Ever attentive to the language of her social milieu, Dickinson probes the nineteenth century's effort to "manage" sexuality and the emotional experience of desire. As an unmarried woman in Victorian America, refused any sanctioned "use" of sexuality, Dickinson records the internalized system of regulation, controlling desire. Her speakers are often psychological accountants, checking the ledger of human emotions, attempting to fix the "price" of desire. Checking their "busy pencil," they face bafflement and perplexity (P 69). The costs are, as we have seen, often morbidly high. When used to regulate the emotions, economic language often goes beyond producing an ethos of sexual frugality, creating instead sexual impoverishment. In this way, Dickinson's writings delineate the cultural language of desire for the Victorian woman in an age that attempted to "rob" the female body of delight.[24]

---

[24] It is no wonder that Mabel Loomis Todd, Dickinson's editor and the mistress of her married brother, a woman who had broken the social mores of her times, eventually found relief in Dickinson's words and a map for her worst fears. In her diary, Mabel Loomis Todd wrote: "The poems were having a wonderful effect on me, mentally and spiritually. They seemed to open the door into a wider universe than the little sphere surrounding me which so often hurt and compressed me—and they helped me nobly through a very trying time," quoted in Bingham, *Ancestor's Brocades*, p. 31.

Emily Dickinson's "Renunciation" and Anorexia Nervosa

Heather Kirk Thomas

Since the death of Emily Dickinson in 1886 of "Bright's Disease" and the publication of what she called her "Snow," biographers and critics have proposed various motives for her nearly forty years of seclusion and renunciation: the unrealistic expectations of a Calvinistic father, the recurrent illnesses of a demanding mother, and the romantic disappointments of the "Master" period. She has been declared an anxious agoraphobic, a latent homosexual, a fixated child, and a restricted nineteenth-century female writer.[1] More often than not, extant personal testimony of her contemporaries, such as this oft-quoted letter from 1881 by Mabel Loomis Todd, portrayed Dickinson as a gentle eccentric: "I must tell you about the *character* of Amherst. It is a lady whom the people call the *Myth*. She is a sister of Mr. Dickinson, & seems to be the climax of all the family oddity. . . . No one knows the cause of her isolation, but of course there are dozens of reasons assigned" (Leyda, II, 357).

As her careless summary of the local gossip confirms—"there

[1] See biographers George Frisbie Whicher, *This Was a Poet* (New York: Scribners, 1939); Thomas H. Johnson, *Emily Dickinson: An Interpretive Biography* (Cambridge: Harvard Univ. Press, 1955); Jay Leyda, *The Years and Hours of Emily Dickinson*, 2 vols. (New Haven: Yale Univ. Press, 1960); Richard B. Sewall, *The Life of Emily Dickinson*, 2 vols. (New York: Farrar, Straus, Giroux, 1974); and Cynthia Griffin Wolff, *Emily Dickinson* (New York: Knopf, 1986). Subsequent references to these editions will appear parenthetically in the text. Also see Sandra M. Gilbert and Susan Gubar, *The Madwoman in the Attic: The Woman Writer and the Nineteenth-Century Literary Imagination* (New Haven: Yale Univ. Press, 1979) and *Shakespeare's Sisters: Feminist Essays on Women Poets* (Bloomington: Indiana Univ. Press, 1979). On Dickinson's homosexuality, see Rebecca Patterson, *Emily Dickinson's Imagery* (Amherst: Univ. of Mass. Press, 1979). Suzanne Juhasz discusses Dickinson and solitude in *The Undiscovered Continent* (Bloomington: Indiana Univ. Press, 1983). Also see Juhasz's bibliographical introduction to *Feminist Critics Read Emily Dickinson* (Bloomington: Indiana Univ. Press, 1983). Finally, see William H. Shurr, *The Marriage of Emily Dickinson* (Lexington: Univ. Press of Kentucky, 1983); he proposes Dickinson was secretly married and pregnant.

American Literature, Volume 60, Number 2, May 1988. Copyright © 1988 by the Duke University Press. CCC 0002-9831/88/$1.50.

are dozens of reasons assigned"—even Todd was not the first
to suggest a theory about the "oddity" of Dickinson. However,
in her own way Todd would contribute to the mythological status of the poet she had so casually unsexed by calling her "It."
After Dickinson's death, and at Austin and Vinnie's suggestion,
she became the first editor of Dickinson's poetry and a much-
admired local lecturer on Dickinsonia.[2] In her lectures Todd
endeavored to ameliorate Dickinson's public image by stress-
ing the poet's creative genius and denouncing stories that she
had been abnormal. Thanks to tributes like those from Todd
and, later, William Carlos Williams, Dickinson subsequently
achieved a quasi-canonization as the "saint" of Amherst, a kind
of New England nun. The "our Emily" school of criticism, with
its veneration of her eccentricities, has continued for nearly forty
years.

Yet in spite of our attempts to dismiss or explain the pecu-
liarities of Dickinson's renunciative life, her puzzle remains un-
solved. Although it is not my intent finally to resolve the enigma
of her behavior or of her art, I suggest that not only does Dickinson's poetry display the obsessive patterns of starvation and renunciation typical of female victims of anorexia nervosa but that
her life and her extant letters present nearly conclusive evidence
that Dickinson herself suffered from this syndrome. Moreover, I
contend that our literary criticism has frequently practiced what
Salvador Minuchin's seminal study of the anorexic family calls
"enmeshment," the process by which the family eventually accepts the anorexic on her own terms and even cooperates to
protect her from the curious.[3] As Dickinson's family once did
for her, her critics have provided a similar "enmeshment" in our
scholarly tradition, and the inception of this protection began
long before her death.

I

Several critics have suggested a metaphorical link between
Dickinson and anorexia but have always stopped short of tender-

    [2] For Todd's lectures on Dickinson, see Polly Longsworth, *Austin and Mabel: The
Amherst Affair and Love Letters of Austin Dickinson and Mabel Loomis Todd* (New York:
Farrar, Straus, Giroux, 1984), pp. 367, 374, 381–82, 384.

    [3] Minuchin, *et al.*, *Psychosomatic Families: Anorexia Nervosa in Context* (Cambridge:
Harvard Univ. Press, 1978). See pp. 30–33 for discussion of "enmeshment."

ing a literal diagnosis. In *The Anxiety of Gender*, Vivian Pollak explores the sexual terror implied by Dickinson's anxious rejection of her femininity; however, in an earlier essay, an analysis of "Thirst and Starvation in Emily Dickinson's Poetry," Pollak furnishes incisive support for the existence of an actual physiological cachexia, a general physical wasting or malnutrition caused by a chronic disease. Pollak establishes Dickinson's fixation with fasting and starving and even concludes that she "resists food in order to survive."[4] Barbara Antonina Clarke Mossberg also confirms the "aesthetics of anorexia" characteristic of Dickinson's figurative language.[5]

Although some may dispute the validity of literary judgments founded upon biographical hypotheses, it may be argued that, as Kenneth Burke maintains in *The Philosophy of Literary Form*, "the poet will naturally tend to write about that which most deeply engrosses him—and nothing more deeply engrosses a man than his *burdens*, including those of a physical nature, such as disease."[6] Thus, Burke continues, "the poet may come to have a 'vested interest' in his handicaps; these handicaps may become an integral part of his method; and in so far as his style grows out of a disease, his loyalty to it may reinforce the disease."[7] Drawing an analogy from the intimate relationship of artist to disease, Burke suggests a writer's style might be effectively named in symbolic physiological terms. Following Burke's example, if Proust's style can be considered "asthmatic," Flaubert's "apoplectic," and Milton's "blind,"[8] I believe that Dickinson's style can be characterized as "anorexic."

Analysis by determination that art imitates life, as Burke also warns, involves no little intrinsic danger; likewise, my identification of the "I" or persona of the poems with Dickinson herself suggests the certain limitations and pitfalls that are inherent to

[4] "Thirst and Starvation in Emily Dickinson's Poetry," *American Literature*, 51 (1979), 43. My study is also indebted to *The Anxiety of Gender* (Ithaca: Cornell Univ. Press, 1984) and to John Cody, *After Great Pain: The Inner Life of Emily Dickinson* (Cambridge: Harvard Univ. Press, 1971).

[5] "Hunger in the House," in *Emily Dickinson: When a Writer Is a Daughter* (Bloomington: Indiana Univ. Press, 1982), pp. 135–46.

[6] *The Philosophy of Literary Form*, 2nd ed. (Baton Rouge: Louisiana State Univ. Press, 1967), p. 17.

[7] Ibid.

[8] Ibid.

this method. Nevertheless, even with these reservations in mind, I believe that a consideration of the connection between the poet and the syndrome will ultimately provide a productive path to her writings. For the final value of a study intended to explore the possibility that Dickinson suffered from anorexia must ultimately lie in any new light that this hypothesis sheds on her poetry.

II

Minuchin defines anorexia as "a psychosomatic syndrome characterized by both physical and psychological symptoms. It is potentially fatal, with reported mortality rates of 10–15 percent."[9] Although often a killer, only in the last twenty years has anorexia received much popular attention, as evidenced by a veritable deluge of books and articles devoted to what appears without doubt to be if not a rapidly spreading condition at least one now more commonly diagnosed.[10] Certainly the very mention of anorexia elicits a universally dramatic response, since it brings to mind a mystical tradition of martyrs and ascetics.[11] A British physician Richard Morton (1637–1698) is generally credited with the first written verification of what he called "phthisis" or the wasting disease, although historical studies indicate the affliction may have been an ancient disorder, even documented in descriptions of early witches. Not until 1874, however, did the Englishman W. W. Gull name the condition *anorexia nervosa*.[12] Unfortunately for its victims, even in the 1980s the etiology remains baffling.

[9] Minuchin, p. 1.

[10] In addition to Minuchin, see Hilde Bruch, *Eating Disorders: Obesity, Anorexia Nervosa, and the Person Within* (New York: Basic Books, 1973) and *The Golden Cage* (Cambridge: Cambridge Univ. Press, 1978); Johanna Krout Tabin, *On the Way to Self: Ego and Early Oedipal Development* (New York: Columbia Univ. Press, 1985); Suzanne Abraham and Derek Llewellyn-Jones, *Eating Disorders* (Oxford: Oxford Univ. Press, 1984); Gloria Rakita Leon, *Treating Eating Disorders: Obesity, Anorexia Nervosa, and Bulimia,* ed. James Butcher (Brattleboro, Vt.: Lewis, 1983); Meir Gross, *Anorexia Nervosa: A Comprehensive Approach* (Lexington, Mass.: D. C. Heath, 1982); Steven Levenkron, *Treating and Overcoming Anorexia Nervosa* (New York: Scribners, 1982); and Susie Orbach, *Hunger Strike: An Anorectic's Struggle as a Metaphor for Our Age* (New York: Norton, 1986).

[11] For a study of Italian nuns and anorexia, see Rudolph M. Bell, *Holy Anorexia* (Chicago: Univ. of Chicago Press, 1985).

[12] For the history of anorexia nervosa, see Tabin, pp. 189–207; Bell, pp. 3–12; and Minuchin, pp. 11–22.

In spite of the confusion over its causes, however, we know that anorexics are not made in a day; they gradually acquire the characteristics we have come to associate with the condition. Minuchin, Bruch, and other leading clinicians have determined that the most commonly shared symptoms are among the following: 1. the rejection of food (though ironically anorexics are often involved in its preparation); 2. amenorrhea, accompanied by a return to childish behavior as a psychological defense against adulthood; 3. the need for secrecy in habit and thought; 4. hyperactivity and related sleeping problems; 5. a confusion in perception of time and space with a tendency to foreground the present over other units of time; 6. hypothermia; 7. a fascination with death or suicide (self-inflicted death symbolizing ultimate control); 8. public denial of the problem; and 9. a withdrawal from accepted patterns of social activity. Some anorexics recover; however, the majority observe a lifelong vigilance against the condition and may experience recurrences. If not controlled, anorexia may cause death as a result of damage to the body. Kidney failure, a diagnosis synonymous with the outmoded term "Bright's Disease" entered on Dickinson's death certificate, is a typically tragic consequence.

Since young men are essentially free to leave an oppressive home environment, cases of male anorexia have been extremely rare. Characteristically, anorexics are intelligent and precocious females, often the second child of middle- or upper-class families. Usually the father dominates the household, and many of the victims are isolated from their mothers at about the age of two, frequently at the arrival of a new baby. (Dickinson was sent to Boston at precisely this age following Lavinia's difficult birth.) This separation during the child's "primary oedipal phase" may sever a girl's bond with her mother and reinforce "the magnitude of the father's importance to the very young child."[13] If the young girl reaches pre-adolescence without identifying with other members of her own sex or views her mother and other female friends as weak or witless, she will grow up with a sense of helplessness because she feels that she, too, is unimportant. An anorexic regains a sense of self-control over her life—and at the same time postpones the sexuality of approaching woman-

[13] Tabin, p. 7.

hood—by denying herself food. Derived from the Greek word suggesting a "loss of appetite," the term anorexia is unquestionably a misnomer, since few patients report a lack of appetite. Instead, they voluntarily starve themselves:[14]

> Undue Significance a starving man attaches
> To Food –
> Far off – He sighs – and therefore – Hopeless –
> And therefore – Good –[15] (439)

An anorexic may perpetuate her starvation to achieve autonomy or a distinct, if tragic, identity. Through her renunciation she may attempt to defeat her mother's role as nourisher ("I never had a mother," Dickinson confided to Higginson [Leyda, II, 152]) or to challenge her father's overprotective control. The disorder often commences when a child attends school away from home, and the ironic result is that the characteristically closeknit family returns the anorexic to a home environment prototypically defined by strong rules. At this time an "enmeshment" takes place, whereby the family mechanism protects the anorexic from peers and the outside world. In effect, the victim's family accepts the autonomy of her new role.

In spite of her illness, the anorexic thinks of herself as healthy and may even appear to derive pleasure in serving other family members, as these domesticities temporarily free her from their concern. In fact, "it is common to find that the anorexic child cooks for the rest of the family, even preparing gourmet meals."[16] Sometimes, as in Dickinson's case, the victim cares for the father because of the mother's illness or incompetence. However, the anorexic's devotion to feeding the "family metabolism" represents a tragically ironic process that involves fattening the members of the unit while starving herself.[17]

III

Dating the onset of the syndrome in any victim's life is a difficult problem; nevertheless, circumstances suggest that Dickinson

---

[14] See Bell, pp. 1–2, and Orbach, p. 13.

[15] *The Complete Poems of Emily Dickinson*, ed. Thomas H. Johnson, 4th ed. (Boston: Little, Brown, 1960). All poem numbers cited in the text are Johnson's.

[16] Minuchin, p. 103.

[17] Ibid., p. 311.

followed the typical pattern and began to manifest symptoms when she went away to school. Although she wrote to Abiah Root in 1846 of her happiness at the prospect of enrolling at Mount Holyoke, her later letters exhibit such depression and homesickness that she would admit to Austin after his visit of October 1847 that "I watched you until you were out of sight."[18] And long before the family had decided to bring Dickinson home to Amherst after her recurrent illnesses, their demonstration of long-distance affection was expressed by packages of food, to which she dutifully responded: "The cake, gingerbread, pie, & peaches are all devoured, but the—apples—chestnuts & grapes still remain & will I hope for some time" (*Letters*, I, 48). Perhaps the passive construction of her reply—"the peaches are all devoured"—is worth noting, as it makes it distinctly unclear who actually consumed the food; and if her family's gesture represents a common expression of affection for an ill and homesick college student, it may also be significant that their reaction was to send nourishment rather than books or bonnets. We know that Dickinson later wrote home to commend the school's food as "wholesome & abundant," presumably to relieve their concern for her health or poor appetite (*Letters*, I, 55).

Eventually, because of the school's dark orthodoxy, her father's solicitude, her homesickness, or her numerous illnesses, Dickinson returned in August 1848 to her home in Amherst. However, "no one of these reasons—health, father, hatred of the regime, or homesickness—fully accounts for Emily's short stay at Mount Holyoke" (Sewall, II, 361). Perhaps her family members observed Emily lapsing into the self-deprivative pattern of the anorexic, but if they did, it is not recorded (a characteristic "enmeshment" response in the families of anorexics). However, one clue furnishes proof of Dickinson's emaciation at the time of her Mount Holyoke experience: Lavinia commented to Austin in an 1849 letter that "I think Emilie is very much improved. She has really grown *fat*, if youll believe it" (Sewall, I, 129).

In the years following her homecoming, Dickinson would gradually inherit the roles of cook and hostess for her father, for by 1850 her mother had lapsed into a recurring pattern

---

[18] *Emily Dickinson: Selected Letters*, ed. Thomas H. Johnson (Cambridge: Harvard Univ. Press, 1958), I, 47. Subsequent references to this edition will be cited textually.

of debilitating illnesses. Kitchen duty was thus the premature obligation of the twenty-year-old daughter whose 7 May 1850 letter to Abiah Root expressed the family's dependence on her skills: "I have always neglected the culinary arts, but attend to them now from necessity, and from a desire to make everything pleasant for father, and Austin" (*Letters*, I, 97). If the tone of Dickinson's letter suggests she resented the sacrifices imposed on a dutiful daughter, then another note to Abiah also implies her guilt for those same feelings of self-pity: "When I am not at work in the kitchen, I sit by the side of mother, provide for her little wants, and try to cheer, and encourage her. I ought to be glad, and grateful that I *can* do anything now, but I do feel so very lonely, and so anxious to have her cured" (Leyda, I, 174–75). In the same letter Dickinson also fretfully acknowledges that her nursing duties kept her from a meeting with a "friend": "Oh I struggled with great temptation, and it cost me much of denial, but I think in the end I conquered, not a glorious victory Abiah, where you hear the rolling drum, but a kind of helpless victory, where triumph would come of itself, faintest music, weary soldiers, nor a waving flag, nor a long, loud shout" (Leyda, I, 175). In fact, the musty odor of martyrdom permeates her correspondence with Abiah, as, "like a martyr," Dickinson writes of her exasperation with the very act of "providing the 'food that perisheth,' . . . [of] being obedient, and kind. *I* call it kind obedience, in the books the shadows write in, it may have another name" (Leyda, I, 176).

The ongoing stress in the Dickinson household is evident when she wrote in 1851 to Austin complaining that "Fathers real life and *mine* sometimes come in collision, but as yet, escape unhurt!" (Leyda, I, 227) Certainly Edward Dickinson's puritanical temperament would have placed heavy demands upon his daughter's ability to uphold her Christian "duty"—to endure adversity and to practice self-denial. Furthermore, since Dickinson had been unable to release herself to the spirit of Christian revival when at Mount Holyoke or later in Amherst, she may now have achieved a quasi-religious personal gratification by self-inflicted renunciative rituals. Many of her letters reproduce the mystical dreams, chills, and sleeplessness typical of medieval saints. One example from 1850 to Abiah Root boasts of her "selfsacrificing spirit" while personifying her common cold as a "cold fantasy" who seemed to possess her, a being from the Alps who "has slept in my bed, eaten from my plate, lived with me everywhere, and will tag me through life for all I know" (*Letters*, I, 87).

These few examples from her late teens and early twenties establish a pattern of unhappy role-reversal for Dickinson. Although in reality still a dependent child, she had prematurely inherited the responsibilities of wife and mother. Moreover, if she was also romantically disappointed during these years, she had ample reason to deny her body and to withdraw more deeply into the imaginative world of her mind. Her letters verify that she resented her quotidian duties as cook and nurse but that she also felt this juvenile resentment was a guilty sin for which she must pay a drastic penance: "I am one of the lingering *bad* ones, and so do *I* slink away, and pause, and ponder, and ponder, and pause, and do work without knowing why—not surely for *this* brief world, and more sure it is not for Heaven" (*Letters*, I, 98–99). Eventually she seemed to value herself as good only when she practiced renunciation. This harsh doctrine of self-discipline placed her own "small" life in a contest of wills she once compared to "Christ's temptations" (*Letters*, I, 98). Her poetry manifests this same tone of zealous self-denial, a terrifying realization that "Renunciation – is a piercing Virtue" (745).

IV

The rejection of food—the most definitive symptom of the anorexic—enabled Dickinson, like other victims of the syndrome, to control, even to feel superior to her environment. Writing to Austin in 1851, she admonished him to take care of himself for "our sakes"; however, what she added to her plea is notable: "I know *my* sake a'nt much, but Vinnie's is considerable—it weighs a good many pounds—when *skin and bones* may plead, I will become a *persuasion*" (Leyda, I, 203). Later that same year Dickinson again jokingly mentioned her own *"slender constitution,"* even suggesting that she *used* her condition to convince "the folks" to let her play hooky from church. However, Dickinson obviously considered physical renunciation akin to spirituality in more than a playful sense: "Give me the aching *body*, and the spirit glad and serene, for if the gem shines

on, forget the mouldering casket!" (Leyda, I, 215) We know
that Dickinson's failure to take nourishment was noted by "Miss
Marian," a seamstress for the Dickinson girls.[19] She remembers
Dickinson ate "like a bird. She scarcely touched her food." In
fact, normally "Emily did not eat at the family table, ever. Her
meals were carried up to her on a tray. She seldom left her
room" (Leyda, II, 480).

Indeed, Dickinson's verse confirms her pride in maintaining
an "aching body": "God keep His Oath to Sparrows – / Who of
little Love – know how to starve – " (690). In (612) she boasts
that "It would have starved a Gnat – / To live so small as I – ."
Declaring herself an "Amber Crumb" (1160), she exists on a
"Dinner for a Bee" (1154) or on "a Berry" (773), but especially on
"a Crumb" (182), (254), (760), (791), (815), and (1659). "Thank
you for Tenderness," she wrote in 1865 to her sister-in-law Sue
Dickinson: "I find it is the only food that the Will takes, nor
that from general fingers—" (Leyda, II, 104).

Dickinson writes like one acquainted with starvation. Not
only does she feel fitter "for Want," she even finds that fasting
can be "Enlightening" (801). Typical of the paradoxical rhetoric
she employs in her most successful poems is her tendency to
compare her victories in self-imposed famine to former weak-
nesses before she acquired sufficient discipline. Her poetry in-
tellectualizes these perpetual trials by temptation:

> Art thou the thing I wanted?
> Begone – my Tooth has grown –
> Affront a minor palate
> Thou could'st not goad so long –
>
> I tell thee while I waited –
> The mystery of Food
> Increased till I abjured it
> Subsisting now like God – (1282)

In a desperate attempt to deny femininity, sexuality, and adulthood, the anorexic often affects the role of a child. Both in
life and in art Dickinson assumed the guise of a childlike persona and confessed it an agreeable state in a letter to Abiah

---

[19] "Miss Marian" is at least one of the women who sewed the shapeless, empire-style
white dresses for Dickinson that were always fitted on Lavinia. See photographs in Jean
McClure Mudge, *Emily Dickinson and the Image of Home* (Amherst: Univ. of Mass. Press,
1975), p. 178.

Root in 1850: "I love so to be a child" (Leyda, I, 186). In this role she spent her spinsterhood, returning her nephew's garments with cookie-filled pockets and serving gingerbread to the neighborhood children with a whimsical arrangement of rope and basket. Her coy pose of childishness was evident when she wrote to Higginson: "I could not weigh myself—myself. My size felt small to me" (Leyda, II, 57). It is well-known that at their first encounter Higginson was amazed by her entry with "a step like a pattering child's," offering a gift of two day-lilies by way of introduction (Leyda, II, 151). Even as late as 1880, at fifty years old, she described herself as "a little Tourist" who "was so small" (Leyda, II, 332); and at her death in 1886, her family memorialized her childishness eternally by burying her in a white casket, a color normally reserved for children.

In her poetry and letters Dickinson occasionally exchanges her female form for the persona of a mischievous little boy who resembles "A little Dog that wags his tail" (1185) or who sings in the "Burying Ground" (Leyda, II, 56). And in her poetic metaphor she repeatedly envisions herself as "small – 'The Least'" (964), even invisible (150). When she uses a child's body, she feels free to stamp her foot at those who would "shut me up in Prose . . . Because they liked me 'still'" (613). Like the anorexic's, Dickinson's childish behavior commands attention.

Mossberg has noted that "hunger is not only at the center of Dickinson's creative consciousness but constitutes her dominant metaphor for herself as the powerless, unloved, and angry child."[20] If the anorexic can control nothing else in her world, she at least feels imperial when she conquers her nourishers. Refusal to eat, after all, is typical behavior for even the least terrible two-year-old. Thus, the anorexic's ritualized starvation accords her weakness strength; in effect, she establishes her own diminutive kingdom: "Too small – to fear – / Too distant – to endear" (283). Consequently, the anorexic stands autonomous in a household where "Deprived of other Banquet" (773) she is forced to court "Want – . . . a meagre Art / Acquired by *Reverse*" (771; italics added). Such is a strategy of power by deprivation that sometimes perplexed even Dickinson herself, although she may have eventually learned to employ it at will.

[20] *Writer*, p. 137.

Another commonly documented characteristic of anorexics is a propensity for secrecy, enacted by hiding from family members or by squirreling away belongings or items of food. Certainly Dickinson's reclusive life typified this pattern. Her need for solitude and seclusion was evident as early as 1852 when she wrote to Susan Gilbert: "And I do love to run fast, and hide away from them all" (Leyda, I, 241). Likewise, Martha Dickinson Bianchi recalled Dickinson's habitual door-locking, even to read a simple note from a neighbor, and her statement that banishment could never enforce discipline in *their* family: "No one could ever punish a Dickinson by shutting her up alone" (Leyda, II, 483).

The closing of doors as a metaphor for the enmeshment practiced by the families of anorexics has been well documented.[21] Likewise, Dickinson seemed to associate safety with her locked front bedroom. Even more than a place of refuge, it seemed a fortress where she could conceal both her body and her mind. A secret once told, she wrote, "Ceases to be a Secret." Better to "continual be afraid" than to fear "Whom you told it to – beside – " (381). Usually Dickinson's room was her ivory tower: an "Escape from Circumstances" (382); a kingdom of "Liberty" (384); or a place where "No Prisoner be – " (720). Hiding there, her "Prison gets to be a friend" (652). But even behind closed doors she was never secure, for psychosomatic fears might instantly metamorphose her safe haven into the domicile of an alien "Assassin" (670) or "A snake with mottles rare" (1670).

Adrienne Rich emphasizes that "it is always what is under pressure in us, especially under pressure of concealment—that explodes in poetry."[22] Dickinson's poetic practice exemplifies oblique concealment ("Tell all the Truth but tell it slant" [1129]), and like the anorexic, she displayed a tendency to hoard. Horrified generally at the thought of relinquishing her poems, she allowed only a few to appear in print in her lifetime. Her statement to Higginson—"I would as soon undress in public, as to give my poems to the world" (Leyda, II, 482)—depicts an especially terrifying analogy for the anorexic. Since she abhorred "Publication" as "the Auction of the Mind" (709), it was

---

[21] Minuchin, p. 65.
[22] "Vesuvius At Home: The Power of Emily Dickinson," in *Shakespeare's Sisters*, p. 102.

understandable that she laid away her poems in fascicles. Yet her practice seems almost obsessive when we consider her total production of nearly eighteen hundred poems. Like other victims of the anorexic syndrome, she was always fearful of being without:

> Our own possession – though our own –
> 'Tis well to hoard anew –
> Remembering the Dimensions
> Of Possibility. (1208)

Dickinson's extraordinarily productive years of the early 1860s suggest the hyperactivity so common to anorexics. Like her letters, much of her poetry seems to have been composed at night. In 1852 she confessed to Austin: "Dont tell them, *will* you Austin; they are all asleep soundly and I snatch the silent night to speak a word to you" (Leyda, I, 228). Her nightly vigils of incessant writing seemed to form a shield against the temptations of the world, a way to exhaust her troubled spirit. "Work," she wrote, "is a bleak redeemer, but it does redeem—it tires the flesh so that cant tease the spirit" (Leyda, II, 287). "Wild Nights" (249) cries out with restlessness, just as "Dying! Dying in the night!" (158) and "Good Morning – Midnight – " (425) portray a child's wide-eyed wakefulness for fear of nocturnal death. When darkness represents a frightening vacuum with too many personal demons to contemplate ("Slow – Night – that must be watched away – " [471]), Dickinson outlasts the long hours through rituals of hyperactive creativity: "Somehow myself survived the Night . . . Henceforth I take my living place / As one commuted led – " (1194).

Certainly the anorexic's confusion of time and space—demonstrated by a tendency to concentrate on the immediate—characterizes Dickinson's poetry. Terms such as "intensity" and "compression" are generally used to describe her style. In her poems of definition, for example, she acutely records the look of "pain" (650) as a condition with a nonexistent past and "no Future," just as she personifies the actual moment of death in the blue, stumbling buzz of a bottlefly (465). Her poetry distills metaphysics by means of an intense focus on the present instant. For Dickinson "Forever – is composed of Nows – " (624). As I have noted, the inclination to value the "now" over the past or future is typical of anorexics.

Although Dickinson's statement of her constant physical chill
was suggested by her 1850 letter to Abiah Root, cited earlier,
a letter to Emily Fowler from 1852 also hints at the hypothermia so common to anorexics: "I cant come in this morning [to
see you], because I am so cold" (Leyda, I, 237). Even more significant than these references, however, is Dickinson's choice of
metaphor for the creative act. She allies the poet with the ability
to induce a kind of permafrost: "If I read a book & it makes
my whole body so cold no fire can warm me I know *that* is
poetry" (Leyda, II, 151). Throughout her poetry "Warmth" is a
metaphor for love and the hearth of home, and "Cold" for the
dead, the lonely, and the miserable. But more often than not she
identified with the "blonde Assassin" rather than the friendly
fireside. Like the little gentian that tried to be a rose and failed,
"the Frosts were her condition" (442). Images of shivering and
chill recreate a frosty landscape in her poetry ([335], [341], [562],
[689], [690], [768]), suggesting a tundra-like environment where
"The Needle – to the North Degree – / Wades – so – thro' polar
Air!" (792), and her condition is "Too cold . . . / To warm with
Sun" (1135). A letter from 1880 reveals her earthly hypothermia:
"I hope Heaven is warm—there are so many Barefoot ones"
(Leyda, II, 332).

Like Dickinson, most anorexics gradually withdraw from
society and most especially from those immediate family gather-
ings and holiday celebrations that focus on food. Dickinson's
reclusive habits are no secret, even to the layman, since many of
her most frequently anthologized poems express the soul's desire
for solitude. She obviously considered her company and thoughts
her uniquely personal possessions and only infrequently shared
either, at least outside her poetry. Even at her father's funeral
in 1874, she sat by herself at the top of the stairs away from
the other mourners. In her art as in her conduct she snapped
a psychological "Belt around [her] life" that constituted a No
Trespassing sign to the world:

> To lives that stoop to notice mine –
> And kindly ask it in –
> Whose invitation, know you not
> For Whom I must decline? (273)

As a physically degenerative syndrome, the progress of anorexia nervosa involves such repetitive cycles of poor health that

victims frequently express a desire for death or may consider suicide as an escape from future pain.[23] Dickinson's many recorded
illnesses are documented in her letters and those of her relatives
and acquaintances. Although we know that as early as 1851 she
visited the "famous homeopathic physician Dr. William Wes-
selhöft" in Boston, we cannot now determine the reason for this
visit (Sewall, II, 435n). However, Austin's letter of the same year
to Susan Gilbert serves as a general illustration of his sister's
chronically poor health: "He [father] says Emily is better than
for *years* since she returned from Boston" (Leyda, I, 218). Besides
these sources, family documents of the 1860s mention Dickinson's problems with failing eyesight, although John Cody has
convincingly argued that her stays in Boston in 1864 and 1865
to consult a Dr. Williams were for psychological treatment and
not for her vision. There is no proof she ever wore glasses.[24]

If she was, in fact, psychologically ill, we can see latent signs
of this disturbance in her poetry, where at times we experience
her morbid fascination with sickness and death and occasionally
observe her entertaining the idea of suicide.[25] Even her early
poems illustrate death's attraction: "What if I say I shall not
wait! / What if I burst the fleshly Gate – " (277). Sometimes
she appropriates her child-persona to evaluate the lure of self-
destruction:

> And if it had not been so far –
> And anyone I knew
> Were going – I had often thought
> How noteless – I could die – (486)

Or in her adult mode, she may welcome death as the final opiate
for the anxiety of living: ". . . to die / Is Nature's only Pharmacy /
For Being's Malady – " (786).

Since Dickinson could not have known what anorexia was, we
cannot expect to know how often she might have disguised or

---

[23] See Greg Johnson, *Emily Dickinson: Perception and the Poet's Quest* (University:
Univ. of Alabama Press, 1985), Part Three: "Death: The Great Romance." Johnson
concludes that Dickinson's anxiety over death recurs so frequently in both her letters and
poems that it must be termed "obsessive" (p. 143).

[24] Cody, pp. 416–42.

[25] See Inder Nath Kher, *The Landscape of Absence: Emily Dickinson's Poetry* (New
Haven: Yale Univ. Press, 1974), pp. 178–228, for the appeal of death in Dickinson's
poetry.

denied her condition.[26] Despite the number of her recorded illnesses, she once compared herself to her perpetually sick mother
as a well person would to the chronically diseased: "We [speak-
ing of herself] are sick hardly ever at home, and dont know
what to do when it comes, wrinkle our little brows, and stamp
with our little feet, and our tiny souls get angry, and command
it to go away" (Leyda, I, 174). She apparently did not wish to be
judged unhealthy, for she wrote to Abiah from Mount Holyoke
of a "treacherous" friend who informed Dickinson's parents of
the "state of her health" against her wishes (Leyda, I, 141).
However, regardless of her epistolary professions of fitness, her
poems record her suspicions that she was the victim of a peculiar condition—that she was mentally abnormal or even "mad"
(410). In fact, many of Dickinson's metaphors represent her attempts at self-diagnosis and are often based on comparisons of
size or weight. This intensely introspective analysis obliges her
to "measure every Grief I meet / With narrow, probing Eyes – "
to judge "if It weighs like Mine – / Or has an Easier size" (561).
In a clever trope Vivian Pollak has suggested that Dickinson
"dines on the discovery of her anorexia and sustains herself on
her witty self-diagnosis."[27] Pollak's apt comment may be nearer
the truth than she and other critics have recognized. If Dickinson, her family, and her physicians did not know *what* to call her
illness, at least the victim herself instinctively recognized that its
terrible prognosis " 'twas Murder by degrees – " (762):

> It knew no Medicine –
> It was not Sickness – then –
> Nor any need of Surgery –
> And therefore – 'twas not Pain –
>
> It moved away the Cheeks –
> A Dimple at a time –
> And left the Profile – plainer –
> And in the place of Bloom
>
> It left the little Tint
> That never had a Name –

---

[26] An April 1987 interview with Dr. Robert Hyatt, M.D., Columbia, Mo., disclosed
that by means of a kind of self-hypnotism anorexics can be adamant deniers of their
body symptomatology. This is in contrast to the bulimic, who is more dramatically hypo-
chondriac in complaint—what the nineteenth century termed a "hysterical personality."
[27] *Anxiety*, p. 128.

You've seen it on a Cast's face –
Was Paradise – to blame – (559)

Dickinson's readers may perceive the poet's quizzical evalua-
tion of her physiological symptoms. But because at her request
many of her private papers were destroyed after her death, only
her extant letters and poems provide clues to her actual physical
and mental health.[28] Moreover, these clues can be elusive, as she
was a writer who had not only mastered the art of concealment
but also knew the significance of the word on the page: "We
must be careful what we say. No bird resumes its egg" (Leyda,
II, 196). In fact, her public voice was not always to be trusted.
In 1862 she demurely responded to Higginson: "You ask how
old I was? I made no verse, but one or two—until this winter—Sir—" (Leyda, II, 56). Dickinson, of course, had written
hundreds of poems by then.

V

The cumulative testimony of Dickinson's literary biography
and of her poetry effectively demonstrates again and again the
symptomology of anorexia, a condition only rarely diagnosed in
the nineteenth century. If these parallels represent more than
mere coincidence, they can provide us with a new kind of access
to the sources of Dickinson's creative act. In fact, other literary
critics besides Mossberg have ascertained that hunger is at the
"center" of her creative imagination.[29] Whether she rejected her
body, as has been suggested, because of gender confusion, par-
ental overprotection, or cultural and artistic limitations, I would
argue that her rejection was as actual as it was metaphoric. To
Abiah, she confessed: "I do not care for the body, I love the
timid soul, the blushing, shrinking soul; it hides, for it is afraid,
and the bold, obtrusive body—Pray, marm, did you call *me*? We

[28] Whether bulimia was associated with anorexia in Dickinson's case would be nearly
impossible to determine from extant documents. The bulimic ritual does not appear
evident in her poetry, but her textbook from the Amherst Academy, Calvin Cutter's
A Treatise on Anatomy, Physiology and Hygiene (Boston: B. B. Mussey, 1850), includes
a complete list of pharmaceutical and vegetable laxatives, emetics, and poisons in its
appendix. Therefore, with her knowledge of herbs or with this text as reference, she
could have induced weight loss artificially. Cutter is cited in Jack L. Capps, *Emily
Dickinson's Reading: 1836–1886* (Cambridge: Harvard Univ. Press, 1966), p. 202.
[29] "Emily Dickinson's Nursery Rhymes," in *Feminist Critics*, p. 59.

are very small, Abiah—I think we grow still smaller" (Leyda, I, 186).

The impulse to hide and stay small and the counter-impulse to confess and reveal herself wage constant battles in her poetry: "Ourself behind ourself, concealed – / Should startle most – " (670). Frequently she lines our way with significant clues that point to her persona or to her meaning. She may use ellipsis; she may employ atypical poetic transitions, punctuation, and rhyme; or she may adopt her ironic rhetorical style to invite her reader to pursue her beyond her concealment and into discovery. An example of the riddle form her poetry would so often assume can be observed in an 1850 letter to Emily Fowler that commences with an *empty* space on the paper. After this elliptical concealment, Dickinson begins with a confession: "I wanted to write, and just tell you that *me*, and *my spirit* were fighting this morning. It isn't known generally, and you must'nt tell anybody. . . . That is'nt an *empty* blank where I began—it is so full of affection that you cant see any—that's all" (*Letters*, I, 90). Later, as we know, Dickinson would suggest the empty spaces but carefully eliminate her explication. Indeed, linguistic paradox is the signature of her work, as she hides behind ellipsis, compression, and lexical idiosyncrasy. She creates a diminutive poetic metaphor for her concealed self as an "Amber Crumb," a "worm," a "wren," a "child," or a "phoebe." And this small self continually courts hunger:

> A little bread – a crust – a crumb –
> A little trust – a demijohn –
> Can keep the soul alive –
> Not portly, mind! but breathing – warm – (159)

Less was more for Dickinson, and this triumph of renunciation informs her poetry with a minimalist's art. Only in her powerful act of denial did she find personal identity. As Joan Burbick notes, for Dickinson "the cost of realizing desire [would be] precisely self-annihilation."[30] Indeed, Dickinson's anorexic outlook seemed to enhance her creative imagination, for when she conquered her physical needs she seemed to receive a corre-

---

[30] "Emily Dickinson and the Economics of Desire," *American Literature*, 58 (1986), 372.

sponding surge in her intellect. This apprehension was so intense that she did not "dare to eat – or sleep – / For fear it would be gone – ." Renunciation may have been the "Difference" that made her "bold" (454).

Her poetry oftentimes seems to emanate from a state of perpetual starvation, even deriving its unique intensity from paring away life's excesses and living hour by hour. When she denied herself nourishment, Dickinson defeated the "not-Me" of the external forces in her world. When she stripped away her own flesh, she reigned supreme in the contest between the world and her lyric "I." She may parody the Christian sentiment "no loss without a gain" when writing to Abiah in 1850 (*Letters*, I, 89), but her uniquely paradoxical sensibility ultimately interprets this doctrinaire euphemism to mean no gain without a loss:

> The hallowing of Pain
> Like hallowing of Heaven,
> Obtains at a corporeal cost –
> The Summit is not given
>
> To Him who strives severe
> At middle of the Hill –
> But He who has achieved the Top –
> All – is the price of All – (772)

Bell has convincingly demonstrated the relationship between anorexia and the ascetic life in *Holy Anorexia*. The hallmarks of a similar asceticism lie deep in Dickinson's work as well: "The Martyr Poets did not tell – / But wrought their Pang in syllable – " (544). She not only writes of martyrs but also studies their lives ("Read – Sweet – how others – strove – "), using their sacrificial example to make her "stouter" and "less afraid" (260). If within Dickinson's cloistered world there was an ongoing power struggle, then her hunger strike became her means to win back her voice. When she was victorious, she could also envision herself as one of the ascetics she so admired; however, this sanctified status was achieved only intermittently and at enormous cost. Moreover, it demanded its terrible toll and torment both physically and intellectually. Just as Dickinson admired the saints for having earned both earthly and heavenly immortality, she also feared them for representing a renunciation she felt in her inordinate modesty, she was too "faint" to match:

> To put this World down, like a Bundle –
> And walk steady, away,
> Requires Energy – possibly Agony –
> 'Tis the Scarlet way
>
> Trodden with straight renunciation
> By the Son of God –
> Later, his faint Confederates
> Justify the Road – (527)

Of course, one cannot supply a definitive medical diagnosis for Dickinson; however, the demonstrable parallels between her condition and that of other anorexics should at least make us challenge statements such as Charles Anderson's that she "was no visionary intent on escaping the prison of this flesh."[31] In her poetry, we can observe her battles with her flesh, perhaps literally as well as figuratively, and we can plausibly if not conclusively link her struggles to those of the typical anorexic. More importantly, such a diagnosis sheds interesting light on her poetry and her creative motivation.

In Dickinson's case, the psychosomatic syndrome that wasted her body may have simultaneously enhanced her artistic consciousness.[32] Re-experiencing her poetry in light of the conclusion that she was a victim of anorexia, one confronts her terror at playing host for years to an unknown, insidious, and potentially fatal condition.[33] Unquestionably, many of her lines testify to her fear that she was abnormal and that she must somehow do penance for this malignancy, paradoxically, with constant acts of renunciation that furthered the condition: "I read my sentence – steadily" (412); "I never felt at Home – Below" (413); "But since we got a Bomb – / And held it in our Bosom" (443). However, unlike many anorexic victims who never escape from their intellectual prisons, Dickinson seemed to find a therapy

---

[31] "Despair," in *Emily Dickinson: Modern Critical Views,* ed. and intro. Harold Bloom (New York: Chelsea, 1985), p. 9.

[32] See poems 414; 430; 443; 490; 497; 531; 565; 883; 1677.

[33] Most modern therapists suggest that a 3:1 death rate for anorexics is more plausible, a ratio markedly higher than Minuchin's or Bruch's original figures. This elevated death rate is based on evidence that many patients suffer recurring symptoms for twenty to thirty years after the syndrome's inception in their youth. When anorexics eventually die from degenerative physical deterioration, the examining physician may not record the cause of death as attributable to anorexia. See Dickinson's poems 458; 574; 701; 1182; 1277; 1285; 1692.

in her writing. If so, then in the victorious achievement of her poetry, she discovered her own sumptuous world of plenty—a place where her creative imagination might actualize "A Word made Flesh" (1651). This healthy harvest served to vanquish the self-destructive state of her physical renunciation. A compelling legacy for her readers, and especially for her fellow victims, these therapeutic "letter[s] to the world" survive as bittersweet testimony to an anorexic's conflict and poetic triumph.

Dickinson's Discontinuous Lyric Self

Margaret Dickie

Iᴛ is the habit of our times to read poetry as if it were prose
perhaps because recent strategies for reading derive from and
are most easily applied to prose. Psychoanalytic, Marxist, feminist models for reading all depend to one extent or another upon
a plot, upon character, and upon extended development. When
these models are applied to a form such as a lyric poem that is
brief, repetitive, and figurative, they fit uneasily and most use-
fully only when the lyric form itself is neglected in favor of the
narrative that can be derived from joining together a number of
poems. It must be admitted that the brevity of the lyric poses
an obstacle to a critical argument because it is equally difficult
to make a compelling point on the basis of a single brief lyric
and, for different reasons, to discuss a series of poems as one
continuous work. Perhaps then what is needed is a critical argument that will start by noticing that the properties of the lyric—
its brevity, its repetition, its figuration—obstruct readings that
are determined by a socially limited understanding of the self or
the subject, by a view of character as expressed in a cause and
effect logic, by an insistence that the poet can be understood
by certain representative attitudes. The lyric poem resists the
totalizing ambition of such readings.

   In trying to formulate a new model for reading the lyric poem,
Emily Dickinson's poetry may be instructive especially because
it has been given a recent and vigorous reading by American
feminist critics who have been reading it for plot, character,
and the extended argument of the work.[1] For example, Alicia

---

[1] It is not only the feminists who have read for the plot. Early and late, narrativizing
critics have worked on Dickinson. See for example Clark Griffith's *The Long Shadow:
Emily Dickinson's Tragic Poetry* (Princeton: Princeton Univ. Press, 1964) which traces
her traumatic relationship with her father as the source of her tragic poetry or John
Cody's *After Great Pain: The Inner Life of Emily Dickinson* (Cambridge: Harvard Univ.
Press, 1971) which uses the poetry as a psychoanalytic case study. Among representative

American Literature, Volume 60, Number 4, December 1988. Copyright © 1988 by the
Duke University Press. CCC 0002-9831/88/$1.50.

Ostriker has commented: "Dickinson genuinely despises publicity and power, prefers the private and powerless life—and the reverse is equally true. We may say the same about many of her poems in praise of deprivation: they reject what they commend, commend what they reject. Their delight, their strength derives from their doubleness" (p. 41). Power and deprivation are themes that interest Ostriker, issues central to feminist criticism; but Ostriker's own claims would suggest that they are not issues equally central or politically determined to Dickinson.

The brevity with which the lyric "I" is presented in Dickinson's poems should suggest that that "I" is not to be known in terms such as publicity and power that might define a character in a novel.[2] The longer life of an individual in the novel, and especially in the nineteenth-century novel, tends inevitably toward steadfastness of character. Even an effort such as Edgar Allan Poe's to undermine the stalwartness of fictional characters by the use of unreliable narrators relies upon a consistency of representation that is foreign to the lyric "I." In a lyric poem, the "I" is known only in limited detail. For a lyric poet of consistent productivity such as Dickinson, this limitation is a deliberate choice of self-presentation, expressive of a particular sense of the self (of herself or a self) as shifting, changing, reforming. Such

feminist readings of Dickinson are Margaret Homans, *Women Writers and Poetic Identity* (Princeton: Princeton Univ. Press, 1980), Joanne Feit Diehl, *Dickinson and the Romantic Imagination* (Princeton: Princeton Univ. Press, 1981), Barbara Antonina Clarke Mossberg, *Emily Dickinson: When a Writer Is a Daughter* (Bloomington: Indiana Univ. Press, 1982), Sandra M. Gilbert and Susan Gubar, *The Madwoman in the Attic* (New Haven: Yale Univ. Press, 1979), and Alicia Suskin Ostriker, *Stealing the Language: The Emergence of Women's Poetry in America* (Boston: Beacon, 1986). Based on a model of binary opposition, these varied readings of Dickinson stress the extent to which she was different because she was made to be by a society that restricted or repressed women's expression. Sacvan Bercovitch in *The Puritan Origins of the American Self* (New Haven: Yale Univ. Press, 1975) explores the strain on the individual from the demands of American individualism in terms that explain some of the difficulties of reading Dickinson's poetry.

References to Dickinson's work are to *The Complete Poems of Emily Dickinson*, ed. Thomas H. Johnson (Boston: Little, Brown, 1957), and *The Letters of Emily Dickinson*, ed. Thomas H. Johnson and Theodora Ward, 3 vols. (Cambridge: Harvard Univ. Press, 1958). References will appear in the text in parentheses.

[2] In talking about the brevity of Dickinson's poems, I mean only to suggest a general characteristic of all lyric poems and not to stress the particular ways in which Dickinson exploited brevity or limitation as a theme. For such treatment, see Jane Donahue Eberwein's *Dickinson: Strategies of Limitation* (Amherst: Univ. of Massachusetts Press, 1985).

a self will be distorted in being described in terms appropriate for either a real-life or novelistic character.

But what terms can be used then? Brevity, repetition, and figuration, I repeat. These qualities articulate a sense of the self as particular, discontinuous, limited, private, hidden. Such a concept of self directly subverts the idea that the self is a publicly knowable, organized, single entity. Thus, it challenges all kinds of narrative explanations of character, not only the feminist and psychoanalytic reading of Dickinson's work but the dominant ideology of self-reliance expressed in the prose of nineteenth-century American culture.[3] Dickinson's poetry has been read typically as an expression of that ideology when actually it is far more revolutionary in its understanding of the self. Its chief means of revolt is its choice of the publicly degraded lyric form.

Only in America, where there was no great lyric tradition and thus no great tradition of reading the lyric, would this easily conventionalized genre be available for subversive expression. Despite Poe's claim for its importance, the lyric was a woman's form, considered insufficient to express the grandness of America and the American individual, the central mission of the nineteenth-century American literary establishment. This insufficiency of form was coextensive with the insufficiency of a self conceived as incomplete, unsure, recalcitrant, and—it must be admitted—female. The precariousness of identity, the un-mappable privacy, and the unacknowledged limitations of in-dividuality could be suggested, evoked, tentatively recognized in the lyric form which shared the very qualities it was called upon to express. Furthermore, the lyric was uniquely available for self-expression in a society where other literary forms for

---

[3] See Sacvan Bercovitch's discussion of Emerson for a complete treatment of his sense of the public self. The whole question of privacy is a central concern of Dickinson. For example, in Poem 1385, she deals directly with the impossibility of publishing the private, making public the secret. Dickinson's privacy is an issue of some debate among her critics. She is charged with being too private by Elinor Wilnor, "The Poetics of Emily Dickinson," *ELH*, 38 (1971), 126–54, and David Porter, *Dickinson: The Modern Idiom* (Cambridge: Harvard Univ. Press, 1981). Robert Weisbuch has defended her habit of privacy in *Emily Dickinson's Poetry* (Chicago: Univ. of Chicago Press, 1975). More recently, Christopher E. G. Benfey has discussed the issue of privacy and secrecy as a longing for invisibility in *Emily Dickinson and the Problem of Others* (Amherst: Univ. of Massachusetts Press, 1984).

such expression (the diary, the letter, for example) had been conventionalized and absorbed by the cultural imperatives of the Puritan tradition.

Dickinson's exclusive choice of the lyric genre separated her from Emerson and Thoreau, but she was also distanced from them in time. She wrote the bulk of her poems in the early years of the Civil War at the very juncture when the ideology of individualism established by its links to an American destiny was beginning to reveal the limits not of its optimism, which was much later in developing, but of its comprehensiveness. The individualism of Emerson and Thoreau was male, white, middle class, and Protestant. It did not extend to the work of a woman. It is no surprise then that in this woman writer, individualism as a concept gave way to the expression of individuality.

The two are not commensurate as we know from reading Emerson, but it is perhaps Nietzsche who most fully articulates the idea that the word individuality is always spoken with a forked tongue. The concept of individuality with its sense of commonality threatens the claims to individuality. Discussing Nietzsche, Werner Hamacher argues:

Individuality is so fully determined as incommensurability that no individual could correspond to its concept if it were at one with and equal to itself, if it were a thoroughly determined, whole form. *Human, All Too Human* proposes, in the interests of knowledge, that one not uniformize oneself into rigidity of bearing and that one not treat oneself "like a stiff steadfast, *single* individual." Only the individual's nonidentity with itself can constitute its individuality. Measured against itself as concept, bearing, and function, the individual proves to be other, to be more—or less—than itself. Its individuality is always only what reaches out beyond its empirical appearance, its social and psychological identities, and its logical form. Individuality is unaccountable surplus.[4]

This unaccountable surplus is what cannot be made uniform, narrated, and organized into a single individual. It is best expressed not in prose but in lyric poetry where a brief and repeated form depends upon the exposure of particularity and

---

[4] "'Disintegration of the Will': Nietzsche on the Individual and Individuality," in *Reconstructing Individualism: Autonomy, Individuality, and the Self in Western Thought*, ed. Thomas C. Heller et al. (Stanford: Stanford Univ. Press, 1986), p. 110.

peculiarity. Such limited details rather than extended narrative development will provide relief from the self-defeating ambitions of a coherent and definitive presentation of the self. The lyric poem does not mythologize the individual as a readable organization, making coherence out of isolated moments and fragmentary experience as the novel does; rather the lyric makes isolated moments out of coherence and restores with words the contingency of the self that has been lost to experience.[5] Unlike the novel, the lyric's "significant form" does not signify social viability.[6]

The brevity of the lyric focuses the sharp edges of details that will be necessarily scant. But the pressure of the brief form also attenuates the detail until it changes under scrutiny. Thus, the lyric's brevity enlarges rather than contracts the possibility of the detail. Such presentation relies on the profligacy of details rather than on their coherence.

The value of profligacy is the subject of Poem 634 where Dickinson represents not a human being but a bird. A riddle or more accurately a quasi-riddle since it is evident from the start that the subject is a bird, the poem demonstrates the way in which the lyric strains the techniques of representation by rendering clear details opaque and then creating out of that opacity the central clarity. The poem's riddling quality is an important element of its representation because it allows Dickinson to present one thing in terms of another as an image and in the instability of the image to suggest thereby the paradox of identity.[7] What we see best, we see least well; what we cannot see or refuse to see becomes clearest evidence. Offering instruction on how to know a bird, Dickinson provides too an inquiry into self-representation.

She starts with alarming confidence in the brief detail: "You'll know Her – by Her Foot." And that particularity presents itself as immediately obstructive since to know *her* by her foot is to know nothing of the conventional feminine beauty of her

---

5 For more on Nietzsche, the self, and contingency, see Richard Rorty, "The Contingency of Self," *London Review of Books*, 8 (8 May 1986), 11–15.

6 I am indebted here to the arguments of Leo Bersani in *The Freudian Body: Psychoanalysis and Art* (New York: Columbia Univ. Press, 1986), pp. 82–83.

7 I rely here on Andrew Welsh's discussion of riddle in *Roots of Lyric: Primitive Poetry and Modern Poetics* (Princeton: Princeton Univ. Press, 1978), p. 30.

face or figure. Nor is it to know much by symbolic extension. The foot, unlike the hand or the heart, does not stand for anything except standing. But, curiously, the first stanza insists on its own particular way of knowing by metaphorical extension, developing in apposition:

> You'll know Her – by Her Foot –
> The smallest Gamboge Hand
> With Fingers – where the Toes should be –
> Would more affront the Sand –

No poet could make these connections without thinking of how she herself is known by her poetic foot, and in the apposition of the foot/hand Dickinson makes a whimsical connection between bird and poet, hand writing and poetic foot, which will be developed in the final stanza where she meditates on an idea close to the Nietzschean surplus in individuality.

Before that, however, the poem appears to be a detailed taxonomy of the bird, identified by particular details—her foot, her vest, her cap. But these typical parts lose their immediate force in the poet's efforts to maintain the metaphor of bird and woman. The bird's foot described as "this Quaint Creature's Boot" is rendered unknowable as either foot or boot when the speaker says it is "Without a Button – I could vouch." That testimony guarantees enigma. Without a button, it is not a boot, and so the vouching undoes the knowledge it would confirm. The excursion seems merely decorative, as does the admission that inside her tight-fitting vest she wore a duller jacket when she was born. This wandering bird-knowledge appears inappropriately applied to a figure described as small, snug, tightly encased, finely plumed.

Like Nietzsche's individual, this bird is something other than its type. Its foot is a boot but not a boot; its orange-brown vest is the opposite of its original jacket; its cap appears from a distance no cap at all and then closer up proves to be a cap that is no cap since it has no band or brim. By the sixth stanza, Dickinson has demonstrated convincingly the extent to which details do not represent the whole, and concomitantly the uncertainty of ever knowing the whole either by knowledge of parts as in synecdoche, by knowledge derived from identifying one thing in terms of another or relating the familiar to the unfamiliar as in metaphor, or by personal testimony or by precise description and careful distinction. Even in combination, such ways do not lead to a satisfactory representation of the whole. But the poem does not end with this conclusion toward which it appears to be drawing. Rather, it presents the bird presenting herself:

> You'll know Her – by her Voice –
> At first – a doubtful Tone –
> A sweet endeavor – but as March
> To April – hurries on –
>
> She squanders on your Ear
> Such Arguments of Pearl –
> You beg the Robin in your Brain
> To keep the other – still –

The "doubtful Tone" that turns into "Arguments of Pearl" is an excessive presentation. And it is perhaps the excess from which the poet imagines the recipient retreating, preferring the idea to this reality.

Such self-presentation as the bird's is always more than enough. It must be excessive if it is to be the expression of an individual, of the "unaccountable surplus" of individuality. This bird of doubtful tone exemplifies Hamacher's description of the Nietzschean individual: "The individual does not live. It outlives. Its being is being out and being over, an insubstantial remainder and excess beyond every determinable form of human life. Instead of being a social or psychic form of human existence, the individual—the self surpassing of type, or genius—is the announcement of what, generally translated as 'superman' or 'overman,' is best translated in this context as 'outman'" (p. 119).

Leaving aside for the moment the absurdity of considering Dickinson's bird an "outman," I draw attention to the way in which the poet presents a bird by brief details and then obliterates these details in the verb "Squanders" where the bird surpasses the type. Thus, the bird is profligate in Nietzschean terms. And the poet behind the bird knows too that, in its squandering, it is casting pearls before swine, claiming individuality in a world that prefers types.

Thus, the brevity of the lyric allows a certain kind of knowing. It demands the excessive patience and attention that only a poet would possess, and it requires an indulgence that Dickinson had every reason to believe her readers would lack. To know by the foot is not a simple knowledge nor is it a different way of knowing something that exists outside the poem; it is rather a form of knowing by excesses only available in brief and metrical form.

Such excesses figure in the brevity of lyric representation by distorting syntax and sense. Knowing by the foot means fitting language to form as in the lines, "Nor is it Clasped unto of Band – / Nor held upon – of Brim." Extracted from the poem, these lines fail to signify anything; they can signify only in an arrangement of language that prizes apposition, parallel structures, or periphrasis, in short, that prizes excessive statement. Or, another example, the opening quatrain with its comparison of foot to a hand that "Would more affront the Sand" is a deictic chaos, made necessary and then managed by the only full rhyme in the poem—"Sand" holds "hand" in place. Here, Dickinson seems to be underscoring the whimsy of knowing in rhyme and rhythm. Like the bird, the poet too is a squanderer and, like the bird's, her squandering is permitted and limited by brief form and the formal repetition it requires.

The lyric's repetition derives from its brevity, but repetition is curiously essential both *to* and *in* the lyric poem. As a way of representation, repetition brought Dickinson's lyrics into conflict with Romantic conceptions of form and subject in nineteenth-century America. A form that depends upon the repetition of its formal elements will not be free nor will it necessarily grow by the principle of organic form. Moreover, the subject presented in repetitive images will not be original and new. It will always be a copy and a copy of a copy.

The vulnerability of the lyric to conventional form and subject is well documented in the history of literature. But for Dickinson, it posed a particular problem. She shared with her fellow Romantics a suspicion of convention. She knew, as they did, the limits of the self that was made and the character that was formed in large and in little by repeating familiar patterns of behavior, by repeated professions of faith, by copying over moral precepts both in school books and in embroidery lessons at home, by duties performed and performed again. She resisted in her own life these means through which one generation inculcated into the next its values, its identity, its way of life, and forced the self through repetition to grow into a presentable self. It was this self that Thoreau hoped to wash off each morning in his dips into Walden Pond. It was this self that Emerson intended to escape by writing "Whim" on his lintel post and departing from family and friends for a day. And it was this self that Dickinson drew and satirized in several poems. But while Thoreau believed in the natural man beyond the social man and Emerson relied on the genius within, Dickinson as a lyric poet had no access to these plots of redemption.

Rather, she was tied by the repetition in and of the lyric to use repetition as the constituent of character. Again, the limits of the genre enlarged her understanding, and when in Poem 443, for example, she takes repetition as her subject she uses it to express ranges of experience inaccessible to narrative organization. The poem has been enforced into such organization by Barbara Mossberg, who reads it as evidence of the duplicity imposed upon women by the dominant patriarchal culture (p. 197). The repetitive language and strategies of the poem reveal, however, a miserable lack of duplicity or division between inner and outer actions.

The repetition in the verb tense—"I tie my Hat," "I crease my Shawl," "I put new Blossoms in the Glass," "I push a petal from my Gown," "I have so much to do"—describes particular habits by which the lyric "I" prepares herself and her house for presentation to the world. Yet they are not aids in self-making so much as subterfuges behind which she hides both from the world and from herself. More crucially, the theatricality of these acts is doubled by the theatricality within; the outer self acting is in danger at every point of being upstaged by the dramatic, even melodramatic, inner self who "got a Bomb – / And held it in our Bosom." By this convergence of outer show and inner show, Dickinson calls into question the nature of identity. What is real? What is cover-up? Or, more to the point, do these questions even apply? Is the self only show?

The repetitive gestures of putting on hats and taking off shawls may be obsessive acts, but no more so than the "stinging work – / To cover what we are," the effort of holding a bomb in the bosom. The speaker justifies her "life's labor" by claiming that it holds "our Senses – on." But on to what? What is the center? What is the periphery here? The speaker's sense that she must "simulate" is, as it must be in the lyric, unexplained. Her boast that she only trembles at the bomb that would make others start suggests a fondness for her own dilemma. She is holding on to "Miles on Miles of Nought" by the same effort of will that nullified the self. Both her inner and her outer life reflect a willingness to act as if "the very least / Were infinite – to me."

Often accused of speaking from beyond the grave, here Dickinson brings the grave into the center of life. This is not a poem in which life as disruption of stasis "seems like an outbreak around which control keeps trying, unsuccessfully, to close" or where "meaning disrupts both vacuous action and the sententia in which such action takes refuge," as Sharon Cameron would have it.[8] It is rather a poem about a life in which control is the only meaning and meaning the only control.

In this poem where the inner self is fashioned by the same patterns of repetition that fashion the outer self, the collapse of the division between inner and outer in the speaker makes it possible to collapse the division between self and other. "I" becomes "we" at the very point in mid-poem where the speaker turns from her daily duties to announce the unique errand that should have distinguished her from all others. It is not that the catastrophe deprives her of individuality but that she divests herself of her individuality by surrendering to this single event. "*We* came to flesh" and "*we* got a Bomb," the speaker boasts, as if she were somehow made more grand, indeed "completed," by this dwindling of life into a single purpose which it is now her duty to memorialize.

In life lived as a duty, there can be no difference between private and public. The repetitive strategies of the lyric are used here to express the dilemma of the self ensnared in its own trap of meaning. The clotting of the lines with internal rhymes, assonance, consonance, alliteration, anaphora, and phrases in apposition suggests the way in which language can be used to impede change, to repeat sameness, even as it seems to press forward.

"I tie my Hat" is not about loss but about the refusal to

---

[8] "'A Loaded Gun': Dickinson and the Dialectic of Rage," *PMLA*, 93 (1978), 431.

give up loss. The speaker in this poem wants to account for the unaccountable surplus of individuality, to explain it in terms of a single completed "errand." But insofar as that "errand" appears undetailed and only abstractly named, it will require endless repetition.

The "Bomb" in the bosom that somehow mysteriously never goes off, that is paradoxically "calm," is pure melodrama, an image that loses its power the second it fixes itself in the imagination or should lose its power. In fact, in critical commentary, it has not. The restitution of order around the bomb evident in the persistent present of the verb "we do life's labor" has come to signify the speaker's martyrdom for critics who want to see in the poem a cause and effect explanation of character, a narrative that will contrast the liveliness of the bomb to the deadliness of routine existence (Mossberg, p. 197). But such a reading provides a plot where plot has been deliberately suppressed by repetitive action; it finds biography where Dickinson has placed only habit.

Dickinson's poems have been particularly vulnerable to narrative explanation, specifically to biographical explication. Vivian R. Pollak justifies this practice by arguing that Dickinson's art of self-display and self-advertisement draws attention to the person behind the poems and so calls for an examination of biographical relationships.[9] What Pollak terms self-display and self-advertisement could as easily be called repression as in "I tie my Hat," where the staged performance of daily duties is an evasion of self-knowledge and even the inner faithfulness to the bomb in the bosom has its element of ritual—a display perhaps, but not of the bared self.

The relationship of poet to speaker is not a simple equation; it is always mediated through and suppressed by the lyric's figurative language. Dickinson wrote to Thomas Wentworth Higginson, the editor who advised her against publishing, "When I state myself, as the Representative of the Verse—it does not mean—me—but a supposed person" (II, 412). In these terms, she points us in a different direction to ask questions that lead away from biography and toward figuration and supposition or,

---

[9] *Dickinson: The Anxiety of Gender* (Ithaca: Cornell Univ. Press, 1984), pp. 18–19.

as in Poem 505, the person supposing. Dickinson's art of self-presentation depends on supposition in "I would not paint – a picture."

The relationship of speaker to Dickinson is intricate and inadequately understood in Adrienne Rich's powerful reading of the poem that identifies Dickinson with the speaker and with the fear of her poetic power.[10] All that is known about the actual person who wrote this poem, about her difficulties in reaching the kind of appreciative audience she imagines in this speaker, about the doubts that she might have entertained over the breathlessness of this speaker, about her attitude toward art in general and her own poetry in particular, all this information must be added to the poem when it is read as a political and social tract. But if such reading seems reductive in its extraneousness, equally reductive is the view of the speaker here as purified of contingency by the lyric. It is a poet, after all, who is writing "Nor would I be a Poet" and imagining what the dower of art would be. Hers is a mixed voice, contaminated by its source and, as we shall see, easily blending into its circumstances.

The speaker of this poem is a person supposing, dwelling in supposition, and, as such, she moves in and out of identities. She figures, refigures, and figures again. Now audience, now artist, she is a creature without a core, free to dwell on and in the creator's feelings and the feelings that creation inspires, as open to elevation as to fixity, both impotent and privileged. The speaker is all feeling here, and her feeling is dependent on what will arouse it. But it is a productive and willing dependency that drives her to superfluous denials and extravagant affirmations. "I would not paint," "I would not talk" are excessive protestations. Denying herself what she most wants, the speaker intensifies its pleasures by doubling them in creating the occasion for the poem. Sweet torment and sumptuous despair are moods of desire prolonged and longingly anticipated, not evidence of Dickinson's passivity as Rich has argued. The speaker's relishing

10 "Vesuvius at Home: The Power of Emily Dickinson," in *On Lies, Secrets, and Silence: Selected Prose 1966–1978* (New York: Norton, 1979), p. 169. Rich gives this much repeated reading its most palatable form because she does understand that for Dickinson there is no split between masculine creativity and feminine receptivity. Other feminists have taken up the split that Rich identifies and then denies and have made much of it. See Diehl, pp. 19–20.

of her own relishing cannot fit into Rich's narrative of female repression because it is perversely an unrepressed narrative— a desire that is always for something else, always reaching out toward something, never satisfying itself except in its repetition and perpetuation. The poet is not frustrated in her desire to be a painter but rather thrilled by the desire to feel what the painter feels. She is not denied art; she has after all "fingers" of her own which stir, as we read, evoking both in the writer and in the reader their own sweet torment.

Again, in the second stanza, the speaker repeats her rapture. Just as in the first stanza where there was an odd disproportion between the "bright impossibility" of paintings and the "fingers" of the painter, so here the speaker as "endued Balloon" launched by "a lip of Metal" presents herself as soaring high from rather low inspiration. The talk of cornets is banal by comparison to the speaker's elevation through "Villages of Ether." The transport of art and the ability to be transported by art thrill the speaker who marvels at her own powers to be moved by "*but* a lip." The cornet player is a performer, not a creator, and his performance is rendered remarkable by the response of the "One / Raised softly to the Ceilings." She, too, is a performer—and on a higher wire.

The final stanza narrows the gap between creator/performer and audience/performer by endowing the speaker with the "Ear" *for* the poet and *of* the poet. Identities blur. The ear of the poet as of her audience is "Enamored – impotent – content," a passive receiver and willing receptacle. It is through the ear that both will be inspired and stunned by "Bolts of Melody." The separate identities of the creator and the reverent appreciator of poetry compose a fantasy that had started disingenuously in the speaker's wondering how the painter's fingers feel and how the musician's lips could inspire her, but it is a fantasy of self-empowerment, not self-diminishment. The speaker also has fingers, also has lips, even as she has "the Ear." "What would the Dower be, / Had I the Art to Stun myself," she speculates, but only after she has presented herself as stunned and stunnable. She has the "Art."

The supposed person that Dickinson might have called the representative of this verse is less a person than the power of supposition. Drawing up a *dramatis personae* for the poem or outlining a narrative continuity of envy and renunciation both diminishes and mislocates the power which names itself only in repetition. "I would not paint," "I would not talk," "Nor would I be a Poet" are repeated affirmations of the always unsatisfied, always to be satisfied desire to create. They celebrate themselves in prolonging the moment of desire just before it is satisfied. If a narrative of sexual longing and consummation cannot be easily generated from these unanchored images, the eroticism of the language here has its oddity.

The description of a painter creating a picture by the "rare – celestial – stir" of fingers is not mimetic. The words move from perceiver to perceived, from effect to affect, along a wayward path that zigzags between sound and sense. Sound alone seems to require the preposterous metaphor "Pontoon" for the self. And finally the wish to know what the dower would be if one could electrify oneself seems willful semantic wandering.

The excess in this language cannot do more than point to the excessiveness in the speaker's fantasy of self. She would be *sweetly* tormented, *sumptuously* despaired, raised and endued, awed and stunned, moved beyond sense. In her state of elevated and extravagant longing, the speaker is wanton with language, disposing lines with abandon as if they were impediments to rather than expressions of anticipated ecstasy. If language cannot speak itself, it must appropriate a channel for its transmission. The channel in lyric poetry need not be a fully developed character defined by birth and death dates, by family and a maturation plot; it can be, as here, a voice that speaks from shifting perspectives, that inhabits various frequencies, that has no center but rather many circumferences.

From the robin to the woman of melodramatic routine to this disembodied power of supposition, the examples I have chosen appear—when placed together—random, discontinuous, and uncentered. They are intentionally so because I want to suggest something of Dickinson's profligacy. It is possible to set the poem about the robin in the context of Dickinson's riddles or of her bird poems and to discuss Poem 505 with other poems in which Dickinson sets out her poetics. Or all three poems could be adapted to one or more narratives of social repression, artistic restriction, romantic deprivation. But although such

order and explanation might justify critical discourse, even my
own, it would have to be superimposed and designed to suppress
or ignore the fact that the poems are discrete forms, perhaps
part of a larger whole that is the poet's imaginative world but
deliberately brief, separate, disconnected units of expression.

Even as I insist on that aspect of the work, I am aware of the
misfit between the brevity of the lyric and the length of my own
commentary. Little can be concluded from one brief lyric or
three. Only the fact that Dickinson chose this form consistently
makes it possible to argue that the form itself is an important
confirmation or creation of her sense of self. Thus, I return once
more to consider the properties of the lyric: brevity, repetition,
and figuration.

The brevity of the lyrics she wrote is a form of artistic restraint that relies paradoxically on excess. In an age of sprawling
masterpieces that followed the laws of nature, chapters prolif-
erating as branches grow from trunks, in Melville's terms, the
brevity, compactness, and convention of the lyric form appear
unnecessarily restrictive. Yet Dickinson could use the brevity
of the lyric to suggest even more freely than Melville the un-
accountability of individuality. Although the lyric speaker can
be conventionalized by the form itself, insofar as she is imaged
in details rather than as a whole, particularized rather than to-
talized, she appears not conventional at all.

Such a speaker presents herself partially, not fully; her whole
existence is, for us, partial. Measured against Ahab, for example,
the lyric speaker suggests a sense of self that is certainly limited
and yet remains paradoxically free from the restraints of social
viability that will be exerted on the novelistic character. The
partial may be, if not all there is, more than we realize. Brevity,
then, may be the soul of character.

The brevity of the lyric form enforces its repetition. It encourages a refiguration of the already figured, and so it permits
a concept of the self not only as partial but as excessive. In
composing over a hundred poems that start with "I," Dickinson
could create and recreate a supposed person supposing one way
and then another. No single "errand" for her, the lyric speaker
is singular, unique, isolated, changeable, not to be made into one
composite person by joining poems together. The lyric "I" is not

the real-life poet or even part of her because she will not share her beginning or her end, her history. She is not a copy of that original either because she is always and conventionally partial.

Formally, repetition encourages a predictability that nonetheless permits disruption and gaps. Dickinson establishes a repetitive rhythm or rhyme scheme or organizing grammar and then breaks it, as she does in "I tie my Hat" when she breaks the rhythm with "Stopped – struck – my ticking – through" and the rhyme in "Too Telescopic Eyes / To bear on us unshaded – / For their – sake – not for Ours" and the grammar in "But since we got a Bomb – / And held it in our Bosom." The disruption, only made possible by the expectations of repetitive form, allows the brief lyric to expand its space, to incorporate blanks, to open indeterminately.

Repetition in the lyric as, for example, in the anaphora of "I would not paint – a picture –" becomes a means of obstructing narrative explanation. It also precludes the organization of events in a causal series. And it leaves open the question of what is original, what copy, as, for example, in "I tie my Hat" in which the repetitive routine gestures of the speaker may imitate a deadened inner life or may be themselves the originator of that life.[11]

Finally, the figurative language of a lyric poem represses one term under another and suggests again the profligacy of such repression. The self is not exposed in figurative language but hidden and shielded and thus freed from social definition. Such freedom allows for the whimsy always available in self-presentation. The lyric character may be called "Pontoon" perhaps only to rhyme with "Balloon" or stuck in the improbable pose of holding a bomb in the bosom or singing not a tune but a "tone." The lyric "I" is free because its relationship to even the "I" of a supposed person is of copy to copy. It can proliferate endlessly. Although Dickinson describes one speaker acting "With scrupulous exactness – / To hold our Senses – on," she actually calls into question the center around which such exactness would accrue both in that particular poem and in a lifetime's accumulation of such poems.

---

[11] I am indebted here to Gilles Deleuze's discussion of repetition in *Différence et Répétition* (Paris: Presses Universitaires de France, 1968), pp. 96–168.

In concentrating on the brevity, the repetition, and the figuration of the lyric form, I have attempted to read Dickinson's poems by the qualities they possess. These terms may
only be useful for Dickinson's work; they will not all serve
Wordsworth's lyrics or Milton's or Shakespeare's, for example.
Thus, they cannot be worked into a model for reading all lyric
poetry. But they are important here because they point to the
essential qualities of Dickinson's work: its interest in the unaccountable surplus of individuality, in repetition as constituent of character, and in figurative excess as essential to self-
presentation.

The problems of interpretation that Dickinson's poetry poses
are essentially problems of narrative readability which have
usually been resolved by the imposition of a master narrative on
the work and the life. Feminist critics of Dickinson who have
brought so much new energy to the reading of her poetry are
only the latest version of this tendency; they have been preceded
by psychoanalytic critics, biographers, and cultural historians.
Dickinson's work evades them because it represents a much
more radical understanding of the self than American feminists,
tied as they are to a social explanation of character, can allow.
Dickinson's lyric speakers have no narrative continuity, no social
viability, no steadfast identity. In their squandering, melodrama,
and excesses, they express an individuality that resists final representation and the control that signifies. Yet Dickinson's lyric
presentation of a self that obstructs narrative reading because it
is discontinuous, profligate, and excessive may be the nineteenth
century's most revolutionary expression of individuality. Thus, it
may offer not only a new model for reading the lyric but a new
and perhaps persuasively feminist model of self-presentation.

Index

Poems cited are listed in numerical order under Dickinson, Emily (poems cited)

Notes on Editors and Contributors

Edwin Cady is Andrew W. Mellon Professor Emeritus in the Humanities and Louis Budd is James B. Duke Professor of English at Duke University. Both Cady and Budd have served on the editorial board of *American Literature* for many years.

Charles R. Anderson (1902–). University of Georgia (1927–30), Duke University (1930–41), The Johns Hopkins University (1941–1969): *Melville In The South Seas* (1939); *Emily Dickinson's Poetry: Stairway of Surprise* (1960); *The Magic Circle of Walden* (1968); *Person, Place and Thing In Henry James's Novels* (1978 Ed. *Sidney Lanier: Poems and Letters,* 1970).

Burbick, Joan (1946–). Washington State University (1978–): *Thoreau's Alternative History: Changing Perspectives On Nature, Culture, And Language* (1987).

Lois A. Cuddy (1934–). Rhode Island University (1978–).

Margaret Dickie (1935–). Illinois University, Champaign-Urbana (1966–87), University of Georgia (1987–): *Becoming A City* (1967); *Hart Crane: The Patterns in His Poetry* (1974); *Sylvia Plath & Ted Hughes* (1979); *On The Modernist Long Poem* (1986).

Betsy Erkkila (1944–). University of Pennsylvania (1980–): *Walt Whitman Among The French Poets* (1980); *Whitman The Political Poet* (1988).

Judith Banzer Farr (1937–). Vassar College (1961–63), St. Mary's College (1964–68), SUNY, New Paltz (1968–77), Georgetown University (1977–): *Twentieth Century Interpretations Of* Sons and Lovers (1970); *The Life And Art of Elinor Wylie* (1983).

Ed Folsom (1947–). University of Iowa (1976–): *Walt Whitman: The Measure of His Song* (1981); *W. S. Merwin: Essays on the Poetry* (1987); *Regions Of Memory: Uncollected Prose of W. S. Merwin* (1987).

Sidney E. Lind (1914–). Rutgers University (1947–50), Brooklyn College (1950–85).

Timothy E. Morris (1959–). Bryn Mawr College (1983–84); Rutgers University (1984–86), Fordham University (1987–88), University of Texas, Arlington (1988–).

Dorothy Huff Oberhaus (19–). Mercy College [Westchester] (1970–).

Vivian Pollak (1938–). Cheyney State University (1970–86), University of Washington, Seattle (1986–): *Dickinson: The Anxiety of Gender* (1984); *A Poet's Parents: The Courtship Letters of Emily Norcross and Edward Dickinson* (1988).

Heather Kirk Thomas (1941–). Has just completed the Ph.D. requirements at the University of Missouri–Columbia.

Anna Mary Wells (1906–). Texas Christian University (1927–28), Wayne State University (1942–45), University of Detroit (1945–46), Douglass College,

Rutgers University (1954–72): *A Talent For Murder* (1942); *Murderer's Choice* (1943); *Sin of Angels* (1948); *Fear of Death* (1951); *Night of May Third* (1956); *Dear Preceptor: The Life and Times of Thomas Wentworth Higginson* (1963); *Miss Marks and Miss Wooley* (1978).

George Frisbie Whicher (1889–1954). *This Was A Poet* (1938); *Walden Revisited* (1945); *The Transcendental Revolt Against Materialism* (1949); *Poetry Of The New England Renaissance* (1950); *Poetry and Civilization* (1955).

Library of Congress Cataloging-in-Publication Data

On Dickinson : the best from American literature/
edited by Edwin H. Cady and Louis J. Budd.
p. cm.
ISBN 0-8223-1014-7
1. Dickinson, Emily, 1830-1886. 2. Poets,
American—19th century—Biography. I. Cady,
Edwin Harrison. II. Budd, Louis J.
PS1541.Z506 1990
811'.4—dc20 89-17004